# The Making of NAFTA

# The Making of NAFTA

## NAFTA

*How the Deal Was Done*

Maxwell A. Cameron
and
Brian W. Tomlin

Cornell University Press    Ithaca and London

Library of Congress Cataloging-in-
Publication Data

Cameron, Maxwell A.
    The making of NAFTA : how the deal was
done / co-authored by Maxwell A. Cameron,
Brian W. Tomlin.
        p.   cm.
    ISBN 0-8014-3800-4 (cloth)
    1. Free trade—North America.  2. Free
trade—United States.  3. Free trade—Canada.
4. Free trade—Mexico.  5. North America—
Commercial treaties—History.  6. Canada.
Treaties, etc. 1992 Oct. 7—History.  I. Tomlin,
Brian W.  II. Title.
    HF1746.C33  2000
    382'.917—dc21
                                        00-008915

# CONTENTS

# TABLES

# ACKNOWLEDGMENTS

**W**e would like to acknowledge the generous support of the Social Sciences and Humanities Research Council of Canada for separate research grants which enabled us to conduct the work that went into the production of this book. Additional research assistance was provided by Carleton University and the University of British Columbia (UBC). We are exclusively responsible for the content of the analysis and any errors or omissions it may contain.

Some of the interviews in Mexico were made possible by the trilateral exchange program between Carleton University, the Instituto Tecnológico Autónomo de México (ITAM), and Georgetown University. The cooperation of the other participants in this program—Maureen Molot, Rafael Fernández de Castro, and John Bailey—is gratefully acknowledged. In addition, the Canadian Embassy in Mexico City assisted in arranging a number of the Mexican interviews, as did the staff in the International Studies program at the Colegio de México.

Able research assistance was provided by Barry Davis, Carey Gibson, Alexis Diamond, Laura Ritchie Dawson, Jonathan Quong, and Margaret Clare Challen. The draft manuscript was inflicted on students in our courses at Carleton and UBC, and their reactions were used in an effort to fine-tune and improve the manuscript.

A number of colleagues read and commented on the draft manuscript, and we have incorporated many of their suggestions for change, though probably not as many as they would like. Special thanks to Michael Hart, Judith Adler Hellman, Michael Dolan, and Claire Turenne Sjolander. Careful copyediting by Mary Babcock improved the quality of the final product.

Above all, we are grateful to the dozens of NAFTA negotiators in all three countries who generously granted their time to help us understand the negotiations. Without their willingness to speak with us, it is no exaggeration to say the book would have been impossible.

# NAFTA CHRONOLOGY

May 23–24, 1991   Congress approves President Bush's request for a two-year extension of fast-track authority for NAFTA and other trade negotiations.

June 12, 1991   The first Trilateral Ministerial Oversight meeting opens in Toronto, marking the formal launch of NAFTA negotiations. Ministers identify six broad issue areas: market access for goods; services; investment; intellectual property protection; dispute settlement; and trade rules on issues such as subsidies and rules of origin. These issue areas are divided among nineteen working groups.

June 28, 1991   Negotiators on market access and trade rules meet in Ottawa.

July 8–9, 1991   Chief negotiators from each country chair a plenary session in Washington. Katz says the United States will not change domestic trade law.

August 18–20, 1991   The second Trilateral Ministerial Oversight meeting begins in Seattle, where the biannual meeting of the Canada-U.S. Trade Commission has just ended, with Canada rejecting the proposed 60 percent auto content rule. Mexico outlines a hard line on energy.

August 20, 1991   U.S. governors offer qualified NAFTA support, with the expectation that there will be joint U.S.-Mexican environmental and labor efforts.

September 19, 1991   The three NAFTA countries exchange initial tariff staging proposals and nontariff barrier request lists in Dallas.

October 9, 1991   Chief negotiators meet at Meech Lake near Ottawa to narrow differences and take stock of developments taking place in multilateral trade negotiations. Katz decides it is time to start drafting text.

October 17, 1991    The Office of the U.S. Trade Representative and Environmental Protection Agency (EPA) release a draft review of U.S.-Mexico Environmental Plan for public comment.

October 25–28, 1991    The third Trilateral Ministerial Oversight meeting is held in Zacatecas, Mexico. NAFTA passes from fact-finding to draft language stage. Negotiators accept Mexican demand that foreign companies be excluded from oil exploration and other risk-sharing activities in this sector.

December 14, 1991    Presidents Salinas and Bush meet privately at Camp David and agree to order negotiators to complete the accord as soon as possible.

December 31, 1991    Composite bracketed texts are completed.

January 6–10, 1992    Meeting is held at Georgetown University in Washington to work on the composite texts.

February 4–5, 1992    Chief negotiators meet in Aylmer, near Ottawa. Work focuses on writing a draft text on financial services.

February 9–10, 1992    At the fourth Trilateral Ministerial Oversight meeting in Chantilly, Virginia, the ministers take stock and instruct negotiators to remove brackets from a composite text. A Canadian proposal to expand the Canada-U.S. Auto Pact is rejected.

February 17–21, 1992    A plenary session in Dallas is chaired by chief negotiators from all three countries. The Mexican team makes major concessions in a number of working groups.

February 26, 1992    President Bush and U.S. Trade Representative Hills discuss NAFTA progress with President Salinas and Minister Serra in San Antonio on the margins of a drug summit.

March 4–5, 1992    A plenary session chaired by chief negotiators is held in Washington.

March 23–27, 1992    A plenary session chaired by chief negotiators is held in Washington.

April 3, 1992    U.S. Trade Representative Hills announces that there are now draft texts from all working groups, except for one dealing with U.S. antidumping and countervailing duty laws. In fact, progress is uneven. The draft text on transportation is nearly done, but negotiations on autos remain intractable.

April 6–8, 1992    Montreal hosts the fifth Trilateral Ministerial Oversight meeting.

April 14–15, 1992    U.S., Canadian, and Mexican negotiators meet in Washington to further examine the establishment of a judicial review mechanism of the three countries' trade remedy laws.

April 17, 1992   Auto negotiators meet in Mexico City to try to clarify a Mexican offer to liberalize its Automotive Decrees (hereafter, the Auto Decrees).

April 27–May 1, 1992   A plenary session chaired by chief negotiators is held in Chapultepec, Mexico City. Canada threatens to pull out of agriculture and textile talks and negotiate separate bilateral deals.

May 8, 1992   NAFTA parties agree to pursue separate bilateral agreements over market access for agricultural products.

May 13–15, 1992   A plenary session chaired by chief negotiators is held in Toronto, at the Four Seasons Hotel.

June 1–5, 1992   A plenary session chaired by chief negotiators is held in Crystal City, Virginia. Talks begin on environmental provisions.

June 17–19, 1992   Chief negotiators meet in Washington.

June 29–July 3, 1992   Chief negotiators meet in Washington.

July 7–10, 1992   Chief negotiators meet to review negotiations in Washington.

July 14, 1992   U.S. and Mexican presidents and trade ministers meet in San Diego and announce the negotiations have entered the final stages. The United States pushes for a trade deal by July 25.

July 25–26, 1992   The sixth Trilateral Ministerial Oversight meeting is held in Chapultepec, Mexico City. Tentative agreement is reached on access to the Mexican auto market.

July 29–August 12, 1992   The chief negotiators meeting is followed by the seventh Trilateral Ministerial Oversight meeting at the Watergate Hotel in Washington. Hope fades for signing a deal before the U.S. presidential election on November 3.

August 12, 1992   NAFTA negotiations are completed after ten consecutive days of meetings among trade ministers. Final sticking points concerned autos, energy, investment, government procurement, trade remedies, textiles, and cultural industries. Various documents, including a negotiated summary of the agreement, are issued.

October 4, 1992   At a speech in Raleigh, North Carolina, presidential candidate Clinton provides qualified support for the NAFTA.

October 7, 1992   President Bush, Prime Minister Mulroney, and President Salinas meet in San Antonio to discuss NAFTA implementation and watch as their trade ministers initial the NAFTA draft legal text.

December 17, 1992   President Bush, Prime Minister Mulroney, and President Salinas sign NAFTA in separate ceremonies. President-elect Clinton reiterates his support for NAFTA and calls for supplemental agreements on the environment, labor, and import surges.

January 20, 1993   Clinton is inaugurated as president, and Kantor is subsequently confirmed as U.S. trade representative.

March 17, 1993  First round of talks on side deals begins in Washington.

April 14–15, 1993  Second round of talks on side deals is held in Mexico City.

May 19, 1993  The third round of talks on side deals begins in Ottawa and breaks up on Friday, May 21, after United States threatens to use trade sanctions to police environmental and labor standards.

May 27, 1993  Canada's House of Commons ratifies NAFTA.

June 8, 1993  Fourth round of side-deal talks begins in Washington, but negotiators concede that nothing concrete is achieved.

June 12, 1993  Kim Campbell becomes prime minister of Canada and expresses support for the NAFTA process.

June 23, 1993  Canadian Senate ratifies NAFTA.

June 25, 1993  Tom Hockin becomes Canadian trade minister.

June 30, 1993  U.S. federal judge rules that NAFTA needs environmental impact assessment.

July 8–10, 1993  Negotiators meet in Cocoyoc, Mexico, for the fifth round of side-deal talks to decide on regional secretariat structure.

July 19, 1993  Sixth round of side-deal talks is held in Ottawa. Negotiators prepare a single bracketed text of draft environmental and labor side accords.

July 26–29, 1993  Ministerial meeting is held in Washington.

August 4–9, 1993  Ministers meet again and extend their negotiations throughout a marathon weekend.

August 11, 1993  Prime Minister Kim Campbell says Canada is unwilling to agree to environmental labor side deals that have been privately approved by United States and Mexico.

August 12, 1993  Ministerial talks resume in Ottawa. Late in the evening agreement is reached on labor and environmental cooperation and on import surges.

August 13, 1993  Agreement is announced by the three governments.

September 14, 1993  NAFTA side agreements are signed in the three capitals.

November 4, 1993  President Clinton sends the NAFTA text and side agreements to Congress.

November 17–20, 1993  U.S. House and Senate pass NAFTA.

January 1, 1994  The NAFTA enters into force. Zapatista rebels start uprising in Mexican state of Chiapas.

---

Sources: Bertrab (1997); *Inside US Trade*, various issues; *Inside NAFTA*, various issues; Grayson (1995).

# The Making of NAFTA

## CHAPTER 1

# Northern Reflections

In the pre-dawn hours of February 4, 1990, a jetliner passed high over the Gulf of Mexico en route to Mexico City from Switzerland. On board, Carlos Salinas de Gortari and Jaime Serra Puche slept fitfully. The president of Mexico and his secretary of commerce, accompanied by other members of the cabinet and Mexican business leaders, were on the final leg of a nine-day mission to Europe. Their trans-Atlantic, red-eye flight was made necessary by an important ceremonial function that the president had to perform that day in the Mexican capital. The previous July, after arduous negotiations, the Mexicans had concluded an agreement with the advisory committee of their creditor banks on terms for rescheduling Mexico's enormous burden of debt. It had taken six months for the individual banks to decide to back the accord and to select one of the three options that had been identified for debt rescheduling. Now, finally, the Mexican debt agreement was ready for the president's signature. This formality represented another step in the reconstruction of Mexico's economy, battered by recession, inflation, and debt for most of the previous decade. Despite the ceremony, however, it was not a major step, because the agreement would only slightly reduce Mexico's debt service obligations. Further action would be necessary, and since Mexico could not count on its creditors for economic aid, it would have to seek capital from foreign investors.

The search for foreign investment had been the purpose of the mission to Europe, and it had been a resounding failure. Potential investors, preoccupied with the economic reconstruction of East European states emerging from decades of communist rule, showed little interest in investing in Mexico. Conversations with Prime Minister Margaret Thatcher of Britain and Chancellor Helmut Kohl of West Germany were sobering to the president and his commerce secretary because they revealed that the Europeans were indifferent to Mexico's urgent need for foreign capital. While attending the World Economic Forum in Davos, Switzerland, Salinas and Serra decided that dramatic action was required to increase the appeal of Mexico to foreign investors. Trade liberalization alone would not guarantee successful integration into the global economy, they reasoned, since other countries were undergoing similar reforms with equal tenacity. The shift in the global economy toward the formation of gigantic regional economic blocks, such as the creation of a common market in Europe, left Mexico with few choices: either remain closed, open the economy unilaterally, or develop a strategy of negotiated liberalization.[1] Remaining closed was not an option, and unilateral liberalization seemed to have few benefits. Set on the idea of negotiated liberalization, Serra and Salinas had approached U.S. Trade Representative Carla Hills during meetings at Davos to determine American interest in establishing a free trade area with Mexico.

As Salinas's jet arched across the coast on its path to Mexico City, it crossed the active volcano belt separating the world's largest metropolitan area from the nation's heartland—the Bajío, an area that had served as the center of a rich colonial economy based on silver mines and was still Mexico's breadbasket. In a village south of Guanajuato, a peasant family also slept fitfully, disturbed by images from the previous day, when local authorities had sent bulldozers to remove squatters from their land.[2] Jorge Rivera had lodged a complaint with local authorities after squatters had erected an adobe hut on the perimeter of his property, and the authorities had upheld his claim. His deed to the land was good, having been paid in cash eight years earlier. For decades he had survived by working as a sharecropper, tilling others' land in return for the right to subsistence on a small plot of earth that was not his own, and by working on communal land, the right to which he disputed with neighbors. Only by borrowing had he accumulated enough money to purchase forty-five acres from a local landlord. Without electricity, running water, or irrigation, Jorge had made his land produce a subsistence minimum, plus a small surplus for the market in Guanajuato, and his wife Amanda's work in a local in-bond factory, or *maquiladora*, supplemented the family income. The Rivera's eldest son was working in California, and he also helped with the occasional remittance.

Life for the Rivera family was not easy or comfortable, and they could hardly afford to lose the investment that their land represented. Nevertheless, they were deeply disturbed by the use of the bulldozers against the squatters. "These people were building on my land. They said it was *ejido* land," insisted Jorge, trying to convince himself he had done the right thing.

Mexico's revolutionary constitution had been written in Guanajuato in 1916–17, and it had created the *ejidal* system of communal land tenure. The promise of land for peasants had been a pillar of revolutionary ideology, but the gross inefficiency of the *ejidos*, combined with relentless population growth, had turned the promise sour. *Ejidatarios* (owners of *ejido* plots) and those who aspired to hold land knew that the mythology of the revolution and the reality of everyday life were discordant. In plain language that captured the Malthusian logic driving the countryside deeper into despair and conflict, Jorge said: "Our ancestors could barely live on the lands they were given. Well, for that matter, they distributed very little. As the years passed, this land was divided among our grandfathers, fathers, uncles, and cousins, and our share of the piece of land has been getting smaller and smaller. Also, when the land was first distributed, what you got many times was limestone, and you couldn't farm because the land was sterile. And if we keep dividing when we inherit, each time the piece is smaller. We don't have a place to harvest, to live"(Hermosillo et al. 1995, 35).

Little did the Riveras imagine that their president had already made a decision that would change their lives irrevocably, altering their future plans in unimaginable ways. When they first heard on the radio about Salinas's idea of a North American free trade area, their initial reaction was ambivalent. The president seemed to be proposing something that went against the grain of Mexico's history and revolutionary traditions, but perhaps that was what the country needed. "Maybe it will serve to get the moneylenders off our backs," Amanda thought optimistically. But when the peso collapsed after Salinas left office at the end of his *sexenio*, or six-year term, the Rivera family was caught up in skyrocketing interest rates. They were forced to sell their land, and move to the city, hoping to find work in the small factories and workshops ringing Guanajuato. Ask what she thinks of the North American Free Trade Agreement (NAFTA), and Amanda will tell you with resignation: "NAFTA was something for the bigwigs. All that people like us can do is to sit back and watch the movie."

The effects of NAFTA would reflect the complexities and paradoxes of Mexican society, the unevenness of its development, and the ambivalence inherent in its relationship with its northern neighbor. Even in remote villages, parabolic antennas provided evidence that many Mexicans, and not just the middle class, were plugged into the five-hundred-channel universe. Rapid industrialization, urbanization, and more recently economic liberalization had transformed Mexico into an increasingly mobile and restless society, with a large middle class and a tiny wealthy elite. But the majority of people had been left out of the prosperity. Whether NAFTA would exacerbate Mexico's problems or provide solutions would depend on changes that were hard to anticipate.

One thing was clear, even in 1990. Salinas had made a momentous decision that would reverse the policies of all previous Mexican presidents since the 1910 revolution and profoundly affect the course of his people's lives. When details of the initiative began to leak to the public in March 1990, reactions among most Mexicans, like the Rivera family, were conflicted. The *New York Times* reported that Salinas, who they routinely described as a forty-one-year-old, Harvard-educated economist, had made a "break with the policy of economic nationalism that has prevailed" in Mexico since the 1910 revolution. This "huge political gamble," wrote Larry Rohter, "has prompted a spirited public debate," and he went on to quote Lorenzo Meyer, a distinguished political analyst in Mexico City, who said: "Our way of life is at stake.... We should take decisions knowing, as much as possible, what we will gain and lose by integrating ourselves with the economy of a great power, one from which we previously considered it our historic and patriotic duty to protect and separate ourselves."[3]

Yet to the surprise of many, polls found strong support for NAFTA among Mexicans of all walks of life, largely because the myths and symbols of the revolution had begun to stand in increasingly sharp contrast to the reality of everyday life for ordinary Mexicans. This optimism also reflected the Mexican government's control over information. Judith Adler Hellman, a Canadian political scientist, spent five months in Mexico conducting extensive interviews in 1990 and 1991. She found that Mexicans showed great sophistication in their views of NAFTA but "lacked experience and hard data on which to base their opinions" (1993, 196). For many entrepreneurs, the benefits of NAFTA would depend on how well the Mexican team negotiated with the United States and Canada. Said a consumer electronics producer, "The way I see it is that the parts industry will grow again if we protect certain areas a little bit, just like the United States protects its areas, just like Canada protects its own. It's just a temporary thing that will end, but it has to be a process...or else the entire industry is wiped out" (cited in Hellman 1993, 198). Others had no illusions about Mexico's bargaining power but still believed that economic integration would be beneficial in the long run: "The United States is going to construct the treaty," said one industrialist. "We will be invited to the bargaining table but...the US will call the shots. We Mexicans are going to end up with two choices: either go to work for the transnational corporations that will move in, or work as busboys and waiters in services. But the important thing is that we Mexicans should have work. I believe the word 'sovereignty' is one we will all come to forget" (cited in Hellman 1993, 199).

Mexican workers, especially those employed in inefficient import-substitution industries (industries created by protective tariffs), braced for greater competition from imports. Much of the trade union hierarchy, linked to the ruling party since the 1930s, tended to support Salinas's initiative, while rank-and-file workers, who instinctively distrusted the government, complained that "the trade unions here are not discussing the matter and they have not been brought into the negotiations" (Hellman 1993, 201). Said a teacher, "There are sectors here that think that there will be a favorable standardization of salaries, levels of well being and so on. This is the expectation that the Mexican government is trying to encourage, in order to promote the idea that we are going to benefit from all that is better or more advanced in American and Canadian society. But to me it looks like the standardization is downward because under the logic of comparative advantage, what Mexico has to bring to the arrangement is cheap labor...." (cited in Hellman 1993, 202).

Several years later, *Newsweek* would note that Salinas had become "Mexico's all-time favorite villain," the country's least popular ex-president.[4] Casual conversations with people in the streets of Mexico City five years after NAFTA was implemented would reveal that many Mexicans believed that the agreement was "for the rich or people in power." Again and again, working-class Mexicans would say things like: "If you want to know about NAFTA, you will have to talk to businessmen or government leaders. Frankly, people like me are as badly screwed as ever."

But in 1990, the mood was different. Salinas was praised as the epitome of the youthful, educated, modernizing technocrat, and Mexicans welcomed how he sharply challenged the corrupt, populist bosses and inward-looking dinosaurs in the bureaucracy who had ruled Mexico for over half a century. What made Salinas's initiative all the more dramatic was his exquisite timing: he proposed NAFTA at a unique historical moment. During a relatively brief window of opportunity between 1988 and 1992, the three North American chiefs of government not only favored closer integration, but also had, or had a good chance of assembling, the domestic coalitions necessary to deliver an agreement. President George Bush had risen to national prominence in the 1980 campaign for the leadership of the Republican Party and had served two terms as vice president under Ronald Reagan. Bush had been elected president in 1988 at a time when the U.S. Congress had become increasingly assertive in the area of trade policy, initiating the first omnibus trade bill to come from the Hill since Smoot-Hawley. Congress continued to delegate broad powers to the executive, but it began to demand more results from international negotiations. Bush came to office at a time of great controversy over trade policy, and because the U.S. political system is based on checks and balances, that controversy inevitably came to concern the competence of and relations between the various branches of government.

Salinas's initiative dovetailed brilliantly with U.S. trade policy objectives. The mix of domestic and international objectives in U.S. trade strategy was captured by the comments of Reagan's secretary of state, James Baker, who believed that bilateralism would harness American market power to get results that were impossible in multilateral negotiations, which would appease congressional demands for results on the trade front. Specifically, Baker argued that bilateral free trade agreements do not undermine multilateralism, extend liberalization into new areas, lower the costs of liberalization by breaking ground with one nation at a time, pave the way for a "market liberalization club" as a possible alternative to the General Agreement on Tariffs and Trade (GATT), provide a lever to exclude states that choose not to open markets, and serve as a counterweight against domestic protectionists. "We can demonstrate a hard-nosed Yankee-trader realism about bargaining: if all nations are not ready [sic], we will begin with those that are and build on that success" (Baker 1988, 40–41).

Canada was the more reluctant partner. Canadian Prime Minister Brian Mulroney had just fought an election on the issue of free trade. In the face of aggressive unilateralism in Washington, Canadian trade policy experts had abandoned efforts to diversify trade relations and focused attention on securing access to the market that mattered most, in the United States. This had opened an acrimonious debate over trade that was resolved in 1988 with the re-election of Mulroney's Progressive Conservative Party. With a commanding majority in parliament—it far exceeded the narrow plurality of the electoral vote—the Conservatives were in a solid position to implement the Canada-U.S. Free Trade Agreement (FTA) and continue to pursue closer economic relations with the United States. In Canada, the prime minister and cabinet are members of both the executive and the legislature, with the result that, as Jackson and Jackson (1990, 282) noted, there is more of an "atmosphere of public political bargaining" in the United States than in Canada. However, an increasingly decentralized federalism meant that in Canada the controversy over trade policy must be seen through the optic of federal-provincial relations.

If Salinas's initiative was brilliant diplomacy, it was also astute domestic policy. Elected in 1988 in a vote tainted by blatant fraud, Salinas began to pursue a path of economic reform that he hoped would restore the hegemony of the ruling Institutional Revolutionary Party's (PRI) sixty-year grip on power, but now under more modern conditions. The decision to pursue what was called "*Salinastroika*" (which wags noted was not accompanied by a Mexican *glasnost*) involved the use of Mexico's authoritarian political system to pursue a whole new approach to economic transformation, with few domestic constraints except for the six-year limit on presidential terms and a prohibition on re-election. Mexico was the country where NAFTA had the greatest consequences, for NAFTA was the centerpiece of Salinastroika.

The three leaders had the will and the means to pursue closer economic relations. Between 1990 and 1992 they devoted themselves to the task of preparing for, negotiating, and implementing North American free trade. It would probably be fair to say that while none of the three even seriously contemplated the idea of comprehensive free trade at the outset of their mandates, NAFTA would ultimately become, for better or worse, the central achievement of their administrations and in the eyes of the public, their most enduring legacy. Only a few years after the NAFTA entered into force did it become clear how unique was the moment when free trade was negotiated. Bush's successor, Bill Clinton, was unable to secure fast-track authority to negotiate the extension of NAFTA to other countries in the hemisphere, a so-called Free Trade Agreement of the Americas (FTAA), thereby crippling U.S. leadership in that extension process. Prime Minister Chrétien proved as assiduous as his predecessor in promoting Canadian business interests and attempted to step in to fill the leadership void, negotiating a free trade agreement with Chile and continuing to press for an FTAA when the United States would do neither. However, Canada lacked the economic and political weight internationally, as well as the political will, to provide the leadership necessary to move the hemisphere to an FTAA. As for Mexico, it was in no position to take the policy lead, as it remained mired in crisis following the collapse of its peso, a peasant rebellion in Chiapas, and uncertain leadership at the top. It seemed that the idea that North American integration would lead to a hemispheric agreement had run out of steam. Given this result, it seems all the more important that we understand how it was that NAFTA was achieved.

### The Key Players and Issues
### The Players

Although NAFTA originated in the economic and political conditions and events of the turbulent decade of the 1980s, it was given its particular expression by key individuals in the three countries, and we will want to examine the roles they played in crafting the agreement. While Presidents Salinas and Bush were the principal players driving the initiative, with Prime Minister Mulroney determined to be along for the ride, these heads of government entrusted their project to members of their respective cabinets for execution. For Salinas, this would be Commerce Secretary Jaime Serra, Mexico's trade minister. Serra was cast in the same mold as Salinas, a forty-year-old economist, with a Ph.D. from Yale, who had entered government from academe in 1986, when he joined the Secretaría de Hacienda y Crédito Público (Secretariat of Finance and Public Credit), the Mexican secretariat of finance, and was named secretary of trade and industrial development by Salinas in 1988. While Serra would be the cabinet official in charge, the actual conduct of the negotiations would be in the hands of the chief negotiator, and Salinas named Herminio Blanco Mendoza to this position. Another forty-year-old economist, this time with a Ph.D. from Chicago, Blanco was subsecretary (deputy minister) of foreign trade in Serra's ministry, but he was Salinas's man. To understand this appointment, it is necessary to know how the Mexican *camarilla* system operates.

Miguel Ángel Centeno (1994, 146) described *camarillas* as "a series of vertically and horizontally interlocking, roughly pyramidal, groups" that operate like professional and political networks. A trade specialist close to the Mexican team noted that "rising stars have coteries of followers who move with them from one position to another." By the time such leaders reach top positions in the government, their vast *camarillas* may extend throughout the bureaucracy and the political system. *Camarillas* are based on a patron-client exchange relationship in which the "patron offers a job or increased influence, the client offers loyalty and trust. At some moments the patron may help a client's career, at others the junior partner might provide resources or knowledge critical to the chief" (Centeno 1994, 146).

Blanco was part of Salinas's *camarilla*, and when Salinas placed him in charge of the negotiations, he allowed Blanco to place members of his own *camarilla* in key positions within the NAFTA negotiating team. This had the effect of undercutting Serra and was intended to ensure that Serra would not rise too quickly as a presidential contender. Blanco was seen in government circles as presidential material (*"presidenciable"*) for the *sexenio* beginning in the year 2000, rather than 1994. Since Blanco was a direct protege of Salinas, his *camarilla*'s grip on the negotiations ensured that Salinas would be able to exercise control over the Mexican team. The team would pay a price for the appointment, however, since Blanco was described by another senior negotiator as "chaotic and autocratic," fond of administering public rebukes to senior members of his negotiating team.

In the United States, George Bush would entrust the negotiations to U.S. Trade Representative Carla Hills, the American trade minister. Formerly a cabinet member during Gerald Ford's presidency, when she served as secretary of housing and urban development, Hills was an extremely successful fifty-five-year-old Washington lawyer when Bush tapped her for the U.S. trade representative position in 1989. Although she was not a trade lawyer, Hills had other attributes to recommend her for the position, being described among trade warriors (Dryden 1995, 352) as "fearless, combative, and uncompromising." Her central preoccupation as U.S. trade representative was the faltering Uruguay Round of multilateral trade negotiations (MTN), where she was engaged in a game of chicken with the European Community over agricultural subsidies. Because of her MTN preoccupation, Hills would enter the NAFTA negotiations only reluctantly. However, once she was in, Hills proved to be a tough bargainer, living up to her reputation in Washington as a negotiator who was reluctant to leave the bargaining table while there was even one more concession left to wring from an adversary.

In 1989, Hills appointed Julius (Jules) Katz as deputy U.S. trade representative, with primary responsibility for the Uruguay Round negotiations. The sixty-two-year-old Katz, a former assistant secretary of state who had represented the United States in numerous international trade and commercial negotiations, including the 1965 Auto Pact negotiations with Canada, was, at the time of his appointment as deputy U.S. trade representative, chairman of a large Washington-based lobbying firm, Government Research Corporation.[5] When Bush decided, over Hills's objections, to proceed immediately with Mexico's proposal to negotiate free trade, Hills decided that the negotiations were sufficiently important to warrant the appointment of Katz as chief NAFTA negotiator for the United States, a job he would carry on top of his continuing responsibility for the MTN. Katz was reputed to be one of Washington's most savvy negotiators: "He's a fox and he knows where all the skeletons are buried."[6] However, according to one old Washington hand, Katz could be cantankerous: "He tends to flare up, but he holds no grudges." The upcoming negotiations would sorely test his patience. The appointment of Deputy U.S. Trade Representative Katz as chief negotiator signaled the importance of the NAFTA negotiations to the Bush administration. In contrast, the American side in the Canada-U.S. free trade negotiations had been led by Peter Murphy, a subordinate official in the Office of the U.S. Trade Representative (USTR) roughly comparable in rank to Canada's chief NAFTA negotiator, John Weekes.

With twenty-five years in the foreign service, the forty-seven-year-old Weekes was an accomplished career diplomat who had served most recently as Canada's ambassador to the GATT talks in Geneva. Canadian Deputy Minster of Trade Don Campbell originally had considered acting as chief negotiator himself,[7] but he concluded that this was not practical, in light of his continuing responsibilities in other trade areas. Nor did he want an independent office to be established for the negotiations, with its head as chief negotiator, as had been done for the free trade negotiations between Canada and the United States. Nevertheless, Campbell's decision to choose Canada's chief negotiator from within the foreign service bureaucracy was a reflection of the fact that NAFTA was less important in Ottawa than in either Mexico City or Washington, D.C. This is not to say that Weekes was not a good man for the job, because by all accounts he was. A trade policy specialist, he had moved rapidly up the ranks of the trade ministry through manifest competence, while demonstrating a rare collegiality. Said one observer, "John's style is very smooth, very congenial, very relaxed and controlled, and without apparent artifice."[8] Weekes's easygoing style provided a sharp contrast to Blanco's despotism and Katz's irascibility: a U.S. negotiator trying to convey the level of tension that developed in the final negotiations in the end game at the Watergate Hotel in August 1992 would comment subsequently, Katz "even got mad at John Weekes!"

Overseeing Weekes from the Canadian cabinet table was trade minister Michael Wilson. After more than six years as minister of finance, and the most powerful member of Brian Mulroney's cabinet, Wilson left finance early in 1991 to head up a combined "super ministry" of trade, and industry, science, and technology. He had been a major proponent of the Canada-U.S. FTA and had been the minister at the negotiating table when the final details of the FTA had been thrashed out during a weekend in Washington in October 1987.[9] Wilson had the absolute trust of the prime minister, and in his new trade portfolio he quickly became the primary political force behind the NAFTA negotiations in Ottawa. A former investment dealer, the fifty-three-year-old Wilson was notorious for his love of detail, an affliction that would serve him well when the ministers became deeply involved in the NAFTA end game at the Watergate in August 1992.

These were the key players in the NAFTA story, and they would be responsible for the critical decisions that shaped the negotiations as they unfolded over a fourteen-month period in 1991–92. If we were to look only at them, however, we would miss the bulk of the action, for below the ministers and chief negotiators, countless officials toiled over the often arcane minutia of trade issues, ranging from agriculture to telecommunications, and technical standards to antidumping duties. These issues, drawn largely off the templates provided by the FTA and the MTN, constituted the subject matters of the various working groups that operated under the direction of the chief negotiators and their deputies. And, of course, there were the lawyers, brought into the action early to ensure that the elements of an agreement, as they emerged from the negotiating process, could be captured adequately in the legal text that would eventually become the *North American Free Trade Agreement.*

## The Issues

An adequate understanding of the NAFTA process requires us to provide answers to a number of questions. First and foremost among these is how free trade came to be on the agenda of Mexican-American relations, despite Mexico's traditional wariness over close ties with the United States? To answer this question, we trace the Mexican decision process and locate the free trade initiative within the political economy of events that occurred in the decade preceding Mexico's overture to the United States. Then our attention shifts to an examination of the ways in which the complexities of trilateral negotiations were handled during the period from June 1991 to July 1992. Specifically, we want to know how the parties attempted to move one another along and advance their individual negotiating agendas, and how the process of convergence was managed, and in some instances mismanaged, through trilateral and bilateral negotiations among the three.

NAFTA was concluded through a dramatic negotiating marathon, held at the Watergate Hotel in Washington in August 1992, and a proper understanding of the agreement requires an examination of how the final deal was crafted, including the principal trade-offs that were engineered and how these were influenced by the kinds of pressures under which the key participants operated. Of course, the Watergate end game did not conclude the NAFTA process. The defeat of George Bush by Bill Clinton in the 1992 presidential election ensured that there would be another episode in the NAFTA story, this one centering on the side deals that were negotiated subsequently on labor and the environment. We describe how these deals were put together and examine the dynamics by which the whole package was put through the grinder of congressional ratification. Finally, we cannot leave the NAFTA story without addressing the turmoil that engulfed Mexico in 1994—assassination, economic crisis, and rebellion. While we make no effort to establish a direct connection between the events of 1994 and free trade, we feel obliged to examine these events and to acknowledge that the immediate aftermath of NAFTA brought tragedy to Mexico, leaving a bitter aftertaste to this historic initiative.

These are the central empirical questions, concerning the "how" and "what" of free trade, that we seek to answer through our investigation. The enquiry is driven as well by a number of theoretical questions concerning the "why" of NAFTA developments and dynamics. First, we observe in negotiations a complex pattern of delayed mutual responsiveness among the negotiating parties, and we want to understand why the pattern emerged as it did in the NAFTA negotiations, in the period between June 1991, when the negotiations began formally, and July 1992, when ministers decided that a dramatic change of pace was necessary, and during the Watergate end game.

Second, the NAFTA negotiations were conducted among parties with highly asymmetrical capabilities, and we want to understand why countries as unequal in power and wealth as Mexico, the United States, and Canada would agree to negotiate the creation of a free trade area. In addition, it is necessary to examine these asymmetries to understand why the negotiations produced the specific outcomes that are embodied in the NAFTA text. Finally, because the three parties were also highly differentiated with respect to their political institutions, we want to use these differences to understand why the parties selected their particular strategic approaches to the negotiations, and the consequences of those choices.

## Studying NAFTA

This book is about how NAFTA was negotiated—where the idea came from, how the players came to the table, how the process of negotiation evolved, and how the final bargain was struck. In many ways, writing the book has been akin to investigative reporting. We began with an informant (who, in deference to the Watergate connection, we referred to as our own "deep throat") in the Canadian government who provided us with essential insider's information about the negotiation process, crucial in determining what questions to ask before conducting extensive interviews with the key players. We were able to use the views of the negotiators in each country to tease out further information from their counterparts in the other two countries. We began in Ottawa. Canada has a highly professional civil service tradition, which meant that although nearly everyone we contacted was willing to talk with us, they tended to be highly circumspect in their remarks and were occasionally reluctant to describe certain bargaining episodes in anything but general language. Nevertheless, they gave us the base information we needed to proceed with our interviews in Washington, D.C. Fortunately, the American negotiators were far more forthcoming, if also more self-congratulatory. Many of the U.S. negotiators were political appointees who left with the change in administration in 1992. We interviewed many former U.S. officials in plush offices in prestigious law and lobbying firms in Washington and found them to be willing to speak, not for attribution, but very openly. Interestingly, the Mexican negotiators were, generally, and with notable exceptions, the most self-critical and often the most informative, especially when they appreciated that we knew the Canadian and U.S. versions of what happened in the negotiation process.

There were a number of advantages to conducting interviews in each of the three countries, as well as spreading them out over the course of a number of years. When an interviewee appeared to underestimate our level of knowledge, we were able to move the discussion to a higher level simply by asking more probing questions based on what previous interviewees (especially our Canadian deep throat) had told us. Such questions would often produce a perplexed pause, followed by questioning as to how we had come by this information (we would never reveal a source), and finally an answer that brought us closer to the information we sought. In more than one instance, negotiators would describe their own behavior and that of the other party, and say to us, "I don't know why [my counterpart] did that—you'd have to ask him/her." We would then take the description of the exchange to the counterpart official and ask for confirmation and an explanation. Often, we would discover enormous differences in the perceptions of government officials from the different countries. The result of this detective work is a comprehensive reconstruction of the entire negotiation process that draws on the perspectives of each of the three negotiating teams.

All interviews were conducted on a not-for-attribution basis. Each interviewee received a letter outlining the nature and purpose of the interview and our assurances that their confidentiality would be respected. All interviewees at comparable levels of authority in their respective negotiating teams were asked roughly the same roster of questions, which enabled us to compare and cross-check responses. One (Brian Tomlin) of us conducted most of the Canadian interviews, we jointly conducted many of the U.S. interviews during visits to Washington, and the other (Maxwell Cameron) of us conducted the bulk of the Mexican interviews (in Spanish) during a period as visiting professor at the Colegio de México, as well as in subsequent research visits to Mexico City. The total number of interviews conducted exceeded one hundred and involved working group heads, chief negotiators, their deputies, and cabinet-level officials. Although most of our information on the negotiations came from these interviews, we also relied on the following public press sources, among others, to reconstruct the negotiation process: the *Christian Science Monitor*, the *New York Times*, the *Wall Street Journal*, the *Washington Post*, *Inside US Trade*, *Inside NAFTA*, *Trade News Bulletin*, *Financiero International*, the *Financial Post*, the *Globe and Mail*, the *Toronto Star*, and the *Economist*.

Our reconstruction of the negotiation process provides a historical record for future analysts, and that alone is sufficient justification for the book. However, we are not content merely to describe the negotiations and offer the perspectives of each of the players. Rather, our interest is in drawing the larger lessons for understanding negotiation strategies and processes, and how institutional mechanisms and ratification procedures shape bargaining outcomes. In the next chapter we discuss a wide range of theories of bargaining from which we derived our own expectations and hypotheses during the research.

As co-authors, we approached the problem of bargaining from complementary perspectives. In previous work, one (Tomlin) of us drew on negotiation analysis in an effort to understand the processes of conflict and its resolution, especially around trade issues, and his work focused on Canada-U.S. relations; the other (Cameron) has used analytical models to explore issues in international political economy, and his work focused on Latin America. In this collaborative effort, we integrate these perspectives to provide a synthesis that builds on the strengths of a number of research traditions.

This book adds to the existing literature by providing the first detailed account of the negotiation process from a trinational perspective. George Grayson (1995) offered a good overview of the negotiations but did not provide a detailed account of the process. Maxfield and Shapiro (1998) discussed a number of sectors and attempted to determine who won in which area, but their work was not based on interviews with negotiators nor did it analyze the negotiation process. Hermann von Bertrab (1997) provided a readable and polemical account of the negotiations, but not one that provides a behind-the-scenes view of the negotiation process. Frederick W. Mayer (1998) complemented our work by analyzing the domestic U.S. politics around the NAFTA negotiation and ratification. However, only one chapter is devoted to the NAFTA negotiations themselves, and one to the side-deal negotiations, and the analysis is heavily slanted to a U.S. perspective with little attention to Canadian and Mexican positions. Moreover, the focus of the book is more directly related to the politics of support and opposition to the NAFTA, especially the debate on fast-track and the ratification process.

Others have written extensively on analytical aspects of the NAFTA negotiations without attempting to reconstruct the actual bargaining process (see Pastor and Wise 1994; Cameron 1997; Ros 1994; Helleiner 1993; and Valverde Loya 1997). None of the existing literature uncovers the most interesting controversies and disputes within the NAFTA negotiations that this book describes, including the fights between finance and trade officials in Mexico; the difficulties in wrapping up the negotiations at the Watergate Hotel in August 1992; Mexico's miscalculations in Dallas in February 1992; Canada's problems with the negotiations over Chapter Nineteen provisions and cultural industries; why the Mexican team was so hierarchical, initially placing single working group heads in charge of multiple working groups; how Canada was "railroaded" in the textile negotiations; and Mexico's unconventional tactical gambit to outnegotiate the United States in the automotive sector.

Although our account is firmly rooted in the story of the NAFTA negotiation process, it is more than a narrative. We have embedded our story of the negotiations within a larger analytical framework that draws eclectically on two-level game theory, approaches to bargaining and negotiation, and theories of international political economy. The next chapter shows how we build on and synthesize these approaches.

CHAPTER 2

# Understanding International
# Negotiation

**W**e argue that the NAFTA negotiations were critically shaped by three factors: (1) asymmetries of power between the three states; (2) sharply contrasting domestic political institutions; and (3) differences in the nonagreement alternatives, patience, and risk orientations of the heads of government and their chief negotiators. To understand the NAFTA negotiation, we need to clarify the meaning of these key concepts, and that is the main purpose of this chapter.

"Market power remains the basic prerequisite to gaining concessions," said Canadian trade negotiator Michael Hart (1990, 41), "the more concessions one has to offer, the more concessions one is likely to gain." In 1995 Mexico's gross domestic product (GDP) of $250 billion represented 3.2 percent of the North American economy; Canada's $569 billion economy was 7.3 percent of the total; and the United States, with a GDP of $6,952 billion, accounted for the remaining 89.5 percent (United Nations Development Programme 1998, 182, 204). This meant that a negotiator for the United States could say to counterparts in Mexico and Canada: "You want access to our $7 trillion market, and you offer in exchange access to your $250 and $500 billion markets? You are going to have to pay for that access, and here is what it is going to cost you…" That is the meaning of asymmetry, and we explore how different theorists of international political economy have attempted to theorize the effects of asymmetry on the chances of successfully negotiating international accords.

As we shall see, however, asymmetries of power do not always lead to asymmetrical results. Domestic institutions also play an important role in shaping the negotiation process and outcome. The key link between international negotiations and domestic politics is the ratification process. Any agreement must be ratified domestically, but ratification procedures vary greatly among nations with different political institutions. The United States and Canada had well-established democratic political institutions, presidential and parliamentary, respectively, while Mexico was a semiauthoritarian system in a process of transition toward democracy. We examine "two-level game theory" for hypotheses about how different domestic institutions might influence the negotiation process and outcome. A key insight from this literature is that negotiators representing a country in which the decision-making process is open and decentralized have more credibility when they say, "We would like to offer you concessions, but we are constrained by our domestic interests and institutions."

Finally, as practitioners know, the patience or impatience of the negotiators and their attitudes toward risk play a key role in the negotiation process. Staggering under a massive debt burden and in desperate need of new sources of capital, Mexico's leadership decided it had few attractive alternatives to a comprehensive trade deal with the United States, and they approached the challenge with great impatience; Canada and the United States had an existing agreement, the Canada-U.S. Free Trade Agreement (FTA), and they were more patient during the negotiation process until, in the U.S. case, the very end of the negotiations. The patient and risk-accepting negotiator can more credibly say no and walk away from the table, thereby placing agreement at risk in order to win important concessions. In this chapter, we examine theories of negotiation that help to explain the role played by these factors in the NAFTA.

It is not enough, however, to provide a laundry list of factors that influenced the outcome of the bargaining. If differences in market size and levels of development, contrasting political institutions, and attitudes toward risk of leaders all played a role in the NAFTA negotiations, how can these disparate factors be integrated into a systematic explanation, one that explores linkages among domestic and international levels of analysis? Our argument, in a nutshell, is that negotiators for powerful, self-reliant states tend to be less responsive to weak states than to domestic constituents, while negotiators for weak states—weak in the sense that they are entangled in ties of asymmetrical interdependence with more powerful states—tend to be more responsive to the demands of powerful states than to the demands of domestic constituents. However, asymmetrical power does not necessarily lead to asymmetrical results, because negotiators in weaker (i.e., asymmetrically interdependent) states, nevertheless, may have attractive nonagreement alternatives and a lower discount rate (i.e., they may be more patient). Negotiators with attractive nonagreement alternatives will be more willing to put agreement at risk by withholding concessions in the negotiation process. Finally, centralized and vertical institutions are often a bargaining liability precisely because weak states tend to be less responsive to domestic constituents, whereas divided government can be a major asset.

The following sections present the derivation and rationale for these arguments. Our goal is to clarify key concepts by reviewing their usage and the debates they have occasioned. We begin with asymmetries of power, then discuss two-level games, and finally review theories of negotiation. At the end of the chapter, we synthesize these theories and state our hypotheses more formally. A glossary of the major concepts used in our argument is presented in Appendix A.

## Asymmetries of Power

Stephen Krasner (1985, 3) argued that Third World states, like all states, "are concerned about vulnerability and threat"; they "want power and control as much as wealth" and will seek to change the rules of the game through international negotiations in ways incompatible with the interests of the advanced industrialized countries of the north. In this neorealist perspective (see Appendix A), conflict rather than cooperation is likely to prevail in north-south relations because Third World states have limited national power capabilities and underdeveloped internal social and political systems, and thus they adopt strategies directed at alleviating their vulnerability, particularly by challenging the principles, rules, and norms of existing international regimes or by creating new ones. They favor authoritative allocation of resources rather than market-oriented modes of allocation because authoritative regimes provide more stable and predictable transactions, free from the external shocks and vicissitudes of international markets, and permit resource transfer to the south.

"Perhaps," Krasner wrote, "no country better illustrates the dilemmas of the Third World and their consequences for foreign policy than Mexico." Mexican leaders were "major critics of the existing order," in spite of their country's impressive economic growth. Mexico's high degree of trade concentration with the United States, dependence on U.S. foreign direct investment, and the enormous gap in the size of the two economies made the country vulnerable. Moreover, Mexico's colonial experience, history of conflict with Spain and the United States, revolutionary ideology, cleavage between the elite and masses, and maldistribution of income provided incentives for policy makers to use foreign policy "to resolve tensions inherent in their political situation," and this was reflected in Third World-ism, non-alignment, support for Cuba, and rejection of the General Agreement on Tariffs and Trade (GATT) (Krasner 1985, 55).

In 1990 Krasner published an article in which he discussed the likely effect of the growth of interdependence between the United States and Mexico. He began by noting that realists suggest that "formal cooperation and the creation of new institutions are very difficult tasks when there are great asymmetries of power between two states" (Krasner 1990, 45), and he contrasted this argument with "theorists of interdependence" who believe greater levels of interaction lead to cooperation. An examination of U.S.-Mexico relations over time and in specific issue areas supports the realist interpretation, according to Krasner (1990, 46). Cooperation between the United States and Mexico has only tended to occur in those periods when basic power capabilities were relatively equal; when power capabilities were distributed unequally, the United States has preferred to act unilaterally, and Mexico has been reluctant to enter into agreements that would make it more difficult to adequately manage, or could increase, vulnerability.

Krasner argued that asymmetry inhibits formal cooperation for six reasons: (1) the more powerful state prefers to act unilaterally and not limit itself by formal accords; (2) the weak state will not enter accords that increase its interactions with the more powerful state, which in the long run increase its vulnerability; (3) even if the terms of an accord benefit the weak state, it will still be reluctant to accept because of a fear of how the accord will be implemented in practice; (4) the weak state's leaders will perceive that greater interactions will alter the distribution of material and human resources within the government, and lead to more and more effort to administer the accord; (5) greater levels of exchange will alter the weaker power's cultural identity and autonomy; and (6) multilateralism is more attractive to weak states because it can build coalitions against the stronger powers (Krasner 1990, 48–50).

Krasner used historical evidence from U.S.-Mexico relations, as well as evidence from negotiations in specific issue areas, to support his interpretation. Based on this record, he (1990, 58) concluded that "there have been some commercial accords between the two countries, but the extreme differences in terms of vulnerability make it very improbable that an agreement as broad as the Canada-United States Free Trade Agreement could be reached." Krasner argued that whereas theorists of interdependence suggest that the United States and Mexico should commit themselves to more formal cooperation, asymmetries of power present a basic obstacle to such initiatives. As noted, Krasner's article was published in 1990, the year of Salinas's NAFTA initiative, a year described by Lorenzo Meyer as decisive in the U.S.-Mexico relationship because it represented a "historical turning-point [giro] in the definition of national interests respecting the powerful neighbor to the north" (cited in Dominguez 1998, 30).

Robert Keohane published a paper on interdependence and asymmetrical relationships in the same volume in which Krasner's paper appeared, but his conclusions were less pessimistic. For Keohane, the problem for analysts is to examine how states in asymmetrical situations can achieve cooperation to distribute the costs and benefits of closer interdependence. He proposed three ways asymmetry can affect large and small countries differently: (1) interdependence implies multiple channels of interaction, which weaker countries may be less able to control; (2) interaction among big powers can affect their relations with weaker powers in unintentional ways; and (3) larger powers often have more bargaining chips to bring to the negotiation table (Keohane 1990, 66–67). The question is, do asymmetries of power necessarily lead to asymmetrical negotiation results?

Regarding the first point, Keohane (1990, 69–70) argued that a larger state can typically erect barriers to flows from the outside world—such as drugs or migration—more easily than a small state, and can afford to disregard the negative externalities of its actions. At the same time, such flows often cannot be controlled completely, as drugs and migration exemplify. Thus, even the strong state may be limited in what it can achieve unilaterally. Next, Keohane noted the crisis of multilateralism and the rise of regional blocks. Competitive trade blocks demanding specific rather than diffuse reciprocity could raise costly barriers for excluded nations, and small countries might have to make concessions to gain access to larger countries' markets. This could force countries to join trade blocks, giving up political autonomy and independence, or risk being left out.

Finally, Keohane pointed out that empirical studies of bargaining between large and small countries, including his own earlier work on Canada and the United States with Joseph Nye, indicate that the smaller state often prevails, and he suggested that this can be explained by the intensity of preferences in each government, which is another aspect of asymmetry (Keohane and Nye 1977). Small countries often approach negotiations with a greater concern for the outcome than do larger countries, and throw more resources at achieving their desired result.[1] Thus, the small country is often willing to bear more costs and fight more intensely for its goals. Moreover, states are not, as neorealists suggest, unitary, and large states are often more fragmented than small ones, creating the opportunity for the small country to pursue alliances with groups in the state or society of the larger country. The United States is sensitive typically to internal lobbies and tends to disregard smaller countries, and this creates an advantage for smaller countries bargaining with an astute negotiating strategy.

Keohane's neoliberal institutionalism (see Appendix A) offered a more optimistic view of the prospects for U.S.-Mexico cooperation than did the neorealists writing in the 1980s. The implications of his view for North American integration seemed clear: the Mexicans might seek an agreement with the United States to avoid being left out of the formation of regional trading blocs; they might use clever strategies to prevail in negotiating the terms of the agreement; and they could demand reciprocity for policies that would provide the United States with more than it might expect to achieve through unilateral actions.

Many of the NAFTA scholars who build on Keohane's neoliberal institutionalism find it insufficiently attentive to domestic forces and call for more analysis through the lens of two-level games, an idea that was embraced by Keohane in his 1990 article. Dominguez (1998, 44), for example, argued that analysts of the international system—whether neorealist or neoliberal institutionalist—tend to neglect internal factors. Although neoliberal institutionalists include some domestic factors, they do not capture the complexity of a relationship such as that between Mexico and the United States. Fernández de Castro (1998, 74–75) made a similar point, suggesting that neoliberal institutionalism should incorporate a two-level game perspective in the study of bilateral relationships.

## Two-Level Bargaining

We now turn to the "two-level bargaining" approach, which seeks to go beyond earlier work in international political economy and provide a more integrative view of the links between domestic and international politics. The two-level game approach invites analysts to explore how bargaining in one arena (the international system, in which institutions are typically weak) interacts with bargaining in another (domestic politics, in which institutions are typically stronger). Robert Putnam (1993) argued that most research has focused on the impact of domestic politics on international politics, or vice versa, providing only "partial equilibrium" accounts. He proposed that when national leaders must win ratification (formal or informal) from their constituents for an international agreement, their negotiating behavior reflects the simultaneous imperatives of both a domestic political game and an international game. At the national level, domestic groups pursue their interests by pressuring the government to adopt favorable policies, and politicians seek power by constructing coalitions among these groups. At the international level, national governments seek to maximize their own ability to satisfy domestic pressures, while minimizing the adverse consequences of foreign developments.

Putnam distinguished "Level I bargaining" between countries' negotiators over a tentative agreement, and "Level II bargaining" involving parallel discussions among domestic constituents over ratification of the agreement. He defined the "win-set" for a Level II constituency "as the set of all possible Level I agreements that would 'win'" in an up or down vote (1993, 439). The likelihood of an agreement among Level I negotiators is largely determined by whether Level II win-sets overlap, and this in turn is influenced by the size of the respective win-sets. Based on this simple logic, Putnam developed three major sets of hypotheses about the size of Level II win-sets: Level II preferences and coalitions, Level II institutions, and Level I strategies.

In the first place, Putnam argued that the size of the win-set depends on the distribution of power, preferences, and possible coalitions among Level II constituents. In particular, "the lower cost of 'no-agreement' to constituents, the smaller the win-set" (Putnam 1993, 443). For large countries like the United States, costs of no-agreement are generally lower for most domestic constituents than in smaller, more dependent countries (Putnam 1993, 443). It follows that more self-sufficient states "should make fewer international agreements and drive harder bargains in those that they do make" (Putnam 1993, 444).

This argument is a version of game theoretic models of alternating offers with "outside options." These models suggest that players with greater bargaining power are those who can walk away from the negotiating table without hurting their own interests. However, such models generally assume unitary actors. Putnam (1993, 444), on the other hand, made a more subtle point: when there are heterogeneous interests at stake (e.g., between labor and capital), negotiators cannot assume that the more they bargain for, the better off they are.

The problem arises not just because of differences between domestic expectations and what can be negotiated realistically. There may be "silent allies" in the opposite camp and silent enemies on the home front. Thus, "transnational alignments may emerge, tacit or explicit, in which domestic interests pressure their respective governments to adopt mutually supportive policies." "In such cases," noted Putnam (1993, 445), "domestic divisions may actually improve the prospects for international cooperation."

One strategy for managing domestic divisions is through issue linkages. Often it is possible not to change the preferences of domestic constituents but to create, through international bargaining, new policy options that were previously beyond domestic control. Putnam (1993, 448) referred to issue "linkage at Level I that alters the feasible outcomes at Level II" as "synergistic linkage." Echoing neoliberal institutionalists, he suggested that economic interdependence "multiplies the opportunities for altering domestic coalitions (and thus policy outcomes) by expanding the feasible alternatives in this way—in effect creating political entanglements across national boundaries."

The second line of argument Putnam made is that the size of the win-set depends on Level II political institutions. Although Putnam's arguments are less well developed on this point, the key link between Levels I and II is ratification procedures. He (1993, 449) suggested that "the U.S. separation of powers imposes a tighter constraint on the American win-set than is true in many other countries. This increases the bargaining power of American negotiators, but it also reduces the scope for international cooperation."

Putnam (1993, 450) suggested that "the stronger a state is in terms of autonomy from domestic pressures, the *weaker* its relative bargaining position internationally. For example, diplomats representing an entrenched dictatorship are less able than representatives of a democracy to claim credibly that domestic pressures preclude some disadvantageous deal." Can Level I negotiators manipulate their counterpart's perceptions of their own Level II win-sets? Peter Evans (1993, 400) summarized the results of a collection of empirical studies based on Putnam's framework and found that the manipulation of ratifiability "is *not* an effective strategy, even for those who head authoritarian regimes. Cross-national informational asymmetries are less prevalent than we first supposed, and mis-estimations within domestic polities are more prevalent." In other words, misperceptions of Level II win-sets are common, but Level I negotiators are about as likely to misperceive the likelihood of ratification in their own polity as in their counterpart's. In short, the "informational consequences of national boundaries" should not be exaggerated (Evans 1993, 409).

Does democracy make a difference in the likelihood of reaching an agreement? According to Evans (1993, 400), democracy is not an impediment: "Authoritarian disenfranchisement is associated with small win-sets that are as great an obstacle to agreement as the boisterous pluralism of undisciplined democracies." However, the ability to drive a hard bargain is an analytically different issue. On this point, Evans (1993, 399) noted that the strategy of "tying hands deliberately is infrequently attempted and usually not effective." Adversaries often just do not buy the argument that their opponent's hands are tied, since they know that executives prefer flexibility. Thus, it is ineffective to try to preserve bargaining room by insisting one's hands are tied.

At the same time, however, efforts to highlight "genuine uncertainty with respect to ratifiability seemed more effective than concocting portrayals of the domestic polity" (Evans 1993, 409). Evans agreed with Putnam that the U.S. domestic arena provides a good example of genuine domestic constraints that allow the executive to play soft cop against Congress's hard-cop routine. Since it is difficult to accurately estimate congressional opposition, this strategy is often effective.

Putnam's third line of reasoning is that the size of the win-set depends on the strategies of the Level I negotiators. He (1993, 450) argued that each Level I negotiator has "an unequivocal interest in maximizing the other side's win-set," since the smaller the win-set, the less likely an agreement and the harder the bargaining. At the same time, collusion between negotiators is almost inevitable: "Level I negotiators are often in collusion, since each has an interest in helping the other to get the final deal ratified" (Putnam 1993, 451).

Moreover, as Evans (1993, 405) noted, once negotiations have begun, negotiators have a stake in their successful completion: "The rising cost of no-agreement based on participation in the negotiations themselves creates COG [chief of government] preferences that clearly cannot be reduced to some sum of constituent interests." Thus, negotiators often try to reinforce one another's standing domestically. Such efforts may be considered positive externalities of negotiation, or "transaction benefits" (Putnam 1993, 452). A major transaction benefit of international negotiations is the opportunity to build international support for efforts to restructure domestic state-society relations. As Evans (1993, 400) noted, intractable obstacles to negotiation are likely to be the target of longer-run restructuring. Chief executives have certain advantages in promoting such restructuring. It is harder for domestic opponents to build international support to oppose these restructuring efforts.

Putnam's argument has spawned a burgeoning literature on the interplay between domestic and international negotiations. However, in seeking to integrate domestic and international levels of analysis, some authors overlooked the distinctiveness of these arenas. For example, Andrew Moravcsik, in his introduction to *Double-Edged Diplomacy* (1993, 4), situated the two-level game approach in relation to "existing efforts to link domestic and international politics theoretically." He began by distinguishing between levels of analysis, but in contrast to neorealists, he did not give much weight to the structural distinction between anarchy and hierarchy. Instead, he argued for the need to integrate the two levels of analysis to overcome the limitations of pure "systemic" theories.

Moravcsik explored, and then discarded, the option of treating domestic politics as a residual source of explanation for international affairs. In criticizing this approach, Moravcsik (1993, 14) suggested that "the decision to begin with systemic, as opposed to domestic theory is essentially arbitrary." This contradicts the neorealist emphasis on the structural distinctiveness of domestic and international politics. Neorealists argue that the anarchic nature of the international system compels states to pursue certain objectives regardless of their domestic attributes. Units in an anarchic system are socialized or selected to act competitively, acting to secure their own survival at a minimum and universal domination at a maximum. This is the "self-help" corollary of anarchy. Choosing the level of analysis is not simply a matter for the whim of the investigator.

We agree with neorealists that anarchy makes cooperation more difficult, and this fact must be confronted by any theory that seeks to integrate domestic and international politics. However, we also believe anarchy inhibits cooperation much less than neorealists might suggest. We can think of three reasons why this might be the case: (1) international institutions may help achieve cooperation under anarchy, (2) anarchy may not constrain state preferences and behavior as much as neorealists think, and (3) states may use domestic enforcement mechanisms to lock in agreements reached internationally.

The first argument is the familiar neoliberal assertion of the importance of international institutions. Neoliberal institutionalists see institutions as "intervening variables" between the fundamentals of world politics (anarchy and the distribution of power) and outcomes (cooperation or conflict) (Keohane 1984, 64). In this view, coordination is possible, and conscious institutional innovation may overcome the limits on cooperation imposed by anarchy. To use the language of game theory, international cooperation is modeled as a noncooperative game in which players choose to create enforcement mechanisms that contribute to rendering cooperation self-enforcing. This is the essence of Keohane's argument about the role of hegemons. "Hegemonic leadership," he (1984, 50–51) asserted, "can help to create a pattern of order." It can do so by supporting and maintaining international regimes. However, Keohane argued that hegemons may be more useful to create regimes than they are to maintain them. Regimes may persist and foster cooperation, "even under conditions that would not be sufficiently benign to bring about their creation."

Alexander Wendt articulated the second argument. He showed that the self-help corollary of anarchy is, at best, an institutional by-product and not an essential feature of anarchy. Anarchy, in other words, does not logically or causally compel states to act competitively by imposing an interest in survival or domination. The interests and identities of states are defined through the process of interaction. Thus, "self-help and power politics are socially constructed under anarchy" (Wendt 1992, 395), and as mechanisms for defining the interests of states, they can be transformed through intentional efforts to change egoistic identities into cooperative ones.

The third argument is implicit in the theory of two-level games. States operating in an anarchic system can achieve cooperation by using domestic enforcement mechanisms to "lock in" international agreements to coordinate policies. In this view, chiefs of government coordinate their policies in a noncooperative game at the international level that is implemented in the domestic arena as an enforceable contract between chiefs of government and their constituents to abide by a given set of policies. There is no presumption here that anarchy is in any way diminished by international negotiations, or that states cannot backtrack away from their international obligations. The international bargain is only as strong as the domestic enforcement mechanisms of the weakest player. If we think of this as an extensive form of the prisoner's dilemma game, we can imagine each domestic game as a subgame of a larger extensive game; however, the domestic subgames are enforceable cooperative games, and they lead to a convergence of policies at the international level, enshrined in an international accord.

In the strategy of "locking in" policy change, domestic enforcement will be the cornerstone of any international agreement, and the strength of domestic enforcement will depend on the solidity of domestic institutions, the reliability of ratification procedures, and the chances of successful domestic implementation. States vary in the degree to which they are highly centralized and hierarchical or pluralist with institutionalized checks and balances.

Thus, the value of "double-edged diplomacy" is not merely that it encourages us to consider various levels of analysis simultaneously in our theories, but that it invites us to explore the dynamics that flow from the integration of two structurally different types of bargaining: international bargaining in a world of anarchy and thus weak institutions, and domestic bargaining in a world of hierarchy and thus well-developed institutions. At the same time, it provides us with an opportunity to examine how domestic enforcement mechanisms might be used to create cooperation under anarchy and, thus, how patterns of cooperation reflect the nature of domestic politics as well as international structure.

Before proceeding, let us recapitulate briefly. We began with a structural question. Why would countries as unequal in power and wealth as Mexico, the United States, and Canada agree to negotiate a comprehensive free trade agreement? In searching for an answer to this question, we found the neorealist argument—that asymmetries of power among states inhibit cooperation—to be wanting. Neoliberal institutionalism answers the question by arguing that asymmetry does not necessarily inhibit cooperation because asymmetries of power do not always lead to asymmetrical results. However, neoliberal institutionalists share with neorealists a neglect of domestic politics as a source of explanation for state policies and preferences. The problem is not so much that neoliberal institutionalism is wrong, but that it is incomplete. Two-level game theory is often presented as a natural successor.[2]

Putnam's two-level game approach is more metaphor than theory, and metaphors can be dangerous if they lead to oversimplification. The integration of domestic and international politics should not erase the distinction between the two levels of analysis. We propose to explore the process through which states cooperate under anarchy in spite of massive asymmetries of power and wealth, and without strong international institutions, by locking in domestic reforms negotiated at the international level. Yet none of the theories we examined explicitly link institution-based concession making or withholding to the bargaining process. For models of the negotiation process, we turn to the broader literature on international negotiation.

## Negotiation Process

Following the work of Daniel Druckman (1986; 1993; Druckman and Harris 1990; Druckman et al. 1991), we conceive the negotiation process in terms of complex patterns of delayed mutual responsiveness between the parties, marked by turning points that move them through various stages in the negotiations. In this process, adjustments in negotiating positions are made following a comparative evaluation of the relative positions of the parties on the various negotiating issues, and at a threshold point where the differences in perceived positions are deemed to be sufficient to warrant a response. This *threshold-adjustment model* requires that we look for patterns of mutual responsiveness to understand how parties reach agreements, but it suggests that these patterns are more complex than what is portrayed by simple models of reciprocal behavior in which bargainers respond to their opponent's immediate past move, matching it in both direction and magnitude.

In analyzing the negotiation process using this more complex model, however, we need additional concepts to assist us in understanding when a threshold in positional differences is likely to be reached and lagged adjustments in negotiating positions are likely to occur, including why the various parties to the negotiation might choose to be responsive, or not, at any particular point in the negotiation process. For this purpose, we turn first to the work of David Lax and James Sebenius (1985, 1986), who argued that the alternatives to a negotiated agreement that are available to the parties will exercise a powerful influence over the negotiation process by establishing the limits to a negotiated agreement (Putnam's win-set). Following from this, we argue that the subjective utility of one's nonagreement alternative (i.e., the course of action that one will follow in the event that it is not possible to reach a negotiated agreement) will influence one's perception of a threshold in positional differences, and the adjustments in negotiating positions that will be made in response. Furthermore, these subjective utilities may change during the negotiation process.

To summarize, we conceive negotiation as a process that follows complex patterns in which the nature and timing of the delayed responses of the parties to positional differences are determined by the subjective utility they attach to their nonagreement alternatives at any particular point in the negotiation process. Why this should be the case requires the addition of another layer of conceptual complexity, this one dealing with risk orientation. Lax and Sebenius (1985, 175), in their discussion of the effects of nonagreement alternatives, stated that "the more risk-prone and cost-insensitive a bargainer is, the more attractive a risky, costly alternative to a proffered deal becomes." We would argue the converse, however, based on research conducted by Max Bazerman and associates (Bazerman and Carroll 1987; Neale and Bazerman, 1985): it is the subjective utility attached to nonagreement alternatives that determines risk orientation, and it is this orientation that in turn determines patterns of mutual responsiveness in the negotiation process.

This approach begins with a basic insight drawn from the work of Zeuthen (1930). As described by Neale and Bazerman (1985, 35), Zeuthen conceived negotiation as a series of mutual concessions where each negotiator decides whether to make further concessions based on the relative "risk willingness" of the parties. In the words of Neale and Bazerman, "the less the negotiator is willing to assume a particular level of risk, the more he or she must be willing to concede in order to promote the certainty of a negotiated settlement." Similarly, they referred to the work of Farber and Katz (1979, 58), who suggested that "the more risk-averse party will concede to the more risk-seeking party because of a greater incentive to compromise to avoid the inherent uncertainty of impasse."

Thus, we expect that negotiators' propensities to make threshold adjustments to their negotiating positions as part of the process of delayed mutual responsiveness will be determined by the degree to which they are risk averse. Bazerman and Carroll (1987, 12), drawing on the work of Kahneman and Tversky (1979), suggested that risk orientation will be determined by the way in which the negotiation problem is framed, in particular whether "outcomes are evaluated as gains or losses from an imputed reference point (part of the 'frame' of the problem), and that most individuals are risk averse for potential gains, but risk seeking for potential losses."

In other words, positively framed negotiators perceive outcomes in terms of potential gains, and they will offer concessions in the threshold-adjustment process in order to obtain the sure (risk-averse) outcome available in a negotiated agreement. Following Lax and Sebenius, we define the imputed reference point for the evaluation of gains and losses in terms of the nonagreement alternatives available to the parties to a negotiation. Furthermore, the subjective utility that a party attaches to its nonagreement alternative at any particular point in the negotiation process will determine its willingness to put agreement at risk by withholding concessions in the threshold-adjustment process. A positively framed negotiator will perceive negotiated outcomes in terms of the potential gains they offer over a nonagreement alternative with low subjective utility.

The definition of negotiators' nonagreement alternatives, their evaluation as having more or less subjective utility, and the role of nonagreement alternatives in setting the limits to any negotiated agreement are crucial elements in the threshold-adjustment process of negotiation. The key to understanding these elements lies in the institutional environment within which negotiators operate as they attempt to manage the negotiation process. The domestic political process, to the extent that it determines which groups are able to delay or stop ratification of a negotiated agreement, becomes a crucial part of the negotiators' environment because, among other reasons, it determines the size of the domestic win-set, clarifying negotiators' nonagreement alternatives, and thus affects the risk orientation of the negotiators. Similarly, interagency or bureaucratic actors are likely to have considerable influence in the negotiation process. Often the toughest part of an international negotiation is assembling an agreement that can be sold politically in the domestic and bureaucratic arena. Players will "look ahead and reason backward" from the implementation and ratification stage during negotiations, since they will not negotiate a deal that they are certain cannot be ratified or implemented.

### Integrating the Arguments

We agree with Keohane that asymmetrical power does not necessarily lead to asymmetrical results. Where the weaker state has more attractive nonagreement alternatives than the more powerful state, or a longer shadow of the future, it may avoid asymmetrical outcomes. The intuition here is that the ability to walk away from a deal is the ultimate source of bargaining power. However, we disagree with Keohane's view that a fragmented state can be exploited by the weaker state, and instead side with Putnam's position that authoritarian disenfranchisement may be a disadvantage if it is associated with larger Level II win-sets, and thus less bargaining leverage. As a result, centralized, vertical national political institutions are a bargaining liability, while divided government is a major strategic asset. Indeed, a fragmented state with strong institutions for domestic enforcement of contracts may demand greater concessions from a state that is unified but lacking strong domestic enforcement powers to compensate for the risks of noncompliance.

In contrast to neorealism and neoliberal institutionalism, we build on the two-level game approach to argue that international negotiators for powerful, self-reliant states tend to be less responsive to the demands of weak states than to domestic constituents, while negotiators in weak (i.e., asymmetrically interdependent) states tend to be more responsive to the demands of the more powerful states than to domestic constituents. This proposition also implies a corollary: that international negotiators in weak states can more credibly use their vulnerability to international pressures to impose painful or costly domestic reforms, often implicitly colluding with the more powerful states against domestic constituents.

This proposition is congruent with our earlier arguments concerning the effects of nonagreement alternatives on the process of delayed mutual adjustment in negotiation, and it locates the determination of the subjective utility of nonagreement alternatives in domestic constituencies. Thus, we can say that the smaller the Level II win-set of a party, and the fewer its number of acceptable Level I agreements, the greater the subjective utility it will assign to its nonagreement alternatives.

To link these institution-based arguments about responsiveness and concession making to the negotiation process, we advance the following propositions. The lower the subjective utility that a party to a negotiation assigns to its nonagreement alternative:

- the more it will perceive a negotiated agreement primarily in terms of the gains it offers over the nonagreement alternative;
- the more risk averse it will be to achieve those gains (i.e., it will have a greater desire for the certain outcome of a negotiated agreement);
- the less willing it will be to put agreement at risk by withholding concessions; and
- the more concessions it will offer in the threshold-adjustment process in order to obtain agreement.

Conversely, the higher the subjective utility that a party to a negotiation assigns to its nonagreement alternative:

- the more it will perceive a negotiated agreement primarily in terms of the loss it entails as compared to the nonagreement alternative (which sets the lower value limit that any agreement must offer);
- the more risk seeking it will be to avoid those losses;
- the more willing it will be to put agreement at risk by withholding concessions; and
- the more it will withhold concessions, or offer smaller concessions, in the threshold-adjustment process.

Table 2.1 summarizes our analysis and how it relates to the literature.

Table 2.1 International Political Economy Theories of Asymmetrical Bargaining

| Hypothesis | Neorealism | Neoliberal Institutionalism | Two-Level Game Theory | Integrated Argument |
|---|---|---|---|---|
| Is cooperation likely among asymmetrical players under anarchic conditions? | No. Asymmetry inhibits formal cooperation because (1) powerful states prefer to act unilaterally, unconstrained by formal accords; (2) weak states avoid entanglements with more powerful states that increase vulnerability; (3) weak states fear how the accord will be implemented; (4) weak states fear greater interactions will alter the distribution of material and human resources within the government; (5) they also fear loss of cultural identity and autonomy; and (6) and they prefer multilateral fora where they can build coalitions against the stronger powers. | Yes. Asymmetry does not necessarily inhibit cooperation. Asymmetries of power do not necessarily lead to asymmetrical results because (1) even large states are limited in what they can achieve unilaterally; (2) smaller states often have more intense preferences; and (3) large states are often more fragmented than small ones, creating the opportunity for the small country to pursue transnational alliances. | Yes. Choice of levels of analysis is arbitrary. Little is said about the distinction between domestic and international politics (anarchy vs. hierarchy). | Yes. Anarchy inhibits cooperation, but cooperation can still be achieved by using domestic enforcement mechanisms to "lock in" domestic reforms associated with an international agreement. Asymmetrical power does not necessarily lead to asymmetrical results because weaker governments can have more attractive non agreement alternatives and a longer shadow of the future. |
| Do domestic institutions vitally shape and constrain international bargaining? | No. This view neglects domestic institutions and processes and how they shape policy preferences. Hence the criticism: "vulnerability is what states make of it." | No. This view, like neorealism, takes state preferences as fixed and seeks to explain state policy as a function of international anarchy rather than domestic politics. It does not begin with the assumption that the primary | Yes. International negotiators play across two game boards. Ratification procedures are the key link between domestic and international levels. The size of a country's alternative to agreement depends on (1) the domestic distribu- | Yes. Negotiators for powerful states tend to be less responsive to weak states relative to domestic constituents, and vice versa. |

| Question | | | | |
|---|---|---|---|---|
| *(continued from previous page)* | | actors in international politics are individuals and groups, rather than states, nor does it examine how state institutions represent subsets of domestic society. | tion of power, preferences, and possible coalitions; (2) its domestic institutions; and (3) the strategies of its international negotiators. National political institutions matter, e.g., authoritarian disenfranchisement is associated with smaller win-sets (fragmentation is an asset). | |
| Are there dominant patterns of delayed mutual responsiveness? | No. This view offers a structural theory of *state* preferences (interests defined as power). This is emphatically not a theory of the bargaining process. | No. This view offers an institutional theory of *state* preferences (i.e., a welfare function), but not a theory of the bargaining process. | No. Concession making is determined by the size of win-sets, but the focus is not on how changes in win-sets are linked to responsiveness and concession making in the negotiation process. | Yes. The lower the subjective utility that a party assigns to its nonagreement alternative; (1) the more it will perceive a negotiated agreement primarily in terms of the gains it offers over the nonagreement alternative; (2) the more risk averse it will be to achieve those gains (i.e., it will have a greater desire for the certain outcome of a negotiated agreement); (3) the less willing it will be to put agreement at risk by withholding concessions; and (4) the more concessions it will offer in the |

## Conclusion

To explore the empirical accuracy of these propositions, in the chapters that follow we set out to reconstruct the NAFTA negotiations, focusing on the positions of the three countries at five crucial moments in the bargaining process: the opening rounds in the negotiations that occurred between June 1991 and early 1992; the negotiating "jamboree" that was held in Dallas, Texas, in February 1992; the post-Dallas period; the end game at the Watergate Hotel in August 1992; and the side-deal negotiations on labor and environmental issues. At each of these junctures in our reconstruction, we present a tabular summary of the positions of the three parties on the major issues in the negotiations, to permit the reader to more easily track, with us, the movement of each party as the triumvirate moves toward the eventual agreement. At each juncture, we also present a summary assessment of the state of the hypotheses, in tabular form, to provide a means for the reader to track their development through these crucial episodes in the bargaining process.

Before proceeding with this analysis, however, we first need to present a summary description of the contents of NAFTA, to provide an understanding of the complex issues that were at stake in the negotiations. This we do in the following chapter. In addition, in Chapter 4 we present an explanation of the events that led these improbable "three amigos"[3] to the negotiating table.

# Assessing the NAFTA Bargain

**N**AFTA is a very big deal. The document itself is 1¹/₂ inches thick, consisting of more than one thousand pages of text organized into twenty-two chapters, with numerous annexes, plus supplemental agreements on the environment and labor. Negotiated in the midst of a severe recession, the agreement touched off a major debate in the United States, where the fears of a flood of goods produced with low-cost labor generated widespread attacks from labor organizations, environmentalists, and import-sensitive industries. It was not Americans who stood the greatest chance of dangerous dislocations as a result of the deal, however. NAFTA broke new trade policy ground because it brought Mexico into a trade agreement that originally had been crafted to govern trade relations between two advanced industrial economies. And yet, although Mexico was afforded some latitude in the agreement for adjustment to a liberalized relationship with these more efficient and productive economies, it was the United States that secured for itself not only broad access to the Mexican market, but also a number of safeguards that would permit it to manage the changing trade relationship in its favor.

Table 3.1 provides a view of NAFTA at a glance by simply listing the titles of the document's twenty-two chapters. A majority of them deal with issues or rules that cut across the entire economies of the three countries, while others deal with specific sectors such as energy, agriculture, and telecommunications. This simple listing reveals just how comprehensive the agreement is and why it is an especially big deal for Mexico, applying broad new disciplines and obligations to the Mexican economy. For the United States and

Canada, on the other hand, NAFTA largely represents an extension and modification of the disciplines and obligations already in place for them in their bilateral Free Trade Agreement (FTA).

## The Basics

The first five chapters of the NAFTA document represent the key elements and principles that are the core of any trade agreement—tariffs, related border measures, and the essential General Agreement on Tariffs and Trade (GATT) principles of national treatment and transparency.[1] Chapter Three provides for the elimination of tariffs on goods from NAFTA parties, either immediately or over agreed five-, ten-, or fifteen-year periods in various sectors. The parties may agree to accelerate these tariff phaseouts, but in any case all tariffs are to be eliminated by January 1, 2008. Special treatment for the automotive and textile sectors is also spelled out in annexes to Chapter Three and in Chapter Four. Two bilateral agreements are used to incorporate Mexico into the largely duty-free automotive trade regime that already existed between the United States and Canada. In return, Mexico agreed to eliminate its domestic automotive regime, embodied in the Auto Decrees, in

## Tariffs and Border Measures
## (Chapters Three to Five)
### Key Provisions

- Principles of national treatment and transparency established and extended.
- Tariffs reduced to zero immediately or over a 5-, 10-, or 15-year schedule.
- Rules of origin established to determine if goods are 60% North American made.
- Mexico incorporated into automotive free trade regime: North American vehicular content requirement raised to 62.5%.
- Yarn-forward rule and triple transformation test established for textiles and apparel.
- United States agrees to increase quotas for textiles and nonwool apparel.

### Issues, Controversies, Gains and Losses

- These are routine elements of any trade agreement, but most significant for trade among parties.
- Rules of origin represent a substantial improvement over those prescribed for the FTA in the sense that they are clearer, but their requirements are also more onerous.
- United States pushed increase in content requirement for automobiles from 50% in FTA to 62.5% over strong Canadian objections.
- Rule and test for textiles and apparel intended to afford greater protection to U.S. industry.
- United States refused Canadian requests for an increase in quota for wool suits.

ten years. This requires Mexico to give up the trade balancing (where vehicle imports are linked to Mexican vehicle sales) and domestic parts content requirements of the decrees, and to lift or phase out import quotas on automobiles, trucks, and buses. The percentage of North American content required for vehicles to qualify for preferred NAFTA treatment was increased from 50 percent in the FTA to 62.5 percent in the NAFTA.

Textiles and apparel also are given separate treatment, in another Chapter Three annex and in Chapter Four, reflecting the sensitivity of this issue in the negotiations. While tariffs on textiles and apparel are to be phased out, products must meet special rules-of-origin requirements to qualify for preferential treatment. The "yarn-forward" rule requires North American content in the actual yarn or fibers from which the fabrics in apparel products are made. In addition, a triple transformation test requires that qualifying goods be cut and sewn from fabric made from North American fibers in a NAFTA country. This is a stricter requirement than the double transformation test in the FTA, which granted preferential treatment to foreign fabric that was cut and sewn in the United States or Canada.

Even as tariffs are removed on trade flows among the three countries, rules of origin are used to ensure that only goods actually produced in the participating countries of the regional free trade arrangement qualify for preferential treatment. Goods that are wholly obtained or produced in North America are considered to originate in North America. Goods containing non–North American content, however, must be "substantially transformed" through further processing in a NAFTA country to qualify for duty-free entry. In practice, this means they must undergo a change in tariff classification. Goods containing non–North American content also may be treated as North American if they have sufficient (60 percent) regional value content, as determined by either the transaction value or the net-cost method. The former was employed in the FTA and deducts the value of nonoriginating material from the transaction value of a good (the price paid or payable) before the percentage of North American content is calculated. The latter method was added to the NAFTA and deducts certain ineligible "nonproduction" costs (e.g., promotion and marketing) from the cost of producing a product before North American content is determined.

### Energy: A Mexican Standoff

Chapter Six governs trade in energy and basic petrochemical products. The equivalent chapter in the FTA created a continental free trade zone in energy products and sharply reduced Canada's control over its energy sector. The FTA prohibited the use of minimum import or export price measures and the imposition of export taxes, unless the same tax is applied domestically. In addition, the FTA stipulated that exports could be restricted for reasons of conservation, but the restrictions may not reduce the proportion exported over the previous three years. In other words, if Canada decided to reduce its energy exports to the United States, then Canadian domestic consumption would have to be reduced as well.

Energy is another matter altogether in Mexico, however. The Mexican constitution prohibits foreign ownership in the petroleum sector, and the Mexicans used this prohibition as a shield to limit their obligations under other provisions in the energy chapter. While NAFTA incorporates the FTA provisions of price measures and export taxes (which reflect GATT rights and obligations), Mexico refused to accept the FTA provision on proportional access; any necessary reductions in supplies will not be shared evenly between Mexican and American/Canadian consumers. In addition, the provisions in the chapter do not apply to the exploration and production of oil and natural gas in Mexico, nor is foreign investment permitted in these areas. Investment in services related to Mexico's petrochemical industry also is restricted. Finally, the chapter constrains the ability of parties to use national security as a justification for quantitative restrictions on the import or export of energy products, but Mexico is not bound by these provisions.

---

**Energy
(Chapter Six)
Key Provisions**

- Builds on existing GATT rights and obligations and on provisions of the FTA.
- Prohibits minimum export or import price measures.
- Prohibits export taxes or charges unless the same tax is applied to energy consumed domestically.
- If export restrictions necessary, Mexico does not agree to maintain the proportion exported prior to restrictions.
- Provisions do not apply to oil and gas production in Mexico.
- Foreign investment not permitted in Mexican oil and gas production or petrochemical services industry.
- Mexico not bound by constraints imposed on use of national security to restrict energy exports or imports.

**Issues, Controversies, Gains and Losses**

- Imposes restraints on the kinds of energy policies adopted by Canada and Mexico in the 1970s and 1980s.
- FTA proportionality clause, designed to enhance U.S. energy security, rejected by Mexico.
- Mexican constitutional prohibition against foreign activity in petrochemical sector used to limit obligations.

---

## Agriculture: Waiting for the Multilateral Trade Negotiations

Agricultural trade has long been the *bête noir* of international trade negotiations. Until recently, agriculture was largely excluded from the GATT regime because countries were unable to agree on even minimal disciplines and obligations in the face of intense pressures from farm lobbies. In this climate, it was a considerable accomplishment when Canadian and American negotiators succeeded in including a limited agreement on agriculture in the FTA. By the time the NAFTA negotiations were underway, however, the temperature on agriculture had risen considerably as a result of a pitched battle

**Agriculture
(Chapter Seven)
Key Provisions**

- There are two bilateral agreements between Mexico and each of the United States and Canada, and Canada-U.S. trade is covered by FTA.
- Eliminates tariffs over 10 or 15 years.
- Parties can reimpose temporary snapback tariffs for up to 10 years on certain products.
- Agreed to tariffication of quantitative restrictions on imports.

**Issues, Controversies, Gains and Losses**

- MTN process facilitated major advances in bilateral agreements on disciplines and obligations for agricultural trade.
- Gains and losses varied depending on specific product.
- Parallel multilateral and bilateral negotiations and U.S. producer sensitivities made negotiations difficult.

between the United States and the European Community over the issue that was occurring in the Uruguay Round of multilateral trade negotiations (MTN) in Geneva.

The fact of parallel negotiations at trilateral and multilateral levels, combined with the very different interests that defined pairwise bargaining in the NAFTA, led the three parties to conclude that no trilateral agreement was possible on agriculture. Instead, market access provisions are covered in two bilateral agreements, one between the United States and Mexico and the other between Mexico and Canada. Canada-U.S. agricultural trade was left under the provisions of the FTA, the two countries preferring to address remaining bilateral issues in the MTN. This was not entirely satisfactory to Canadian negotiators, who had hoped to address the harm being done to Canadian producers as a result of U.S. subsidization of grain exports in third markets. However, the Americans were unwilling to agree to disciplines on grain subsidies in a forum that did not include the European Community.

Mexico and the United States agreed to eliminate tariffs on a wide range of agricultural products immediately, with most of the remaining products becoming duty free over a ten-year period. For certain especially sensitive products—corn and beans for Mexico, and sugar and orange juice for the United States—the transition period is fifteen years. Even with these phase-in periods for adjustment, American negotiators, in particular, insisted on additional safeguards against the possibility of a surge of certain Mexican products. For a period of ten years, if imports of these products reach a specified level, the importing party may increase the tariff to its original rate (referred to as a "snapback"). As had occurred in the MTN, the NAFTA parties agreed to convert quantitative restrictions on imports of certain sensitive products into tariff rate equivalents (tariffication). Chapter Seven also contains extensive provisions to ensure that sanitary and phytosanitary (SPS) measures to protect against pests, diseases, and contaminants are used for health reasons and not as nontariff barriers to trade.

## Government Procurement: Incremental Change

Governments have guarded jealously their right to use their purchasing power to support domestic industries, and Mexico and the United States, in particular, approached this issue very cautiously in the trilateral negotiations. Prior to NAFTA, Mexico had refused to become a signatory to the optional GATT Code on Government Procurement. For its part, the United States had the largest procurement market by far and had demonstrated its reluctance to free up this market to any significant degree in the FTA, which offered only modest gains in access for Canada. Both countries moved considerably in 1992.

The procurement provisions of the NAFTA go significantly beyond those of the FTA, to cover new entities and sectors and to include services. In addition, the United States agreed to waive application of its Buy America requirements on purchases covered by the chapter, although its small- and minority-business set-aside requirements remain in place. The threshold amount for purchases of goods and services by covered federal government entities was raised from the FTA level of U.S. $25,000 to $50,000—any purchases above this amount are open for competition—and the threshold for federal government enterprises was set at U.S. $250,000. The inclusion of the latter enterprises was especially significant for Mexico because it permits competitive access to purchases of goods and services by major state-owned energy operators, such as PEMEX (Petroleos Mexicanos) for petroleum and CFE (Comisión Federal de Electricidad) for electricity.

The potential for trilateral controversy over this chapter was never fully realized. Due to confusion over appropriate objectives for a procurement agreement, Canadian negotiators sidelined themselves, allowing primary negotiations to proceed between the United States and Mexico. Faced with the prospect of a bilateral Mexican-American procurement deal, Canada finally got back in the game sufficiently to permit a trilateral agreement.

## Government Procurement
## (Chapter Ten)
### Key Provisions

- Agreement covers entities and sectors, including services, not covered in other agreements.
- Purchases above threshold of U.S. $50,000 for federal government entities are open for competition.
- United States waives Buy America requirements but retains small- and minority-business set-asides.
- Purchases above threshold of U.S. $250,000 for federal government enterprises are open for competition.

### Issues, Controversies, Gains and Losses

- Deal goes significantly beyond FTA provisions.
- Threshold raised from U.S. $25,000 in FTA.
- Gives competitive access to procurement by major state-owned energy enterprises in Mexico.
- Trilateral deal rescued at last moment after Canada brought back in.

### Investment: A Giant Sucking Sound

In constructing the NAFTA chapter on investment, the parties played out a profound irony in the negotiations. A primary Mexican goal in negotiating a North American free trade agreement was to establish conditions that would make Mexico attractive as a destination for badly needed foreign investment. Therefore, the more concessions they made to American demands to eliminate restrictions on foreign investment and establish a wide-open investment market, the better the agreement would be in terms of the principal Mexican goal. In the negotiation process, however, the Mexican strategic posture was to resist U.S. efforts to open their investment market. American negotiators, on the other hand, were acutely aware that a primary vulnerability of NAFTA in the United States stemmed from domestic fears about an outflow of investment to Mexico (the "giant sucking sound" described by Ross Perot in his attacks on NAFTA). Ironically then, while the United States was pushing for a liberalization of the rules on investment and the Mexicans were resisting that liberalization, those positions ran counter to domestic imperatives on this issue.

The result was a far-reaching investment agreement that goes considerably beyond the comparable FTA chapter. First, the prohibition on investment-related performance requirements was strengthened in NAFTA and broadened to include subnational governments. Second, the United States was determined to secure protection for American investors against discriminatory treatment during expropriation. In practice, this meant that compensation for expropriation had to be "prompt, adequate and effective," a U.S. standard developed initially in response to Mexican expropriations of American petroleum interests in the 1930s. This specific language had to be avoided, however, owing to Mexican sensibilities, but the agreement uses equivalent language requiring the parties to pay compensation at fair market value without delay. Finally, the United States wanted to secure Mexico's agreement to include investor-state arbitration in the investment chapter. The significance of this provision lies in the ability it affords foreign investors to take complaints about a breach of obligations by a NAFTA party to an international arbitration body. This is an important departure from traditional practice whereby only states are capable of bringing international legal proceedings.

Overall, the United States was able in the NAFTA to achieve the investment agreement it could not get in the FTA, thanks in part to Mexico's determination to do whatever it took to attract foreign investment. Contrary to U.S. desires, however, the chapter does give Canada and Mexico the right to

---

## Investment
## (Chapter Eleven)
### Key Provisions

- Prohibitions on investment-related performance requirements strengthened and broadened to include subnational governments.
- Protects foreign investors against discriminatory treatment during expropriation.
- Investor-state provisions allow investors to bring complaints about governments to international arbitration.
- Mexican review threshold for direct acquisitions set at U.S. $25 million for 10 years.
- Mexico retains restrictions on foreign investment in petrochemical industries.

### Issues, Controversies, Gains and Losses

- Because of domestic fears about an outflow of investment to Mexico, the better U.S. negotiators did in opening the Mexican investment market, the worse the agreement looked.
- Allowing the United States to force open the Mexican investment market served Mexico's goal of attracting foreign investment.
- Canada convinced Mexico of the need to retain the right to review major direct takeovers.
- Salinas had already unilaterally liberalized Mexico's foreign investment regime in an effort to secure foreign investment.

review direct acquisitions by foreign investors that exceed a threshold amount. Canada retained its FTA right to review major foreign takeovers, above Can$150 million, although acquisitions below this threshold in the oil, gas, and uranium sectors can be reviewed. The Mexican threshold for review was set at U.S. $25 million for a ten-year period, and Mexico retained restrictions on foreign ownership in its petrochemical sector.

### Services: Securing a Beachhead

The significant treatment of services in a trade agreement was undertaken for the first time in the FTA, largely as a result of pressure from key service sector firms in the United States, especially American Express. It was in the Uruguay Round negotiations, however, when the United States pressed hardest for an agreement to open up service markets, and it was the resulting General Agreement on Trade in Services (GATS) that cleared the way for many of the provisions in the service chapter of NAFTA.

Whereas the FTA covered only the providers of commercial services that were explicitly listed in the agreement, the NAFTA chapter applies to all service providers except those that are specifically identified as not covered by the chapter. The latter include telecommunications and financial services (covered in separate NAFTA chapters) and air services (covered in separate bilateral agreements), plus government purchases and subsidies. For all other service industries, the parties agree to treat providers from other

---

**Services
(Chapter Twelve)
Key Provisions**

- National treatment and most-favored-nation principles extended to all service providers except those identified as not covered.
- Prohibits residency requirements.
- Includes land transportation services.

**Issues, Controversies, Gains and Losses**

- Key U.S. agenda item, also pressed in the MTN where a GATS agreement was achieved.
- MTN experience permitted a more comprehensive agreement than was possible in the FTA.
- Transport services had been excluded from the FTA, owing to lobbying by U.S. marine industry and unions.

---

NAFTA countries the same as providers in their own country (national treatment principle), and no less favorably than providers in any other country (most-favored-nation principle). The chapter also prohibits the parties from requiring the establishment of an office, or residency, in the country in order to be eligible to provide a service. Finally, transport services had been excluded from the FTA because of opposition to inclusion from the marine industry and unions. The problem was avoided in the NAFTA by including an annex to the service chapter dealing with land transportation exclusively.

## Telecommunications and Financial Services

Whereas telecommunication services were dealt with in an annex in both the FTA and the GATS, the importance of communication networks in a more fully integrated North American market is recognized in the inclusion of a separate telecommunication chapter in the NAFTA. As with the more general chapter on services, the original FTA commitments are expanded significantly as a result of the progress made in this area in the GATS, which provided the basis for many of the provisions in Chapter Thirteen. Although the operation of public telecommunication networks and services is not covered by the chapter, it does oblige the parties to provide reasonable access to and use of the public network. In addition, radio and television broadcast and cable distributions are not covered by the agreement.

The financial service chapter, too, represented an expansion on the FTA, extending obligations in a limited number of areas to apply to all financial institutions and services, including banking, insurance, and securities, and to subnational governments. The chapter also differs from the FTA in allowing exceptions to the fulfillment of obligations by the parties for "prudential reasons," such as ensuring the stability of the financial system and maintaining the soundness of financial institutions. So, while the scope of the chapter was expanded considerably, so too were the allowable exceptions open to the parties. Finally, whereas FTA dispute settlement provisions did not apply to financial services, the NAFTA provisions are applicable.

As was the case in the FTA negotiations, the United States wanted to secure for American banks the right to establish branches in Canada and Mexico that would be accorded national treatment, allowing them to operate like their Canadian / Mexican counterparts. However, a reciprocal national treatment obligation granted by the United States would not yield the same benefits to Canadian and Mexican banks that might be established in the American market. This was because of the greater regulation of banks in the United States by state governments, and the fact that the American banking system under the Glass-Steagall and McFadden acts was much more decentralized and fragmented than the Canadian or Mexican systems. In the FTA, Canada made concessions to the United States in exchange for a commitment that Canadian banks would be accorded the same national treatment as American banks in the event of future amendments to Glass-Steagall. Since no amendments, and hence no prospect of reciprocal benefit, had been forthcoming, Canada and Mexico agreed in the NAFTA only that they would review market access for financial services if and when U.S. law was amended to permit substantial expansion by banks in the American system. Because each country had a different regime for regulating financial services, the chapter contains a number of country-specific commitments. These are intended to further the aims of transparency and access while at the same time maintaining regulatory diversity and local control over domestic banking systems. Canada and the United States agreed to incorporate their FTA commitments into the NAFTA, and Mexico was given a transitional period in which to phase in rights of establishment for financial service providers from Canada and the United States.

---

### Telecommunications and Financial Services (Chapters Thirteen and Fourteen)

**Key Provisions**

- Obliges parties to provide access to telecommunication networks and services for entities from other NAFTA countries.
- Obligations apply to all financial institutions and services and to subnational governments.
- Exceptions permitted for prudential reasons.
- Dispute settlement provisions apply to financial services.
- Does not provide right of establishment for bank branches.

**Issues, Controversies, Gains and Losses**

- Obligation does not apply to provision of public networks and services.
- Radio and television broadcast and cable distribution not covered.
- Mexico and Canada will review market access for American financial institutions if U.S. Glass-Steagall Act is amended.

---

### Competition Policy: A North American Market?

This chapter did not appear in the FTA, but nevertheless its roots can be traced to that earlier agreement. In 1986–87, Canada had been unsuccessful in its efforts to persuade the United States to negotiate changes in its trade remedy laws governing the application of antidumping and countervailing duties. The former are aimed at dumping, which occurs when goods are sold into an importing market at prices below those prevailing in the home market or at prices below the cost of production. Dumping is actionable (i.e., antidumping duties may be imposed) if it causes or threatens material injury to an industry in the importing country. A countervailing duty is a special duty levied for the purpose of offsetting any subsidy provided to an industry in an exporting market that permits the below-normal pricing of imports and causes or threatens injury to a domestic industry.

Unable to reach any agreement on changes to the American trade remedy regime, Canada and the United States put in place a system of binational panels to adjudicate the propriety of applications of existing national trade remedy laws. They also agreed to continue negotiating for another five to seven years in an effort to develop common rules governing subsidy-countervail and dumping. In those negotiations, which concluded without success, Canada argued that the use of trade remedies is inappropriate in a free trade agreement because they can disrupt the market in the free trade area unnecessarily and can inhibit market integration at the firm level. Antidumping rules, in particular, are inappropriate because they have the potential to penalize business practices that would be normal in a single domestic market but that could attract antidumping duties when goods originate in a foreign market. However, Canadian negotiators argued that these business practices were already governed by the competition policies in place in each country to promote fair competition within the marketplace. A harmonized system of competition policies would be much more appropriate in a free trade area and therefore, should replace the antidumping rules. The Americans did not agree.

---

## Competition Policy
## (Chapter Fifteen)
### Key Provisions

- Provides limited obligations for the operations of monopolies and state enterprises to ensure fair competition.
- Allows negotiations to continue for 5 years on the development of common competition policies among the parties.

### Issues, Controversies, Gains and Losses

- Mexico and Canada failed to persuade United States to substitute competition policy for antidumping rules.

---

In the NAFTA negotiations, Mexico and Canada continued to argue in favor of substituting competition policy for antidumping rules, again to no avail. However, Chapter Fifteen does recognize the importance of competition policy and establishes some limited obligations for the operations of monopolies and state enterprises. Also, following the FTA model, the parties agreed to continue negotiations for an additional five years on the subject of competition policy in a free trade area.

## Intellectual Property: The American Empire

Intellectual property rights was one of the items on the agenda of new trade issues that the United States was advancing very aggressively in the Uruguay Round negotiations. Determined to secure improved protection for the rights of American holders of copyrights and patents, as well as other forms of intellectual property, the United States pressed for an agreement on trade-related aspects of intellectual property rights (TRIPs) in the MTN, and this, plus other international treaties on intellectual property, provided the foundation for the NAFTA chapter. When Canada and the United States were negotiating the FTA, the MTN negotiations were not far advanced, and the United States was unable to convince Canada to break new ground in this area on a bilateral basis. As a result, there was no chapter on intellectual property in the FTA.

However, both Canada and the United States were signatories to the major international treaties on intellectual property, such as the Berne Convention, which defines obligations for countries concerning the treatment of copyright, and both countries had well-developed and relatively similar systems of policies and laws for the treatment of intellectual property. So, even without an FTA base, the two countries were not negotiating something completely new. This, however, was not the case for the Mexicans. Mexico had only a rudimentary domestic legal system dealing with patent and copyright, and the country was not a signatory to the Berne Convention. Thus, the comprehensive requirements for the parties to protect intellectual property rights that were agreed on in Chapter Seventeen represent a considerable new commitment for Mexico.

The chapter requires parties to adhere to the obligations set out in the four major international conventions on intellectual property, including the Berne Convention, and stipulates specific protections for copyright and patent holders, as well as for trademarks and industrial designs. The chapter also prohibits patent infringement through the use of compulsory licensing, a practice followed by both Canada and Mexico to permit the manufacture of generic pharmaceuticals and one that was fiercely opposed by the United

States on behalf of the American pharmaceutical industry. Finally, the principal controversy over this chapter centered not on the elements outlined above, but instead on the aspects of intellectual property that would not be covered by its provisions. In negotiating the FTA, Canada had insisted on and achieved an exemption for Canadian cultural industries. This fight was joined again in the NAFTA and was fought out primarily under the umbrella of the intellectual property negotiations. To the bitter disappointment of U.S. negotiators, the Canadian cultural exemption was preserved in Annex 2106 of the NAFTA, despite the strenuous objections of the powerful American motion picture and recording industries.

---

### Intellectual Property
### (Chapter Seventeen)
### Key Provisions

- This is a key U.S. agenda item, also pressed in the MTN, where a TRIPs agreement was achieved.
- MTN experience permitted a comprehensive agreement, whereas there is no comparable chapter in the FTA.
- Requires adherence to major international conventions and specific legal protections for copyrights, patents, trademarks, and industrial designs.
- Prohibits compulsory licensing.

### Issues, Controversies, Gains and Losses

- Represents comprehensive new commitments for Mexico and requires reforms to its domestic legal system.
- Mexico and Canada cannot use compulsory licensing to promote development of generic pharmaceutical industry.
- Intellectual property obligations do not apply to Canadian cultural industries, which are exempt from NAFTA provisions.

---

## Dispute Settlement: Hobbling the Hegemon

Two chapters in the NAFTA document deal with institutional mechanisms for managing the agreement and for settling disputes. Chapter Twenty creates a number of institutions to oversee the implementation and operation of the agreement and prescribes procedures for the settlement of disputes between the parties. Building on procedures used in the GATT, but going further to reflect changes adopted for the World Trade Organization,

Chapter Twenty establishes a system for the settlement of disputes between the parties by panels composed of national nominees. The parties also agreed to the establishment of the Free Trade Commission, composed of cabinet ministers from each party, which will oversee the work of committees and working groups, as well as a NAFTA secretariat to service the commission and other NAFTA bodies.

The dispute settlement provisions regarding the application of rules on subsidy-countervail and dumping are contained in Chapter Nineteen. The origins of similar provisions in the FTA were described earlier, in the section dealing with the chapter on competition policy. Unable to agree on changes to trade remedy laws dealing with dumping and subsidy-countervail, Canada and the United States instead agreed to create a system of binational panels to adjudicate the propriety of applications of existing national trade remedy laws. This system was carried over into NAFTA Chapter Nineteen to replace each country's judicial review process for countervail and antidumping cases with binational review procedures. Instead of final antidumping and countervail orders being reviewed by the regular courts in each country, any of the three countries can request that they be reviewed by a binational panel composed of two panelists named by each party from an established roster plus a fifth panelist selected by consensus. Panels are empowered to determine on a binding basis whether existing trade laws were applied correctly and fairly. Panels also may be used to determine whether legislative changes in trade remedy laws are consistent with the NAFTA and the GATT. Finally, Chapter Nineteen includes an extraordinary challenge procedure through which a party may secure a review of a panel decision on the grounds that there was gross misconduct on the panel or that it violated a fundamental rule of procedure or exceeded its powers.

The Chapter Nineteen provisions are significant on three counts. First, Mexico did not have in place the same trade remedy system as existed in the United States and Canada, and in particular lacked the legal infrastructure necessary for the claim and appeal process. As a result, at the outset of negotiations, it was not clear that Mexico could even qualify for the application of these dispute settlement provisions. Their inclusion in the final agreement was possible only because Mexico agreed to substantially overhaul its domestic trade law regime to bring it into accordance with those of the United States and Canada. Second, there had been considerable unhappiness in the U.S. Congress over the original inclusion of the binding binational dispute settlement panels in the FTA, and American negotiators suggested, to the immense discomfort of their Canadian counterparts, that there was no guarantee of their continuation in the NAFTA. Finally, when it had been agreed in principle that these provisions might be included in the NAFTA, and that a way might be found to secure their application to Mexico as well, the Americans proposed changes to the extraordinary challenge provisions that very nearly blew the negotiations out of the water. In the end, the FTA language on this issue was left largely unchanged, at Canadian insistence, and Canada and the United States carried their disagreement over into their respective Statements of Administrative Action, interpretive documents that normally accompany the legislation implementing trade agreements.

---

### Dispute Settlement and Institutional Arrangements (Chapters Nineteen and Twenty)
#### Key Provisions

- Maintains the replacement of judicial review by domestic courts of countervailing and antidumping final orders by binational panels.
- Panels empowered to rule whether national trade remedy laws applied correctly, and whether legislative changes are consistent with NAFTA and GATT.
- Applies to general administration of NAFTA and to dispute settlement, except for investor-state and financial service disputes.
- Establishes the Free Trade Commission, composed of cabinet-level officials and a secretariat.

#### Issues, Controversies, Gains and Losses

- Requires substantial reform of Mexican domestic trade law regime.
- Removes potential threat of sunset termination of countervail and antidumping review in FTA.
- United States unsuccessful in efforts to change extraordinary challenge provisions.

---

## Exceptions and Final Provisions

The final two NAFTA chapters deal with (1) exceptions, which are the conditions allowing the three governments to follow policies that are inconsistent with their obligations under the agreement; and (2) the process by which additional members can be added to the agreement. Most of the exceptions are similar to those contained in the GATT and the FTA, and the most controversial of these, that dealing with cultural industries, has already been addressed. The terms and conditions of admission of new members are to be determined by the Free Trade Commission, the cabinet-level body created by the agreement. The Free Trade Commission's decisions are by consensus, suggesting that the three parties must be unanimous in their choice of additional members. On the other hand, Chapter Twenty-two also states that a party may stipulate that the agreement does not apply between itself and an acceding country, suggesting that accession might occur over the objections of one of the original three.

---

### Exceptions and Final Provisions
### (Chapters Twenty-one and Twenty-two)
### Key Provisions

- Canadian cultural industries are exempt from the provisions of the agreement.
- Accession of new members decided by consensus.
- Party may state that the agreement does not apply between itself and an acceding country.

### Issues, Controversies, Gains and Losses

- Is an issue of major conflict between Canada and the United States; the latter maintained that cultural industries are "entertainment" businesses, like any other.
- Combination of consensus and nonapplication creates uncertainty over right of parties to veto new members.

---

The NAFTA represents a reaffirmation, albeit in expanded form, of a trade agreement already in place between the United States and Canada. What was, for Canadian decision makers, a radical policy departure four years earlier had become almost routine trade policy by the time NAFTA was negotiated. For Mexico, however, the agreement remained a bold, even blind, leap of faith. Never before had countries with such disparate levels of economic development merged their economies with so few conditions attached to the merger. Mexican dictator Porfirio Díaz once lamented that Mexico was "so close to the United States and so far from God." For better or worse, Mexico would now be even closer to the United States.

## CHAPTER 4

# Getting to the Table

The decision to seek free trade with the United States was a momentous choice for Mexico, just as it had been for Canada in 1985. Both countries had instituted policy regimes designed to control, or moderate, the effects of American economic and political influence in their affairs. In Mexico's case, however, negative public attitudes toward the United States were more widespread and deeply felt than in Canada, and Mexican policies were far more autarchic. Despite these differences in scale, the two countries traveled remarkably similar paths on their respective journeys from the rejection of explicitly protectionist strategies to the adoption of formal economic integration with the United States.

An examination of Mexico's journey toward North American free trade is important to understand the origins of this fundamental shift in Mexican public policy, one that could not have been anticipated at the outset of the decade of the 1980s; in fact, it was not even considered to be an option by policy analysts as the 1990s approached. As indicated in Chapter 2, neorealists like Stephen Krasner argued that Mexico would not negotiate a bilateral agreement with the United States because this would increase its vulnerability. Even liberal economists saw a comprehensive bilateral agreement as, at best, a remote possibility (Schott 1989). All observers, without exception, were taken aback by Salinas's initiative—no one predicted it. However, the fact that the decision was made at the World Economic Forum in Davos, Switzerland, is extremely suggestive. Mexico's leaders were about to embark on a wholesale transformation of the Mexican domestic economy, and they needed to demonstrate how the new constellation of social forces, patterns of production and trade, and the relationship between state and society would be embedded in a more supportive international environment.

## The Prenegotiation Process

An analysis of the decisions and interactions that occurred on the path toward negotiation—the prenegotiation process—is important to an understanding of the process and outcomes that characterize the negotiations themselves. The dynamics of prenegotiation contribute in important ways to the establishment of the parameters within which negotiations subsequently unfold (Stein 1989, 252). These parameters may change once negotiations are underway, but the initial definition of their scope in the prenegotiation phase can have significant effects on the process and outcomes of negotiation.

Prenegotiation includes the interval between a decision on the part of some or all of the parties to seek negotiations over a set of issues and the formal start of negotiating sessions. In this period, the parties are likely to try to define negotiation parameters and shape the agenda to suit their needs. We must go back further than the actual decision to negotiate, however, to review the factors that led the parties to consider negotiation as a policy option in the first place, since these too may influence the course of the negotiations. Our problem here lies in knowing exactly how far back we should go in the analysis of interactions and events that occurred before the decision to negotiate was made. Prior conditions and relations are undoubtedly important (Saunders 1985), but we need to avoid infinite regress in efforts to explain the negotiation process and its outcomes. To do so, the prenegotiation phase should be defined so as to clearly mark it as a prelude to negotiation and distinguish it from the longer-term pattern of relations among the parties. To accomplish this, we adapted Druckman's threshold-adjustment model of negotiation for application to the prenegotiation process.[1]

As described in Chapter 2, Druckman conceived negotiation in terms of patterns of delayed mutual responsiveness between parties, marked by turning points that move the parties through various stages in the negotiation process. When applied to prenegotiation, the model suggests that the phase be conceived as that period in relations when negotiation is considered, and perhaps adopted, as a policy option by some or all of the parties. The onset of the phase is likely to be marked by a turning point, either a change in relations between the parties or the occurrence of an event or change in conditions experienced by one or more of the parties that prompts a reassessment of alternatives and adds negotiation to the range of options being considered by at least one of the parties. After onset, the prenegotiation phase, like the subsequent negotiations, will unfold as a process marked by turning points that move the parties through various stages of prenegotiation, concluding, if all stages are completed, with the start of formal negotiating sessions.

This framework provides an organizing set of concepts for an examination of the prenegotiation process that will highlight important stages and events as the parties move toward negotiation, or fail to move forward, and behavioral patterns that may be important to an understanding of the subsequent negotiations. Application of the framework to the case-specific details of the NAFTA prenegotiation phase will provide a systematic description of the decision processes and behavior of the three parties during the prenegotiations, as well as the pattern in relations among the three as they moved toward the start of formal negotiations.

## Prenegotiation Stages

Prenegotiation centers on that period in relations among parties when negotiation is considered, and perhaps adopted, as a policy option by some or all of them. We expect that the onset of the prenegotiation process is marked by a turning point, when negotiation is added to the range of options being considered by one or more of the parties. The occurrence of this initial turning point is best understood through a strategic analysis of the effects of the change in events or conditions on the relative array of outcome values of the parties. This approach focuses on the comparison of decisions to negotiate with decisions not to do so in terms of the restructuring of evaluations of different outcomes by one or more of the parties.

For this initial turning point to occur, a problem must be identified: one that results from the change in events or conditions. Therefore, the first stage in the prenegotiation process is problem identification. The onset of this stage is brought about by an event or change in conditions that first, causes a restructuring of the values attached to alternative outcomes by one or more of the parties in a relationship, and second, results in the addition of a negotiated solution to the array of outcomes under consideration by at least one of the parties. The stage is characterized by an assessment of the problem produced by changing events or conditions and a preliminary evaluation of alternative responses that may or may not add negotiation to the range of policy options. If that addition does occur, then a turning point is reached, and the prenegotiation process moves to its second stage.

In the second stage of the prenegotiation phase, the search for options, one of the parties has under active consideration a negotiated solution to the policy problem identified in stage one. The nature of the search for alternative solutions to the problem identified will vary, depending on the complexity of the policy subsystem that is used to deal with the problem and the severity of the constraints the subsystem faces. Less complex subsystems have few decision makers and a simple organizational setting that is closed off from the influences of other policy actors. Constraints on the subsystem are less stringent when the decision-making problem is well defined, information is relatively complete, and time is available. Howlett and Ramesh (1995, 148) stated:

> The complexity of the policy subsystem affects the likelihood of attaining a high level of agreement or opposition to an option within the subsystem. Some options accord with the core values of the subsystem members while others do not, thereby structuring decisions into hard and soft choices. Similarly, the making of decisions is constrained to varying degrees by information and time limitation, as well as the intractability of the problem.

In this model of decision making, less complex and constrained subsystems are more likely to engage in rational searches for alternatives that entail major change than to adopt incremental adjustment strategies. Whether through adjustment or search, in the event that negotiation is chosen as the preferred policy alternative, another turning point in the prenegotiation process is reached.

The third stage of prenegotiation, commitment to negotiation, marks the shift from a consideration of whether to negotiate to what will be negotiated. In this stage, the policy process is still largely directed inward as each party assesses how far it may have to go on the negotiation path. At first, minimalist solutions may be preferred as parties attempt to implement the decision to negotiate incrementally. As a result, this stage probably will be characterized by the consideration of alternative negotiating scenarios, reflecting varying degrees of scope for the potential negotiation, and possibly by successive steps toward increasing commitment to negotiation as a solution to the policy problem.

It is in this third stage of prenegotiation, however, that the focus of policy makers becomes directed more outward, as the preoccupation with internal decision dynamics gives way to increased concern for the other party (or parties) to the policy problem. Druckman's framework emphasizes the monitoring activity that is undertaken by the negotiating parties, especially when attempting to define the scope of the negotiation. Monitoring involves determining the interests of the various parties, including the domestic interests within the principals (i.e., the negotiating parties). Monitoring is undertaken during prenegotiation as well, especially in stages one through three when the primary interest coalitions may have to be constructed within, rather than between, parties. At some point in stage three, however, attention will shift to a consideration of the interests of the other parties to the potential negotiation, particularly because the desire to undertake negotiations (of still undetermined scope) is likely to be made explicit at this stage.

It is the communication of a desire to negotiate from one of the parties to another that marks the turning point to stage four in the prenegotiation process: agreement to negotiate. It is in this stage that the parties must formally commit themselves to pursue a negotiated solution to the policy problem that gave rise to the desire to negotiate in the first place. Their dominant focus in this stage will be directed outward as they attempt to come to terms with the desirability of negotiation as an approach to the problem, while reserving any commitment concerning the scope of the negotiation itself. The achievement of an agreement to proceed with negotiations is the turning point marking the passage to the fifth, and final, stage of the prenegotiation process.

As previously noted, Druckman's model of negotiation conceives the parties to be engaged in complex patterns of mutual responsiveness that move negotiation through a series of turning points. The first stage in his model consists of behavior through which the parties attempt to define the scope of, or agenda for, the negotiation by establishing or altering the parameters within which the exchange and convergence process that characterizes negotiating will occur. In fact, this structuring activity is likely to occur even before formal negotiations begin, as the parties attempt to position themselves for an advantageous start.

It is this activity, intended to influence the scope or agenda of the negotiation, that predominates in the fifth stage of the prenegotiation process: setting the parameters. In this stage, the attention of the parties will remain directed outward in an effort to define the initial scope of the proposed negotiation and to attempt to establish the parameters, whether limited or expansive, for the negotiation process to follow. This stage also provides the parties with an important opportunity to assess the extent of congruence in their respective agendas prior to the formal negotiation. Although the parties may not reach agreement on appropriate parameters in stage five, their agreement to proceed with formal talks means that this final stage of the prenegotiation process will simply merge into the first stage of formal negotiation.

An analysis of the prenegotiation process, using the stages and turning points just outlined, will permit a reconstruction of the sequence of decisions and interactions that lead two or more parties to attempt to negotiate joint solutions on a set of issues. As with Druckman's threshold-adjustment model of the negotiation process, application of this framework of prenegotiation stages will provide order and organization to an analysis of the flow of activities leading up to the formal negotiation. In addition, the concept of turning points serves to focus the analysis on the transition from one stage to another in the process. It also guides the search for the events and conditions that facilitate or impede the movement of the parties through and between the stages of the prenegotiation process.

Druckman argued that the movement of the negotiation process through its various stages is marked by a series of turning points. The achievement of these turning points represents progress from one stage to another, progress that may be impeded by impasse or crisis. Resolution of the impasse or crisis is then necessary before progress to the next stage can occur. This argument can be applied to the prenegotiation process as well, where deadlock in the policy process (impasse) or intensification in the problem that gave rise to the onset of prenegotiation (crisis) may prevent or promote movement through the successive stages toward negotiation. The analysis that follows focuses on the events and conditions that impeded and promoted progress through the turning points of the five stages of prenegotiation on the path to North American free trade.

Druckman asserted that while securing an agreement to negotiate is less problematic between friendly nations seeking to reinforce and extend their relationship, it is more difficult for nations seeking to redefine their relationship. For Mexico, the decision to negotiate free trade represented a basic redefinition of its relationship with the United States, not only because of the long-standing suspicion that marked relations with the United States, but also because of the significant asymmetries in power and interdependence between the two countries. As a result, the Mexican prenegotiation process is longer and more complex than that of either Canada or the United States. For this reason, we begin our analysis with Mexico, linking the prenegotiation progress of the other two parties to that of Mexico at appropriate points.

## The Decision to Negotiate North American Free Trade
### Mexico

The journey toward North American free trade began for Mexico, as it had for Canada, in the punishing recession of 1981–82. In the 1970s Mexico gambled that the price of oil would remain high and interest rates would remain low. The gamble was lost on both counts. The collapse of industrial production and markets in the world's advanced economies resulted in a sharp decline in demand for oil, resulting in a supply glut, with a concomitant drop in price. A sharp increase in interest rates raised Mexico's already substantial debt burden. All of this was very bad news for Mexico, so heavily dependent on oil exports to fuel its economy and particularly to finance its foreign debt.

*Stage One: Problem Identification*

The recession and the collapse of oil prices decimated the Mexican economy and brought the country to the brink of default on its foreign debt. Mexico's fiscal deficit had more than doubled between 1978 and 1982, financed largely by expansionary monetary and credit policies. The growing deficit in turn contributed to rising inflation, larger current account deficits, loss of international reserves, and increased indebtedness. After riding high for a decade on oil, the economy, with its highly protected domestic market, was in deep trouble. On August 13, 1982—"Black Friday"—Mexico's banks were closed by government edict. The Mexican government was forced to turn to the International Monetary Fund (IMF) for help, and in late 1982, Mexico successfully negotiated an IMF loan to address the foreign debt problem. In the bargain, however, they were forced to accept the IMF structural adjustment prescription for the Mexican economy, which included reduced public spending, tax increases, and tighter monetary policy.

This economic crisis triggered the start of a prolonged policy shift by Mexican authorities as they attempted to deal with the profoundly changed economic world that emerged from the global recession. The shift was begun under the administration of Miguel de la Madrid Hurtado, who assumed the Mexican presidency in December 1982, and was led by the man he chose as his secretary of planning and budget, Carlos Salinas. Together, de la Madrid and Salinas began the process of liberalizing the Mexican economy—dismantling regulatory regimes, opening markets, removing restrictions on foreign investment, and privatizing state enterprises. The measures were insufficient, however, as oil prices deteriorated farther and the Mexican debt crisis deepened. In 1985, additional funds were supplied to the major debtor nations, including Mexico, under the Baker Plan (proposed by U.S. Treasury Secretary James Baker), but in exchange Mexico was required to intensify its adjustment processes and speed up the opening of its markets.

As part of the latter initiative, Mexico sought membership in the General Agreement on Tariffs and Trade (GATT) in 1986. This action represented a reversal of a previous Mexican decision on GATT membership. Mexico originally had applied for membership in the GATT in December 1978 and had negotiated successfully a draft protocol of accession by early 1979. President López Portillo allowed his cabinet official responsible for the Secretariat of Trade and Industrial Development (SECOFI), Jorge de la Vega Domínguez, and his deputies, Héctor Hernández Cervantes (undersecretary of SECOFI) and Abel Garrido (director of international negotiations, SECOFI), to negotiate a protocol of accession that in the words of the president, was "the best of the protocols that might have been obtained" (Story 1986, 138). The protocol provided a twelve-year transition period, allowed export subsidies and import controls, gave permission to use tax incentives to promote industries, permitted protectionist policies in agriculture, and let Mexico ignore GATT codes on nontariff barriers that conflicted with Mexican law (Grayson 1984, 124).

In spite of a generous protocol of accession, a number of factors contributed to López Portillo's decision not to join the GATT. First, Mexico was confident that oil income would provide the wherewithal to pursue a statist strategy to promote its local industries. Second, the president allowed an unprecedented public debate on whether to join the GATT in which opponents of the GATT were more forceful in their views than were advocates. Even within the López Portillo cabinet there was dissent. Foreign Minister Jorge Castañeda and his officials emphasized the dangers posed by GATT to Mexico's sovereignty, stressing the influence of powerful and wealthy countries within the GATT and arguing that Mexico should persist in supporting other developing countries instead. In this view they were supported by the National College of Economists and other prominent members of the intellectual elite.

"After receiving various contradictory opinions," said López Portillo on March 18, 1979, "I have resolved that it is not the opportune moment" to join the GATT. The date of his decision was significant—it was the forty-second anniversary of the nationalization of the oil industry. Respecting tradition, advocates and adversaries closed ranks behind the president (Grayson 1984, 133). López Portillo's decision was not final, however, and as Michael Hart (1990, 33) put it, "[t]wo years later the roof fell in." When oil prices began to decline in the early 1980s and interest rates shot up, Mexico found itself vulnerable to U.S. trade remedy actions at a time when it needed to generate hard currency through nonoil exports. In 1985 Mexico "unilaterally declared commercial disarmament by initiating a massive reform of its trade regime and re-applying for GATT membership" (Hart 1990, 34).

In August 1985, Héctor Hernández Cervantes, now the secretary of trade, met with members of the Mexican Congress to outline the government's trade strategy. In spite of the bruising experience of 1979, he was more convinced than ever that Mexico had to join the GATT. Opposition among small and medium-sized businesses (represented by the powerful Cámara Nacional de la Industria de la Transformación [CANACINTRA]) remained strong, but business support for the GATT was growing in chambers of commerce across the country. And this time, the secretary of trade had the determined backing of the president. Knowing that there would be fervent opposition from trade unions, left-wing political parties, and factions within the Institutional Revolutionary Party (PRI), de la Madrid decided against holding a public consultation on the decision. But he made it clear that low oil prices had contributed to a huge (U.S. $98 million) foreign debt, and Mexico needed an alternative source of foreign exchange.

The terms of the 1986 protocol reflected Mexico's loss of bargaining power. The protocol, approved on July 15 by over two-thirds of the ninety-one GATT members, represented a major step down for Mexico, which agreed to a wide range of concessions that it had not accepted in 1979. Viewed against the backdrop of this previous rejection of membership, the 1986 GATT accession decision can be seen as a turning point in the Mexican prenegotiation process: key decision makers, confronted with a profound economic crisis, assessed the problem and concluded that in response Mexico would have to consider negotiating a reduction in its barriers to international trade. This did not mean free trade with the United States, however. That option for Mexico would take some further time to surface.

*Stage Two: Search for Options*
As Mexico proceeded with the negotiations that would result in its accession to the GATT in August 1986, the de la Madrid administration was turning its attention to its most important trading partner. In 1987, the United States and Mexico signed the *Framework Understanding on Trade and Investment*, which identified negotiating agendas in a number of areas between the two countries. These included key bilateral trade sectors such as agriculture, steel, and textiles, as well as issues that the United States was seeking to address through the GATT Uruguay Round of multilateral negotiations, such as intellectual property and investment. Trade liberalization received an additional boost in 1988 when Carlos Salinas was elected president. Salinas accelerated initiatives to open up the Mexican economy, reducing tariffs and restrictions on imports, mainly quotas. By 1989, Mexico's average weighted tariff was 6.2 percent, and 96 percent of Mexican imports were free of quotas.

However, in 1988, Salinas was thinking liberalization, not bilateral free trade: "I am not in favor of such a proposal," he said. "I believe that through the GATT we have a multilateral way to deal with our neighbors. There is such a different economic level between the United States and Mexico that I don't believe such a common market would provide an advantage to either country."[2]

Two years before his government's decision in 1985 to pursue negotiations with the United States, Canadian Prime Minister Brian Mulroney also had declared his opposition to bilateral free trade. In this, and a number of other important respects, the paths taken to free trade with the United States by Mexico and Canada were remarkably similar. For example, in May 1989, less than a year before taking its free trade initiative, the Salinas government announced a sweeping liberalization of its foreign investment regulations. It revoked measures that prevented majority foreign ownership and opened to foreign investment some areas that previously had been off limits altogether. Canada also unilaterally had liberalized its foreign investment regime in the run-up to its free trade initiative. In giving away such important bargaining chips before entering free trade negotiations, each country was demonstrating an incrementalist and fragmented approach to policy change: not having yet arrived at a decision to seek negotiations, neither government was concerned to withhold its investment chips for strategic negotiating advantage later.

Nevertheless, as Mexico proceeded with its major multilateral liberalization under the auspices of the GATT, bilateral trade negotiations with the United States also were moving forward. The 1987 framework agreement with the Americans served as an umbrella for working group negotiations during 1989 on steel, intellectual property, and textiles, and in August 1989, the two parties agreed to accelerate the pace of these negotiations, although under the auspices of the Uruguay Round. At this stage then, Mexican-American trade negotiations still were framed within the context of Mexico's general shift in the direction of multilateral liberalization. This would change, however, during a meeting between Salinas and U.S. President George Bush in Washington in the autumn of 1989.

Bilateral negotiations under the broader framework talks between the two countries had produced a number of agreements—on textiles, steel, beer and wine, and (outside the framework) civil aviation—in time for a summit meeting between Bush and Salinas on October 3, 1989. Mexico also agreed to provide increased intellectual property protection for U.S. corporate patents and to eliminate a 40 percent tax on the export of capital. For its part, the United States agreed to major increases in the quotas granted to Mexico for exports of steel and textiles to the American market. More importantly, the two presidents agreed to initiate longer-term comprehensive talks on market access and trade and investment facilitation in specific sectors—in other words, sectoral free trade arrangements. The plan called for the identification of specific sectors by the following month, with sectoral negotiations scheduled for completion by July 1990. Salinas indicated his designs were on textiles, steel, and agriculture, stating, "The permanence of Mexico's economic opening depends on our having reciprocity in other markets, which is why it is so important to have an agreement by sectors with the United States."[3] In response to this further Mexican step in the direction of liberalization, the United States was careful not to push too hard. Although American trade officials are generally not enthusiastic about sectoral arrangements, they were prepared to sit down with the Mexicans on the issue and were careful not to suggest that it would necessarily lead to any more comprehensive arrangement. An administration trade official commented, "What we have is a series of negotiations in specific product sectors, which, of course, could develop their own momentum, but any free-trade agreement between the two countries is a long way off, if ever."[4]

In its decision to initiate sectoral free trade negotiations with the United

States, Mexico followed almost exactly the path to free trade that had been traveled by Canada earlier in the decade. In August 1983, Canada too had announced its intention to enter into sectoral free trade negotiations with the United States as a means to secure access to its major market and to adequate supplies of U.S. investment dollars. And like Canada, Mexico would find that this half step along the free trade path was not the solution to its policy problem, because complementary sectors could not be identified. Nevertheless, with sectoral free trade identified as the preferred Mexican policy option, another turning point in the prenegotiation was reached, and the process entered its next stage.

*Stage Three: Commitment to Negotiation*
Mexico's decision to pursue sectoral free trade and the United States's willingness to enter into sectoral negotiations moved the prenegotiation process into its third stage as the two parties moved toward a commitment to negotiate. In the aftermath of the Washington summit, U.S. Commerce Secretary Robert Mosbacher revealed that Mexico and the United States already had held informal discussions on the subject of a comprehensive free trade agreement. Predicting that the two eventually would negotiate an agreement similar to that between the United States and Canada, Mosbacher told the Senate Banking Committee, "We should not try to push them too fast, too hard, but they are interested, extremely interested, in moving toward this— they want to take it a step at a time."[5] Subsequently, Mosbacher's interest in a bilateral free trade agreement would be instrumental in determining the U.S. response to Mexico's next step down the free trade path. That step would be taken at the 1990 meeting of the World Economic Forum in the ski resort of Davos, Switzerland.

The forum, the brainchild of Klaus Schwab, a Swiss professor of business administration, began in 1971 with a gathering of the chief executives of prominent European firms to discuss business strategies in the international marketplace. By the 1990s, the forum boasted a membership of one-thousand leading global companies, and its annual week-long meeting in Davos had become the place to be, not only for chief executives, but also for government leaders, high-ranking officials from intergovernmental and nongovernmental organizations, and naturally, the media. Its original business-economic focus had been broadened substantially to include presentations on such diverse topics as demographics, medicine, and war. It also had gained a reputation for diplomatic drama. In 1988, the prime ministers of Greece and Turkey stepped back from the brink of conflict and signed the "Davos Declaration" at the annual meeting, and in 1994 Israeli Foreign Minister Shimon Peres and Palestine Liberation Organization (PLO) Chairman Yasser Arafat reached a draft peace agreement at Davos.

While there was no similar dramatic breakthrough at the annual gathering in January 1990, an article in the *Economist* described the meeting as "a celebration of the great events in Eastern Europe," adding, "Sheer numbers of statesmen begat still more statesmen, until at one moment during the Davos weekend there were 70 ministers, prime ministers and heads of state among the delegates at the bunker-like conference center."[6] Among them were Mexican President Carlos Salinas and Secretary of Trade and Industrial Development Jaime Serra.

The two, along with other members of the Salinas cabinet plus Mexican business leaders, had left Mexico on January 25 for a nine-day mission to Europe, which included stops in Britain, Belgium, and Germany, as well as Switzerland, and meetings with fourteen heads of state. The trip had been planned in July 1989, a date of some significance because in that month Mexico's debt negotiators reached an agreement with the advisory committee of their creditor banks on terms for rescheduling Mexican debt. There was still a need, however, to address the other key dimension of Mexico's capital equation, namely the requirement for increased amounts of foreign investment to finance Mexican industrial development. The Salinas mission to Europe was intended originally to raise Mexico's profile as an investment destination. Not only was foreign investment critically important to the country's prospects for economic growth, but tracking by the Bank of Mexico (Mexico's central bank) during 1989 revealed that investment flows were substantially below government expectations. The dramatic changes in Europe lent the mission an additional sense of urgency, however, because by the time the Mexicans arrived in January 1990, they faced stiff new competition for European capital from the reforming countries of Eastern Europe.

With Europe's gaze directed east, the Mexicans found it difficult to attract investor interest. As one senior member of the Salinas cabinet put it, "Mexico was simply not a player, and we noticed that in Davos, that we were not attractive enough." Throughout a series of meetings at the Swiss resort, the Mexicans were unable to generate any enthusiasm among the Europeans about the attractions of Mexico as an investment destination. Given Mexico's enormous need for private investment, the message received at Davos profoundly discouraged the Mexicans. If foreign investment continued to lag, Mexico would be forced to raise domestic interest rates to attract capital, and this would increase the government's already heavy debt burden. For Mexico to meet its requirements for foreign capital, another way would have to be found to make the Mexican investment environment more attractive. Salinas and Serra realized in Davos that the idea they had been considering for several months—the establishment of a bilateral free trade area with the United States—offered a way to make Mexico a more attractive site for foreign investment. They also realized that the negotiation of NAFTA would provide an opportunity to strengthen relations between the Mexican government and the private sector. A prominent businessman, Juan Gallardo Thurlow, was named to preside over the Business Coordinating Council for Foreign Trade (Coordinadora de Organismos Empresariales de Comercio Exterior [COECE]), which would rally Mexican business behind the idea of free trade negotiations with the United States.[7] Thus did the shift in Mexican preferences from sectoral to comprehensive free trade occur.[8]

U.S. Trade Representative Carla Hills was another of those in attendance at Davos. Seizing the opportunity to probe the idea further, Salinas and Serra met with Hills and expressed their interest in the possibility of negotiating a bilateral free trade agreement. Hills, while properly noncommittal, agreed to float the idea in Washington. The probe launched, Salinas returned to Mexico on February 4, 1990, aboard a trans-Atlantic red-eye flight that arrived just hours before the president was due to sign the debt rescheduling agreement (the Brady Plan, named for U.S. Treasury Secretary Nicholas Brady) that had been negotiated the previous July. As for trade, there was some irony in the fact that the overture to Europe planned by the Mexicans in July 1989 proved, little more than six months later, to be the genesis of North American free trade.

The initiative taken, Carlos Salinas did not waste time reflecting on the idea. "Around the beginning of February 1990, Salinas called George Bush and proposed the free-trade pact. The President and his close friend, Secretary of State James Baker, immediately accepted the idea, viewing it as a grand chance to stabilize Mexico as a free-market, democratic nation, while providing trade expansion for American exporters" (Dryden 1995, 369). The free trade proposal subsequently came in writing from Salinas in early March. Mexico's decision, finally, to commit itself to the pursuit of bilateral free trade negotiations with the United States marked the turning point to the next stage in the prenegotiation process.

*Stage Four: Agreement to Negotiate*
This stage would center on events in the United States, as various elements in the American system of divided powers took up the issue. First, however, Canada would be caught up in the prenegotiation process, as the Mexican decision created a problem to which Canadian policy makers were forced to respond.

## Canada

Canada was a reluctant partner at the start of the negotiations to create NAFTA. Canadian trade and investment ties with Latin America and Mexico have been weak historically, providing little commercial incentive to enter into free trade negotiations with the Mexicans. In addition, the government was not eager to reopen the bitter national debate that had occurred over Canada's bilateral free trade deal with the United States. In the end, however, Canada entered NAFTA because key policy makers believed it had little choice if it was to protect its interests in the North American market.

*Stage One: Problem Identification*

In March 1990, Canadian Prime Minister Brian Mulroney was en route to Mexico for a state visit when he received an in-flight telephone call from Derek Burney, Canada's ambassador to Washington. U.S. Secretary of State James Baker had just called Burney to say that the United States had received a formal request from Mexican President Salinas for bilateral free trade negotiations with the United States. Salinas planned to inform Mulroney during his Mexican visit. Burney and Mulroney agreed that the prime minister would simply ask to be kept informed of developments while Canada examined the issue internally. Mulroney, as usual, went further in Mexico City, emphasizing that Canada already had its free trade agreement with the United States in place, implying that Mexican-American negotiations would not be of direct interest to Canada (a position that subsequently would lead the Mexicans to suspect Canadian motives). Nevertheless, Mexico's action clearly was going to require a decision (or nondecision) by Canada, and the addition of prospective trilateral negotiations to the Canadian menu of trade policy options provided the turning point to move Canada's prenegotiation phase to its second stage.

*Stage Two: Search for Options*

To conduct the internal Canadian examination, a small task force was created within the Department of External Affairs to address the implications of a bilateral Mexico-U.S. free trade agreement for Canada. The task force secured impact analyses from a variety of other government departments, including departments of energy, mines and resources, agriculture, and industry, science, and technology. The agriculture and textile sectors were the only ones singled out as specific problem areas. In general, the impact analyses indicated that Mexican access to the Canadian market posed no threat, although in the longer term Mexico would provide moderately serious competition for Canada in the U.S. market. While there was little cause for concern here, however, there was also little at stake for Canada in the Mexican market. Of far greater significance to Canada was the access it had already secured to its major market through the bilateral Free Trade Agreement (FTA) with the United States.

By the end of April 1990, the task force had prepared a draft memorandum on the issue, ready for submission to the cabinet. First, however, the draft was circulated to other government departments for comment, and the Department of Industry, Science and Technology identified a potentially serious problem for Canada in a Mexican-American deal. Department of Industry, Science and Technology officials pointed out that the U.S. presence in two bilateral free trade agreements on the continent—referred to as the hub-and-spoke model—could lead to a diversion of investment dollars to the United States as the only platform from which to serve all three North American markets.[9]

The Department of External Affairs memorandum was taken to the cabinet on May 22, 1990, by Minister for International Trade John Crosbie. The cabinet document sketched the impact of a Mexico-U.S. FTA on various Canadian stakeholders and sectors and put forward two options for cabinet consideration. The first option, tantamount to doing nothing, called for Canada to simply monitor developments. The second, recommended by the task force, called for the government to seek agreement from the United States and Mexico that Canada be provided an opportunity to participate in exploratory discussions, without prejudice to any subsequent Canadian decision on whether to join the negotiations. The cabinet adopted the second option and directed the task force to prepare a fuller report on the impact of a Mexico-U.S. free trade agreement on Canada. In effect, the government wanted to keep its options open while it studied the issue further. As the task force continued its work during the summer of 1990, it became clear to Canadian officials that Mexico and the United States were committed to negotiations, and pressure mounted for a Canadian decision.

A second memorandum to the cabinet was considered by the Priorities and Planning Committee of the cabinet on August 29, 1990. This time, four options were presented for consideration: continue to monitor developments, seek observer status at bilateral Mexican-American negotiations, negotiate a bilateral Canada-Mexico free trade agreement, or join Mexico and the United States in trilateral negotiations. The task force recommended the fourth option because it addressed all of Canada's interests in the issue: it offset the danger of investment diversion in a hub-and-spoke model, it prevented Mexico from getting preferential access to the U.S. market through a better free trade agreement than the Canada-U.S. FTA, and it offered access to the growing Mexican market. With the presentation of two negotiation options, bilateral and trilateral, to the cabinet, the prenegotiation process moved to its third stage during which Canada would have to consider exactly what should be negotiated.

*Stage Three: Commitment to Negotiation*
Although Crosbie and his Department of External Affairs officials on the task force now favored the trilateral option, the powerful Department of Fi-

nance had strong reservations, and the key ministers who sat on the Priorities and Planning Committee paid careful attention. Political considerations were also important for ministers. They realized that a trilateral agreement would likely emerge in time to provide a contentious issue for the next federal election. While the Mulroney government had won the so-called "free trade election" in 1988, defeating the opposition Liberals who campaigned on a platform opposing the Canada-U.S. FTA, the economic times had begun to turn by 1990, as the approaching recession gathered momentum in Canada. As a result, few ministers relished another defense of free trade in the new circumstances. On the other hand, the government was floundering in the aftermath of the failure of the Meech Lake Accord, a major initiative to satisfy Quebec's demands for constitutional reform. Blame for the failure, and the national malaise that resulted, was being pinned squarely on Brian Mulroney and his Conservative government. What was needed was a significant policy initiative around which government forces could rally. Crosbie argued that free trade was an issue they had won on in 1988 and on which they again could join political battle with the opposition parties. In the end, ministerial combativeness, coupled with the reality that Canada could not prevent a bilateral Mexico-U.S. deal and could influence the terms of Mexico's access to the North American market most directly by being at the table, led to the decision to seek participation in the negotiations.

In summary, Canada's decision to join the trilateral negotiations was prompted by a concern that a separate bilateral Mexico-U.S. free trade agreement would give the United States an advantage in attracting investment as the only country with access to a continental market, and might result in preferred access to the American market for Mexico. Once the negotiations were underway, Canada's principal objective would become the negotiation of improvements to the Canada-U.S. FTA in areas such as rules of origin, government procurement, financial services, and dispute settlement provisions concerning the application of countervailing and antidumping duties. In the decision to seek participation and in the negotiations themselves, access to the Mexican market was a secondary, although not completely unimportant, consideration for Canada.

The Canadian decision to join the trilateral talks marked a turning point that moved the prenegotiation process to its next stage. Agreement to negotiate would require the concurrence of Mexico and the United States, however, and neither would be won easily.

*Stage Four: Agreement to Negotiate*
In the matter of relative disinterest, Mexico eventually would repay in full the Canadian compliment. The Mexicans, after all, had requested free trade negotiations with the United States and had little commercial interest in

Canada. Nevertheless, when Canada sought agreement in May for an opportunity to participate without prejudice in exploratory discussions while they weighed their options, the Mexicans did not refuse. In fact, in June, Jaime Serra met with John Crosbie in Montreal, and he assured the Canadians that they would have a seat at the table if they wished.[10] Crosbie rebuffed Serra's initiative, however, stating that the government still needed to consult with the provinces, plus business and labor organizations. He also indicated that the decision for Canada hinged on whether or not it needed to be at the table to prevent Mexican competition from eroding gains made by Canada in the FTA.[11] Thus spurned, Mexico's stance shifted to opposition to trilateral talks during the summer of 1990. As the Canadians played Hamlet, wondering whether to be or not to be (at the table), Mexican officials became wary about Canada's indecision, suspecting (rightly) that the Canadians could find few commercial incentives to enter into free trade negotiations with the Mexicans. After all, Brian Mulroney had indicated at the outset, in March 1990, that a Mexican-American negotiation would not be of direct interest to Canada. With the Canadian conversion in September, the Mexicans suspected that the Canadians had discovered a negative reason to be at the table, namely to play the role of spoiler and prevent Mexico from getting the same access to the American market that Canada enjoyed. Mexico worried that Canadian participation would cause delays; that Canada might be a deal spoiler, walking away from the negotiations or failing to pass the implementing legislation; and indeed, that a change in government could lead to a disruption in the negotiations. As a result, the Mexicans decided to oppose Canadian participation in the talks.

Having taken six months to convince themselves that it was in their interest to be at the table, the Canadians were surprised, and more than a little frustrated, to discover that their belated interest in Mexico was unrequited. They got little more than expressions of sympathy from American officials over their plight. Mexico's interest was in the American market, after all, and a bilateral negotiation with the Mexicans would provide the United States with the most direct path to its regional economic goals, free of the confounding effects that might result from the addition of a third party to the negotiation equation. While they expressed sympathy for the Canadians over their dilemma, U.S. officials maintained that this was a Mexican decision and there was little they could do to help.

However, U.S. officials had not accounted for Canada's favorite flanking maneuver when faced with bureaucratic noncooperation in Washington. In this situation, on an issue that mattered (as this one now did), the Canadians resorted to a direct approach to the president. Canada's prime minister made it his career's work to ensure that when the times required it, he could confidently approach the president. As he had done with Ronald Reagan, Brian

Mulroney assiduously cultivated as close to a personal relationship with George Bush as was possible between two heads of government. And when Mulroney appealed to Bush to gain Canada entry to the upcoming negotiation, Bush acceded, directing his officials to make it clear to the Mexicans that the United States wanted Canada in.[12] The Mexicans had little choice but to go along with the president's wishes, but they insisted on adding a rider to Canadian participation: should Canada's presence at the table subsequently prove to be an obstacle to a bilateral Mexico-U.S. deal, then the Canadians would withdraw from the negotiations.

Canada's decision and Mexico's acceptance completed the loop, as all three parties indicated their desire to proceed with free trade negotiations. However, the Canadian and Mexican actions were not sufficient, in themselves, to constitute a turning point that would conclude stage four of the prenegotiation process with an agreement to negotiate. This point could be turned only by an act of the U.S. Congress, and it was into this crucible of American trade politics that the fate of the trilateral talks was delivered.

## The United States

The Mexican request and American acceptance, in principle, to pursue free trade touched off a debate in Washington over the appropriate timing for negotiations. On June 10, 1990, Presidents Bush and Salinas, meeting in Washington, announced their determination to move in a "timely manner" to establish a comprehensive free trade agreement between the two countries, and they instructed Carla Hills and Jaime Serra to undertake the consultations and preparatory work needed to initiate such negotiations. The problem was that Carla Hills did not wish to proceed, at least not right away. She and her deputy, Jules Katz, were preoccupied with the Uruguay Round of multilateral trade negotiations (MTN), which they expected to conclude in December 1990. This expectation was driven by the requirements of the fast-track negotiating authority under which the U.S. administration was conducting the MTN. Fast track enables the president to negotiate an international trade agreement but requires him to notify and receive approval to negotiate from Congress and to consult with Congress during the negotiations. In return, the Congress will move the agreement through committee on an accelerated timetable, prohibit amendments, and limit floor debate, thereby ensuring that the agreement will be voted up or down without amendment within a fixed period of time.[13]

Trade officials calculated that legislation to implement a multilateral agreement would have to be submitted to Congress by March 1, 1991, ninety days before fast-track authorization for the MTN was scheduled to expire. However, they also had to allow time to build support in Congress for the legislation. Therefore, the final Uruguay Round ministerial meeting had been scheduled for December 1990. Hills, supported by Agriculture Secretary (and former U.S. Trade Representative) Clayton Yeutter, argued that the administration ought to concentrate its attention on the MTN and delay the congressional debate about NAFTA until after the Uruguay Round results had been considered, which would mean sometime in late 1991. Labor Secretary Elizabeth Dole also opposed an early start to the NAFTA talks, reflecting the opposition of organized labor to free trade with Mexico. Also reportedly opposed was Illinois Democrat Dan Rostenkowski, chairman of the House Ways and Means Committee, which would have to grant fast-track authority for any NAFTA negotiation.[14]

During the summer of 1990, Hills and Yeutter argued inside the administration that NAFTA was a good idea that should not be pursued until after the conclusion of the MTN.[15] Opposing them was a Texas triumvirate—Secretary of State James Baker, Secretary of Commerce Robert Mosbacher, and Lloyd Bentsen, chair of the Senate Finance Committee, which would also have to approve fast-track negotiating authority. Mosbacher already had pronounced a free trade agreement with Mexico inevitable the preceding autumn, and in February Baker had urged President Bush to seize the opportunity to stabilize Mexican reforms and provide an expanded market for American exports. Support for the Republican initiative from Democrat Bentsen, while not without precedent, was testimony to the generally positive orientation toward free trade with Mexico that prevailed in the U.S. Southwest. Reflecting this view, the Texans wanted to move forward immediately with a request to Congress for fast-track negotiating authority on NAFTA.

By August, the president had been persuaded to proceed, and the White House announced that Bush would soon notify Congress of his intention to negotiate a trade pact with Mexico. With a clear path finally established, President Salinas communicated a formal Mexican request for bilateral free trade negotiations to the United States in a letter dated August 21, 1990. This set the stage for the administration to submit a request to the Senate Finance Committee and House Ways and Means Committee for fast-track negotiating authority. Under fast-track procedures that had been put in place in the Trade and Tariff Act of 1974, and amended in 1984 in anticipation of U.S. bilateral free trade agreements with Canada and Israel (Koh 1992, 148), the committees would have sixty legislative days to consider the president's request, providing them with an opportunity to stipulate conditions that they would attach to their approval of any agreement subsequently negotiated. However, the Omnibus Trade and Competitiveness Act of 1988 had toughened fast-track requirements, to give Congress more power to influence the administration's conduct of trade negotiations.

The 1988 act stipulated that fast-track consideration (legislation would be voted up or down without amendment within a fixed period of time) could be applied to legislation implementing a trade agreement that was submitted within the next three years (i.e., up to May 31, 1991) with the possibility of a two-year extension.[16] A decision on extension would be made by a one-house disapproval rule: "the Fast Track procedure could be applied to implementing bills submitted after May 31, 1991, but only if, before that date, the President requested an extension with reasons, and neither house of Congress adopted a nonamendable 'extension disapproval' resolution [that had been] reported out of the Senate Finance Committee and jointly by the House Ways and Means, and Rules Committees" (Koh 1992, 151).

Thus, not only was the Bush administration required to secure approval for fast-track negotiating authority for NAFTA, but also they would need to seek congressional approval for an extension of the authority before formal talks had even begun.[17] The dual requirement is significant because it introduced a second front on which the Democratic Congress could battle the administration on trade policy.[18]

The first battle was joined on September 25, 1990, when George Bush notified the Senate Finance Committee and the House Ways and Means Committee of his intention to negotiate a trade pact with Mexico and requested fast-track negotiating authority. With sixty legislative days (which could stretch out over several months) available to consider the request, the committees were in no hurry to act. So, for the short term, the administration had the NAFTA stage largely to itself. In late October, Robert Mosbacher and Jaime Serra orchestrated a series of conferences across the United States designed to sell the American business community on free trade with Mexico. While they received support from industries seeking expansion into the Mexican market, including computer manufacturers and wine producers, they also uncovered strong opposition from industries facing competition from low-wage Mexican producers, such as apparel manufacturers and produce growers.

Even as the fast-track process began its slow movement toward a decision, the parties started maneuvering to influence the parameters of the proposed negotiation, edging into the fifth stage in the prenegotiation process in anticipation of American agreement to negotiate. On September 20, 1990, trade ministers Carla Hills, Jaime Serra, and John Crosbie met in New York City for a preliminary discussion of how a trilateral negotiation might proceed. They agreed to open a consultative process that would extend to January 31, 1991, and would involve regular meetings between chief negotiators, as well as monthly ministerial meetings to assess progress. This contrasted sharply with the Canada-U.S. FTA negotiating process, for which ministers were brought in to the substance of the negotiations only during the end game, in

Washington, in October 1987. This time, the Canadians wanted the political input of ministers throughout the negotiations, and Mexico and the United States agreed.

At a meeting in San Diego in October 1990, Guillermo Guemez, executive director of COECE, suggested that as a developing country, Mexico should be eligible for a longer period in which to phase out its tariffs in certain sectors than would be granted to the United States. He also indicated that while Mexico was not likely to open the door to U.S. investment in oil refinery operations, there could be some room for give on this issue.[19] The Mexican constitution prohibits foreign ownership or direct investment in oil production, and Mexican officials had asserted repeatedly that oil must be excluded from the negotiations.

At a meeting in Houston in November 1990, the chief negotiators made some basic decisions concerning negotiating parameters on these and other issues. First, and most importantly, they agreed that Mexico would not be treated as a developing country in the negotiations, meaning that it would not receive preferential treatment in matters such as transition periods for the elimination of tariffs. In addition, they agreed to proceed top down on tariffs, meaning that the agreement would cover all tariffs except those that were identified specifically for exclusion. To Mexico's surprise, Jules Katz glossed over the issue of energy during the meeting, not even posting a marker of U.S. interest in access to Mexico's energy sector. On the labor issue, however, he was much more forthcoming, bluntly telling Herminio Blanco that if Mexico intended to push for the inclusion of the free movement of labor in an agreement, there would be no free trade deal. Finally, they agreed that the subsidies-trade remedies issue, which had been so contentious in the Canada-U.S. free trade negotiations, should be deferred to the MTN.[20]

On November 26, 1990, when Presidents Bush and Salinas met in Monterrey, Mexico, oil was on American minds, however, not least because of the potential for conflict in the Persian Gulf as a result of the Iraqi invasion and occupation of Kuwait, a major oil-producing country.[21] In Monterrey, the United States announced that Mexico had agreed to allow access to their oil fields for American companies specializing in oil-drilling services. The issue of Canada's role in the negotiations also was raised. Mexico continued to oppose trilateral talks, but its resolve on the issue was weakening. While Mexican officials continued to suggest that Canada might be present only as an invited observer, President Salinas included in his Monterrey speech a reference to "a possible free-trade agreement with the United States and Canada." As mentioned previously, Mexican objections to Canadian participation ultimately were undone by Mulroney's appeals to Bush for a seat at the table, and in February 1991, Bush notified Congress that the negotiations would include Canada as well.

Events took an unexpected turn in December 1990 when the GATT ministerial meeting, during which the United States originally had anticipated a conclusion to the Uruguay Round of MTN, took place in Brussels. Instead of the end game resulting in agreement that had been planned, the meeting produced an impasse when the United States, unable to convince the European Community to move substantially on agricultural issues, announced that it would not negotiate further on the other issues on the table, and the talks collapsed. With the MTN deadlocked, the proposed negotiations with Mexico assumed greater urgency and a higher profile in the Washington trade game, encouraging opponents of the administration's request for fast-track authorization to focus their attack on NAFTA. Their opportunity came on March 1, 1991. Since it was now clear that the Uruguay Round negotiations were not going to be completed by May 31, 1991 (after which date the fast-track authorization granted in the 1988 act would expire), President Bush was required to submit to Congress a request for a two-year extension of fast-track negotiating authority, to June 1, 1993. It is important to note that the request, in accordance with the 1988 act, was for a general fast-track extension, which would apply not only to the MTN, but also to NAFTA.[22] According to Koh (1992, 155), the language in the 1988 act that prescribed the wording for a one-house extension disapproval resolution "did not appear to contemplate that Congress could disapprove extension of Fast Track procedures for implementing bills for *some* trade agreements, but not others." This meant that members of Congress could not approve an extension for the MTN, which had relatively broad congressional support, but not approve one for NAFTA, against which organized labor, environmental groups, and the farm lobby were already mounting significant opposition.

Bush's request landed in a Congress controlled by Democrats, who held 55 to 45 and 266 to 165 majorities in the Senate and House of Representatives, respectively.[23] Extension disapproval resolutions were introduced almost immediately in both the Senate and the House. In the Senate, the principal sponsor was South Carolina Democrat Ernest Hollings who, along with Strom Thurmond, his Republican colleague from South Carolina, was a leading opponent of a resumption of multilateral negotiations that might hurt the interests of his state's textile industry. The principal sponsor of the House resolution was North Dakota Democrat Byron Dorgan, who wanted to use fast track as a point of leverage to secure protection in any international agreements for his home-state wheat farmers. Because the 1988 act required that these resolutions had to be reported out of the Senate Finance Committee and the Ways and Means and the Rules committees of the House before they could be voted on the floor of either chamber, it was possible for the committee chairs to simply bury the resolutions, not allowing them to be reported out for a vote by the full membership of the Senate or House. In this circumstance, the two-year extension of fast-track authority would have been granted automatically. However, Destler (1992, 99) reported that congressional leaders decided that this procedure, while legal, would discredit both the process and any agreements reached.[24] Therefore, the disapproval resolutions would be sent to the floor of each chamber to be voted up or down, with passage in either resulting in the denial of extension. It goes without saying that going this route would also provide an opportunity to assert the authority of Congress over trade negotiations, and permit the Democratic leadership in Congress to attach conditions to any prospective agreement.

They wasted no time in doing so. On March 7, 1991, House Ways and Means Committee Chair Rostenkowski and Senate Finance Chair Bentsen wrote to the president to request, as the price for fast-track extension, an administration action plan to address "the disparity between the two countries in the adequacy and enforcement of environmental standards, health and safety standards and worker rights." These issues would have to be addressed either within the trade agreement itself or through some alternative context within the same time frame as the negotiations. House Majority Leader Richard Gephardt followed up with a similar letter asking the administration to spell out its plans to deal not only with these issues, but also with wage disparities and worker adjustment programs. Recognizing its vulnerability, the administration replied with alacrity. U.S. Trade Representative Carla Hills had already, on the day the fast-track request was made, stated in an interview that an environmental treaty negotiated with Mexico concurrently with the trade talks was an idea that ought to be explored. Now, she indicated that the administration shared congressional concerns and would work with congressional leaders to design a plan to address the concerns—the said plan to be ready by May 1.

All of this was simply "trade politics as usual" in Washington, where the players were acting out their expected roles. The need for members of Congress to appear to be serving constituency interests as part of their effort to retain office explains the division between Democrats Hollings and Dorgan, on the one hand, and Bentsen on the other, where the latter was playing to the benefits his Texas constituents would receive from increased commerce with Mexico that would result from free trade. But Democratic congressional leaders also had to be seen to be sensitive to the concerns of a large number of their members about the potential negative effects of free trade with Mexico, hence the demand for a presidential action plan. As for the administration, it too was playing an accustomed role, mollifying the Congress on specific issues sufficiently to obtain negotiation authorization, and using the congressional pressure to justify the demands that it would make on Mexico as the price for a free trade agreement. For his part, Gephardt was playing the trade issue for a constituency in his home base in St. Louis, Missouri, and beyond. Restricting trade had been a major plank in his unsuccessful presidential campaign in 1988 and was expected to be so again 1992.

As with other elements of the NAFTA story, this fast-track scenario was developing in the spring of 1991 in much the same way a similar episode had unfolded five years earlier, in the spring of 1986, when Congress was asked to authorize a fast track for free trade negotiations with Canada. At that time, strong opposition from lumber interests, coupled with congressional dissatisfaction with the Reagan administration's conduct of trade policy, led congressional leaders to demand a presidential commitment to address members' specific concerns in the negotiations. In 1986, however, administration complacency almost scuttled the negotiations: a motion before the Senate Finance Committee requiring the resubmission at a later date of the request for fast-track authorization failed by a vote of 10 to 10, and the tie narrowly granted the president his authority to begin negotiations. By contrast, while there was significant opposition to fast-track extension in the Congress in the spring of 1991, few observers believed that congressional leaders would allow disapproval of an extension. Bentsen, while he would not bury Hollings's resolution in the Finance Committee, would ensure that a vote was taken on the measure at a time when it was sure of losing. Nor did Gephardt want to take the president on in a losing fight, and there was sufficient support for fast track in the House to make its defeat an uphill battle. In the end, it was expected that he would talk trade but back away from Dorgan's resolution.

Even if the extension was likely to be approved, there was still a political game to be played out, and the battle would prove to be heated. While most Republicans were solidly behind extension, Democrats were badly split on the issue. Members from rust-belt states joined forces with those from textile and farm states in an effort to prevent extension, in opposition to their own leadership on the issue. They were responding to pressure from trade unions in the American Federation of Labor and Congress of Industrial Organizations (AFL-CIO), protectionist lobbies like the American Textile Manufacturers Institute, the Consumers Federation of America, and environmental nongovernmental organizations (ENGOs) like Greenpeace and Friends of the Earth. The labor-environmental coalition got an early jump on proponents of a deal with Mexico, beginning its lobby against free trade in the autumn of 1990. The U.S. business sector was slow to respond with a lobby of their own in support of extension. Finally, in March 1991, House Ways and Means Committee Chair Rostenkowski warned a group of business leaders that fast-track was in trouble, saying, "If you want to win this thing, move your ass."[25] Business responded by establishing the Coalition for Trade Expansion, an umbrella group of major corporations and business associations, including the Business Roundtable, the U.S. Chamber of Commerce, and the National Association of Manufacturers, among others, and began a very aggressive lobby of Congress. The Mexicans, too, entered the fray with a vengeance. In April, Carlos Salinas undertook an American tour, meeting with business leaders and the media in a number of U.S. cities to present the Mexican case for free trade and assuage concerns about Mexico's labor and environmental regulations. More important, the special office established by Mexico in Washington mounted a full court press on members of Congress. To do so, they hired a phalanx of top Washington lobbyists, with Republican and Democratic connections, and including many of the major firms in the business.

On May 1, the administration, in a letter to Bentsen and Rostenkowski from the president, unveiled the promised action plan. The plan contained a number of provisions intended to address the concerns raised by Bentsen and Rostenkowski in their letter, among them: a program of assistance for dislocated workers; retention of the right to limit entry of Mexican products that fail to meet U.S. health and safety standards; exclusion of U.S. immigration policies from the negotiations; an integrated environmental plan for the Mexican-American border that would curb pollution, strengthen environmental enforcement, and appoint ENGO representatives to government trade advisory bodies; safeguards against surges in imports of Mexican fruits and vegetables; and rules of origin that would prevent third countries from funneling their goods through Mexico to evade U.S. tariffs, including a domestic content rule of more than 50 percent (the FTA level) for automotive imports. The action plan achieved its intended objective, allowing congressional leaders to acknowledge the president's bow in their direction. Bentsen and Rostenkowski pronounced themselves satisfied with this demonstration of administration sensitivity to congressional concerns, as did Democrats Max Baucus and Sam Gibbons, chairs of the trade subcommittees of the Senate Finance and House Ways and Means committees, respectively. Only Majority Leader Gephardt was silent, for the moment, reportedly desirous of tougher commitments on labor and environmental standards but anxious to avoid being labeled (again) a protectionist.[26] However, Dan Rostenkowski believed that Gephardt's presidential ambitions would carry the day, stating, "If Dick Gephardt is a candidate for president, he'll be for it [fast track extension]."[27] On May 9, Gephardt proved Rostenkowski right by announcing his support for fast-track extension and free trade with Mexico.[28]

Gephardt's defection was a bitter disappointment for opponents of fast-track extension, especially organized labor,[29] and it effectively sealed the fate of the two disapproval resolutions.[30] Observers predicted that the administration was headed for a lopsided victory on fast track, and on May 15 the Senate Finance and House Ways and Means committees voted overwhelmingly to reject the extension disapproval resolutions, by votes of 15 to 3 and 27 to 9, respectively. However, Gephardt and Ways and Means Chair Rostenkowski then co-sponsored a resolution in committee calling on the administration to adhere to its May 1 action plan in the negotiations and indicating that the House would try to amend any agreement that did not include the promised labor and environmental protections. Michigan Senator Donald Reigle, a member of the Finance Committee, similarly raised the prospect of a Senate amendment of an eventual agreement and received some support for the proposal from Senate Majority Leader George Mitchell. On May 23, the full House of Representatives voted 231 to 192 to reject Dorgan's resolution disapproving the administration's request for a two-year extension of its fast-track negotiating authority. House Democrats were sharply divided on the issue, with 65 percent voting against their own leadership in support of the disapproval resolution.[31] The House then voted overwhelmingly for the Gephardt-Rostenkowski resolution, with Gephardt stating, "We give this authority conditionally. We're going to be looking over the shoulders of our negotiators."[32] As long-time observers of trade politics in Washington could attest, there was nothing new in this, except that Gephardt would be saved the trouble because U.S. trade negotiators were accustomed to looking back over their own shoulders at the Congress.

Since opposition to fast-track extension had been strongest in the House, with its large Democratic majority, the 59 to 36 Senate vote against Hollings's disapproval resolution on May 24 was anticlimactic.[33] Nor did the Senate follow Gephardt's lead in attaching conditions to the fast-track renewal. In fact, when Reigle vowed at a press conference to press on with his efforts to enable the Senate to amend any agreement that might be negotiated, contrary to the rules governing fast track, chairmen Bentsen and Baucus said they would oppose any such attempt. Failure of the House and Senate to disapprove the administration's request for a two-year extension of fast-track negotiating authority was the turning point that moved the prenegotiation process into its fifth and final stage, where the parties would attempt to influence the scope or agenda of the negotiation to come.

*Stage Five: Setting the Parameters*
While the U.S. executive and legislative branches were engaged in their fast-track decision process over whether to agree to negotiate NAFTA, the parties were already engaged in efforts to influence the parameters of the prospective negotiation. In fact, the U.S. decision process itself could be seen partly as a contest between Congress and the administration over what the parameters should be, in particular, whether they would include issues related to labor and environmental standards. In other areas as well, the parties were positioning themselves for the upcoming negotiations. On the issue of intel-

lectual property, U.S. recording and software industries were pressing for improvements to Mexico's system of copyright protection. In January 1990, the Mexican government, threatened with American action under the so-called Super 301 provisions of the U.S. Omnibus Trade Act,[34] had promised to undertake revisions to Mexico's intellectual property laws. However, more than a year later, the promised changes still had not been enacted, and although the Mexicans promised action sometime in the spring, it was apparent that the changes would have to be secured through negotiation. Mexico was more forthright on the energy issue, which, it never tired of repeating, was not on the table at all. Oil was a Mexican constitutional preserve, and negotiators would not be empowered to provide foreign investors access to the oil fields, nor would Mexico offer supply guarantees to American consumers.

Canada, for its part, was also busy identifying what would not be on the negotiation agenda. At a conference held to discuss North American free trade in April 1991, Canadian Trade Minister Michael Wilson[35] declared that Canada was not about to renegotiate its bilateral free trade agreement with the United States as part of the trilateral negotiations: "Canada is not going to let the United States get through the back door [NAFTA] what it failed to get through the front [FTA] door."[36] More specifically, Wilson said that Canada was not prepared to reconsider the exemption for cultural industries that it had secured in the FTA, nor did he see any reason to reopen the Auto Pact provisions that were included in the bilateral agreement, especially those setting the level of North American content in automobiles at 50 percent.[37] Jules Katz answered for the United States at the same conference. Not only the Auto Pact, but also the entire bilateral FTA would probably have to be replaced by a North American agreement, said Katz, although the United States did not intend to renegotiate substantive parts of the FTA. However, content rules would have to re-examined across the board, he said, including for automobiles. In addition, Katz stated that the United States still saw Canadian protection of its cultural industries as a violation of the spirit of free trade, and pointed out that Canada's right to protection was matched by an American right, embedded in the FTA, to retaliate with measures of equivalent commercial effect in other sectors. In a speech to the Canadian Manufacturers Association in Ottawa in early June, John Weekes indicated that Canada would be seeking greater access to the U.S. financial service sector, and he set Canadian sights on a larger share of the U.S. government procurement market, with Buy America programs the intended target.

For their part, U.S. officials contented themselves with the mantra that everything was on the table in the negotiation, including sensitive issues such as oil and culture. It was largely left to the American private sector to speak to individual items on the putative negotiating agenda. The Business Roundtable, speaking for the chief executive officers of two hundred major

U.S. corporations, said that the negotiations should seek a comprehensive removal of restrictions not only on trade, but also on flows of investment, and greater protection for intellectual property. Fruit and vegetable farmers in California, Florida, and Washington State expressed concerns about the need for negotiators to protect their industries from damage by low-cost Mexican producers. As a spokesman for Florida's citrus and vegetable farmers put it, "When negotiations occur, we just want to make sure Florida farmers aren't chunked out the window."[38] And so it went for the myriad of American interests that would be affected by a North American trade agreement, as each tried to influence the scope of the coming negotiations by moving issues on, or off, the table. As we shall see, the areas of incongruence in the respective negotiating agendas of the three parties would surface as problems throughout the negotiating process and fourteen months later would provide the major plot lines for the drama that would unfold in the negotiation end game at the Watergate Hotel in Washington, D.C.

## Organizing to Negotiate

These problems were yet to be discovered, however, as the parties moved through the last stage of the prenegotiation process, and their attempts to set parameters blurred into the formal negotiation process itself, scheduled to begin in Toronto on June 12. Throughout the final stages of the prenegotiations, each party had been putting in place the organizational machinery that would take it through the negotiations. The extended debate over fast-track authorization in the United States threw a wrench into Jules Katz's planned timetable for the NAFTA negotiations. Katz had intended to use the period between September 1990 and the end of January 1991 for extensive consultations to exchange information, so that once the negotiations began, they could move forward rapidly toward a conclusion by the end of 1991. This proved impossible, to Katz's great frustration. It was largely fast track, and to a lesser degree the debate over Canadian participation, that held up progress, but another reason for the slow start was Mexican disorganization.

The Mexicans initially were unsure about how to organize their team. After examining the Canadian experience in the FTA, and taking into account Mexico's own political and bureaucratic circumstances, the president decided to opt for a highly centralized negotiation structure. Responsibility for the entire negotiation would be given to SECOFI, under the cabinet authority of Jaime Serra. The chief negotiator would be a subcabinet official, who worked with a deputy and chief lawyer. Below them were a number of directors general who would be responsible for various working groups. Officials from other secretariats could participate in some areas of the negotiations, but final authority rested, at least nominally, with SECOFI.

While structure was important, personnel mattered more, and Mexican vulnerability in this regard was revealed early on and slowed up the consultative process considerably. At the meeting of chief negotiators in Houston in November 1990,[39] the Mexicans were drawn into a discussion of matters of substance by Katz, and it quickly became apparent to all those present that Mexican chief negotiator Herminio Blanco was not prepared for substantive discussions on the issues. The Mexican negotiating team was just being assembled, and Serra and Blanco had decided that the individuals in the various secretariats responsible for the issues were not adequate for the task at hand. As a result, they decided to bring in a cadre of lead negotiators who were known to them and trusted and who were personally interconnected. However, they were also very inexperienced. The exchanges between Katz, a savvy and experienced negotiator, and Blanco, who had little negotiation experience, convinced the Mexicans that the pace of the prenegotiation consultations had to be slowed while they did their homework.

The highly centralized negotiation structure in Mexico contrasted sharply with the U.S. model, in which various government departments were brought in to handle the negotiations in their respective areas. Thus, the Department of Commerce managed the automobile chapter, the Department of Agriculture headed up the negotiations on agriculture, and Treasury Department officials took the lead on financial services. Carla Hills, the cabinet official in charge, and the chief negotiator and his deputy were all from the Office of the U.S. Trade Representative, but this relatively small bureaucracy played a crucial coordinating and leadership role rather than dominating the discussions in all working groups.

Canada was somewhere between the two. Having opted for the centralized model in the Canada-U.S. free trade negotiations, the Canadians determined that this time there would be no independent chief negotiator with a private line to the prime minister's office. Instead, the chief negotiator, John Weekes, was drawn from the trade ministry, as was his deputy, and he would report to the trade minister. Lead negotiators, and their staffs, were drawn from either the Trade Ministry or other government departments, as appropriate, and Weekes established a small coordinating unit to monitor and help him manage developments across the various issue areas. The structure and members of the negotiating teams for each of the three countries are presented in Appendix B.

With fast-track authorization secured and the negotiating teams of the three countries in place, the formal negotiations were set to begin. To meet the timetable of the upcoming U.S. presidential election, the Americans calculated that the negotiations had to be completed within roughly one calendar year, by May 30, 1992, so that implementing legislation could be put before the Congress in time for passage before the House and Senate finally adjourned for the November 1992 elections. The slow progress that had dogged fast track and the prenegotiation consultations would persist, however, with profound effects on the negotiation process and ratification of the agreement.

## CHAPTER 5

# Opening Rounds

The North American free trade negotiations formally opened in Toronto, the center of Canada's financial and industrial heartland, on June 12, 1991. The times were not propitious. The economies of the United States and Canada were struggling, having entered a severe recession in 1990; conditions had been particularly harsh during the winter of 1990–91, with recovery proving to be unusually slow. Under the circumstances, opening up markets to Mexico would not be a popular course in either country. In contrast, the Mexican economy enjoyed continued growth. The economy would turn out to be the soft underbelly of the Bush administration, making the president extremely vulnerable on the issue of NAFTA.

The potential for trouble as negotiations got under way was masked partly by the huge popularity enjoyed by George Bush and his administration during the Persian Gulf War. However, approval ratings on how Bush was handling his job as president, which peaked at close to 90 percent, began to decline in March 1991. Throughout the NAFTA negotiations, his approval ratings continued to drop, as disapproval ratings began to rise. By January 1992, as negotiations were about to enter their most serious phase in Dallas, disapproval rates equaled approval rates for the first time, and thereafter the gap widened, with disapproval growing and approval declining as negotiations moved toward their climax in August 1992 (Pomper et al. 1993, 42).

Bush's vulnerability on the economy was revealed in the fact that even throughout the Gulf War, approval of his handling of the economy was substantially lower than either the more general rating on his role as president or his handling of foreign affairs (Black and Black 1994). And as recovery of the U.S. economy continued to sputter throughout 1991, approval ratings on the economy dropped further. To add to his problems, in June 1990 Bush had agreed, as part of a deficit reduction deal with congressional Democrats, to an increase in taxes. In so doing, he broke an explicit 1988 campaign pledge and further undermined his reputation on economic matters.

## Opening Gambits

At the inaugural meeting in Toronto, Carla Hills, accompanied by Jules Katz, sat down with Michael Wilson and John Weekes, and Jaime Serra and Herminio Blanco. The ministers agreed to divide the negotiations into six broad areas: market access for goods; services; investment; intellectual property protection; dispute settlement mechanisms; and trade rules on subsidies, dumping, and rules of origin. In doing so, they followed the broad pattern established in the Canada-U.S. Free Trade Agreement (FTA). They also agreed to establish nineteen working groups to handle the various issues within the six major areas and to seek initial progress simultaneously in all nineteen groups. This decision would create logistical problems subsequently, since membership in the groups overlapped. Mexico, in particular, had problems because several individuals had been named to head more than one working group, making the scheduling of group meetings a complex task.

Beyond these procedural matters, ministers moved quickly at this first meeting into substantive areas, as the positioning that had characterized the prenegotiations continued, signaling the issues that would re-emerge repeatedly throughout the negotiations. Table 5.1 summarizes the opening positions of the three parties on the principal issues in the negotiations. As expected, Hills raised the issue of Mexico's oil, and Serra quickly declared it nonnegotiable. American negotiators were undismayed, however, since they were confident that a means would be found to negotiate some U.S. entry to the Mexican petroleum industry. Canada had its own nonnegotiable issue and attempted to remove culture from the table at this inaugural meeting. The United States opposed this, naturally, with Hills insisting that everything was on the table. To Canada's distress, Serra indicated that culture was not an important issue for Mexico and could be discussed or not, as the others wished. When Canada supported the U.S. position for a discussion of oil, President Salinas subsequently corrected Serra, reaffirming Mexico's desire to preserve cultural safeguards (Economist Intelligence Unit 1991, 12).

Table 5.1 Opening-Round Positions by Issue

| Issue | Canada | Mexico | United States |
|---|---|---|---|
| Trade Rules | Entrench Chapter 19 of the FTA in NAFTA.<br><br>Did not want to keep Mexico out of Chapter 19, and quietly supported Mexico's efforts to eliminate U.S. trade remedies. | Remove antidumping rules and nontariff barriers, including countervailing duties.<br><br>Opening position was a proposal to replace antidumping rules with harmonized competition law. | Resists Mexican efforts.<br><br>Will discuss the trade rules issue but not negotiate. |
| Market Access | Negotiators focus on a few key sectors (forestry, fish, telecommunications, wood, aluminum, paper, footwear, prefabricated housing).<br><br>Water was so sensitive Weekes does not allow his negotiator to discuss this issue. | Wanted recognition of asymmetry between the U.S. and Mexico in terms of levels of development of respective industries.<br><br>Realizes that because its tariff levels are highest, it will have to make more concessions on access to its market than Canada and the U.S.<br><br>Starts with conservative offers. | Wants as big a package as possible with no exceptions (i.e., as many tariffs eliminated as soon as possible).<br><br>Needs to neutralize sensitive sectors, rather than trade them off against other sectors.<br><br>Market access provisions could be different, depending on rule of origin. |
| Energy | The FTA would be the basis for NAFTA; Mexico could not opt out. | Refuses to negotiate.<br><br>Initial position: no working group; oil is nonnegotiable. | Wants to negotiate energy; is prepared not to press for Canada parity.<br><br>The FTA would be the basis for NAFTA, and Mexico could not opt out. |
| Rules of Origin | Low rules of origin.<br><br>Cost-based equation.<br><br>Proposes common external tariff on computers after 10 years. | Prefers transaction-based equation.<br><br>Permanent duty drawbacks.<br><br>Rules of origin that are neither too restrictive nor too liberal; use value-added tests. | Prefers high rules of origin.<br><br>Ambivalent on method of calculation.<br><br>Proposed that the motherboard, screen, and hard drive be required for computers to be North American. |

Table 5.1  Opening-Round Positions by Issue (*continued*)

| Issue | Canada | Mexico | United States |
|---|---|---|---|
| | Duty drawbacks: wants 5-year extension. | | No extensions on duty drawbacks for Canada; Mexico gets 4 years of duty drawbacks. |
| Agriculture | Protect dairy / poultry farmers and supply management. | No quotas for access to U.S. market. | Safeguards for producers. |
| | | Maximum reciprocity. | Open up Mexican market; comprehensive liberalization. |
| | | | Weaken FTA provisions on subsidies. |
| Financial Services | Access to Mexican market. | Initial position: financial services not on the table. | If no financial services chapter, then no NAFTA. |
| | Establishment of subsidiaries. | | |
| | Exemption from Glass-Steagall and McFadden acts. | Modified position: permanent caps on foreign ownership; low levels of market share for foreign banks, phased in over a long time. | Strengthen financial service provisions of the FTA. |
| | Improvements to the FTA (national treatment and dispute settlement provisions). | Insists on subsidiaries (not branching). | Branching into Canada and Mexico. |
| | | | Access to Mexican market; no permanent caps. |
| Textiles | No separate textile chapter. | Sides with Canada on rules of origin but is ambivalent. | Yarn-forward rule of origin proposed. |
| | Fabric-forward rule of origin (as in FTA). | Wants to lower U.S. barriers, dubbed "Himalayas." | A Caribbean Basin Initiative–type deal for Mexico (i.e., a system of special quota preferences). |
| | Slow liberalization, with long phaseout periods. | Liberalize clothing and apparel (remove quotas). | |

| | | | |
|---|---|---|---|
| Autos | 50% rule of origin; clarify customs procedures. | Initially supported Canadian view that FTA should be the basis of discussion. | 70% rule of origin. |
| | If rules of origin increase, Canada wants a long transition (i.e., 10 years). | 50% rule of origin; clear and transparent rules. | Eliminate Auto Decrees in a way that would not adversely affect the competitiveness of U.S. firms in Mexico; as rapid a phaseout as possible, but slow enough to allow assemblers (i.e., the "Big Three") to adjust. |
| | Preserve the Auto Pact. | Slowest possible transition to protect the parts industry; initial position: 15-year phase out. | 4–6-year transition period. |
| | Fix the "Honda problem." | Eliminate the Auto Decrees after 10 years and replace with safeguards like those in the Canada-U.S. Auto Pact. | Opening position reflects initial demands of Big Three auto producers. |
| | | Eliminate the chicken tax (25% duty on light trucks). | |
| | | Access to the U.S. market equal to Canada. | |
| Investment | An FTA approach, with improvements. | No investor-state mechanism, upholds the Calvo clause. | A BITs-based approach (based on BIT with Argentina). |
| | Preserve screening. | Problems with language on compensation. | A maximalist treaty that defines investment very broadly. |
| | Resists U.S. efforts to define investment broadly. | On expropriation, wants language of "fair market value." | Clearer rules and fewer restrictions on investment in Mexico. |
| | Maintain attractiveness of Canada as a host. | Improve conditions for attracting capital by creating clear rules and fewer investment restrictions. | Investor-state arbitration. |
| | Open the Mexican market. | Felt U.S. definition of investment was too broad, without reservation. | Wants language of "prompt, adequate, effective" compensation for expropriation. |
| | | Wants strong disciplines within limits of constitution. | "The better we do, the worse we look." |

Table 5.1 Opening-Round Positions by Issue (*continued*)

| Issue | Canada | Mexico | United States |
|---|---|---|---|
| Intellectual Property Rights | A deal similar to TRIPs. | A deal similar to TRIPs. | TRIPs plus (i.e., wanted provisions it did not get in TRIPs, to show it was possible to go beyond the GATT). |
| | Seeks exemption for culture. | Consolidate and facilitate the changes they had already undertaken with their intellectual property legislation. | No exemption for culture. |
| | NAFTA is less important than the GATT TRIPs negotiation. | Reach an agreement consistent with Mexico's legal traditions, which gives greater importance to the rights of the author (in the U.S., rights of the producer are paramount). | Pipeline protection. |
| | | | Wants Mexico to expand U.S. patent protection, especially concerning plant breeder rights. |
| | | Culture is a nonissue. | Stop Mexico from using modified decoder chips to get free signals. |
| Procurement | Eliminate small-business set-asides in the U.S. | Opening position was "universal coverages, disciplines on everything, everything on the table." | Small-business set-asides not on the table. |
| | | | Lock in Mexican reforms; use the procurement chapter to create internal disciplines. |

| | | | |
|---|---|---|---|
| Services | A rules-based approach; add Mexico to the FTA and improve the FTA. Wants to include maritime services. | Make NAFTA a regional GATT deal. Liberalize with reciprocity. | An irritants-based approach. According to Canadian negotiators, the U.S. focused on irritants confronting U.S. producers in the Canadian and Mexican markets rather than on a rules-based approach. Wants maritime issues set aside (no changes to the Jones Act, which restricts national cabotage—the ability of a foreign country to carry cargo from port to port within the U.S.). |
| Transportation | No strong demands on land transportation. Same access to Mexico as the U.S. | Initially does not want to talk about transportation. Wants to give away as little as possible, and get as much reciprocity as they can for what they give away. Wants recognition for asymmetry in the structure of the firms in their operational capacities; differences in enforcement in rules; and the development of infrastructure, finance, and assurance. Wants the U.S. to open first, then Mexico. | Opening with Mexico (U.S. already has a long-standing agreement with Canada on transportation). Wants access to Mexican truck and bus operations, to move rail liberalization as far as possible, open ports. Shorter phaseout periods. |

BITs = bilateral investment treaties; TRIPs = trade-related aspects of intellectual property rights.

## Trade Rules

With the opening ministerial meeting completed, negotiators moved quickly to begin discussions in each of the six broad areas. First off the mark were the negotiators on market access and trade rules, who met in Ottawa on June 28, while the remaining groups held their meetings throughout July 1991. As Canada had done during its bilateral negotiations with the United States in 1986–87, Mexico was demanding that the Americans agree to changes in U.S. domestic trade laws, specifically rules governing the application of antidumping duties, on the grounds that the duties constituted nontariff barriers (the Mexicans were less concerned with U.S. countervailing duties, aimed at subsidies). Their opening position was to replace antidumping rules with competition law, an approach they bolstered with the question, "Why do we have to have these rules in a free trade area?" In a statement in Washington on July 8, 1991, Jules Katz insisted that the U.S. administration was not going to assume the political risks associated with asking Congress to pass changes to domestic trade law.

Although the Canadians had been down this dead-end path before and had paid heavily for the trip (Doern and Tomlin 1991, Chapter 7), they nevertheless supported Mexican efforts to persuade the United States to reform its antidumping rules. For the next several months, this situation would prevail: Mexico, with discrete support from Canada, demanded that the Americans negotiate changes in their trade remedy laws, and the United States insisted that it would not or could not do this. Jules Katz was willing to discuss the issue, but he would not negotiate a change in the U.S. position. Although the Canadians felt they were supportive of Mexico's position, they were nevertheless skeptical of the Mexican belief that they could do any better than Canada had done in the FTA negotiations. For their part, the Mexicans were frustrated with the Canadians because they appeared to be sitting back, letting the Mexicans battle it out with the United States.

When the Canadians had recognized in the 1987 FTA negotiations that the battle was lost on changing U.S. trade laws, they negotiated, as a substitute, a system whereby binational panels were empowered to decide whether the respective trade laws of each country had been applied properly (Chapter Nineteen of the FTA). This provided Canada with a separate, binational route of appeal in cases where it believed U.S. countervailing or antidumping duties had been applied improperly against Canadian exports. It would be a natural step to integrate the Chapter Nineteen provisions into NAFTA. In fact, the Canadians were eager to take this step, because a difference of opinion was emerging between the United States and Canada over the lifespan of the FTA Chapter Nineteen provisions. The FTA stated that they were to prevail for five to seven years, during which time the two countries would negotiate a new trade remedy regime. These continuing negotiations had not been successful, however, and were unlikely to be so within the prescribed time frame (negotiation of the trade remedies issue had been shifted to the Uruguay Round of the General Agreement on Tariffs and Trade [GATT]). Under those circumstances, lawyers from the office of the U.S. Trade Representative (USTR) were hinting subtly that the Chapter Nineteen provisions would expire, and the binational panel system would cease to operate. Although the Canadians insisted that the panel system would continue, even in the face of a failure to negotiate a new regime within the five- to seven-year time frame, they were eager to establish the Chapter Nineteen provisions in a new agreement with no implication of a time limit, however tenuous. The Mexicans thought they could do better. However, it was not clear at the outset of the negotiations whether they could achieve even the binational panel system. Early in August 1991, the U.S. Commerce Department indicated that Mexico would have to make very significant structural changes in the administration of its law and judicial review process before the United States could consider the inclusion of a binational panel system to review countervail and antidumping cases. The Canadians, too, would press the Mexicans for these needed changes to ensure that the Chapter Nineteen provisions could be embedded in a trilateral agreement.

## Energy

On the energy issue, some progress was made during July 1991. Mexico agreed to discuss the "energy sector" in the negotiations, including existing restrictions on foreign investment in the sector, but would not agree to establish a working group. "The working group existed, but we did not recognize it," said a Mexican negotiator, who admitted only that Mexico was willing to listen to what the United States and Canada wanted but would not give up energy for reasons that involved Mexican history, its constitution, and its sovereignty. For its part, the United States indicated that it intended to press for guaranteed access to Mexican oil in times of emergency, access it had secured to Canadian supplies under a provision contained in the Canada-U.S. FTA. Under that provision, Canada agreed that in times of emergency, exports of oil to the United States would only be reduced proportionately to reductions to Canadian consumers. The proportionate access provision of the FTA had been very controversial in Canada, and the Mexicans wanted no part of it. They pointed to the terms under which Mexico entered into the GATT, terms that acknowledged a special role for petroleum in the Mexican economy. At least initially, the United States did not play hardball with Mexico on the energy issue because the major oil companies were being "pretty sophisticated," as a senior American negotiator put it, in that they wanted to open up Mexico's energy sector but knew that Mexico would not do this at the behest of the United States. The main argument that both Canada and the United States used to pressure Mexico was that the FTA would be the basis for NAFTA, and Mexico could not simply opt out of those chapters it did not like. Since there was an energy chapter in the FTA, there would have to be one in NAFTA.

### Rules of Origin

Rules of origin were bound to be an important issue in this free trade nego- tiation, as the parties maneuvered to establish a definition of what would constitute a "North American" product, eligible for preferred entry to their national markets. These rules for determining origin are important because they can confer significant advantages and disadvantages on industries within the three countries, thereby influencing investment decisions. Cana- dian negotiators argued for low rules of origin, to be calculated using a cost- based equation, and they argued for a five-year extension of duty draw- backs.[1] Mexico wanted rules of origin that would be neither too restrictive nor too liberal; an optimal rule would be the one that would attract the most foreign investment. Mexico preferred a value-added equation for calculating rules of origin and proposed a system of permanent duty drawbacks. The United States wanted higher rules of origin and initially went back and forth on the method of calculation, listening to the arguments made by Canada and Mexico. On duty drawbacks, the U.S. negotiators' views were strong: they argued for their elimination on the grounds that they act as an export subsidy and offered no extension for Canada and a four-year transitional pe- riod for Mexico (the same as Canada received under the FTA).

A product of special sensitivity for the United States was computers. What parts should be produced in North America for a computer to be considered North American? The U.S. negotiators' initial proposal was that the com- puter should include the motherboard, screen, and hard disk. However, when IBM heard about this, they reportedly "had a fit" because they had to be able to source their components internationally.

Domestic content rules on textiles and clothing also proved to be ex- tremely contentious, because varying the content rules to include or ex- clude different inputs to a final product could provide an advantage for producers in one country over those in the other two. Under the terms of the FTA, for example, fabric had to be woven in Canada to meet content rules for cloth garments, but the yarn used to weave the fabric did not have to originate in Canada or the United States. Importing their yarn from third countries permitted Canadian clothing firms to manufacture at costs below those of their American competitors because U.S. producers are vertically integrated, producing their own yarn domestically. Under these conditions, Canadian firms were able to increase significantly their sales into the U.S. market under the FTA. To eliminate this advantage, the U.S. industry was insisting that North American content rules should apply to all inputs from (including) yarn forward. This meant moving from a "double" to a "triple transformation rule."

Canadian negotiators opposed the U.S. position and fought to retain the FTA rules of origin. From the outset, they identified textiles as a problem area. Indeed, the original Canadian position was that textiles should be negotiated under market access—there was no need, in the Canadian view, to have a special chapter devoted to textiles in the NAFTA. They wanted the slowest possible opening for their producers and the greatest access to the U.S. market possible. Mexico initially sided with Canada, to the Canadians' relief, and agreed that the double transformation rule in the FTA should be the basis of discussion. Mexico's other objectives were to reduce the tariff spikes (the Mexicans called them "Himalayas") that disadvantaged Mexican producers, to liberalize clothing and apparel, and to establish safeguards. The textile sector was a "win sector" for Mexico, and they knew that Mexican gains in this area would be painful for the United States. However, they argued that the United States was better off losing jobs to Mexico than to Asia, since Mexico imported more goods from the United States than did Asian countries. The United States appeared ready to offer some sort of preferential access to its market along the lines of its agreement with the Caribbean nations, known as the Caribbean Basin Initiative.

The working group on rules of origin was able to agree by the end of July 1991 that they would adopt the FTA principle of "substantial transformation" in determining the origins of products, meaning essentially that there had to be a minimal, defined degree of processing of a product in one or more of the three countries in order to consider it to be North American in content. At the urging of the United States, they also agreed that decisions concerning what would be considered substantial in controversial areas such as textiles and automobiles would be left to those working groups.

### Automobiles

The domestic content rule for automobiles would prove controversial. The FTA required 50 percent North American content to qualify for duty-free access into Canadian and American markets, and Asian transplant producers in Canada had taken advantage of this to increase exports of cars assembled in Canada, but with substantial offshore content, to the United States. American automobile producers, and parts manufacturers from both countries, were demanding that negotiators define a higher-content requirement for

NAFTA, a development Canadians feared would force the Asian transplants to move their manufacturing facilities from Canada to the United States.

Canada's opening position was to maintain the 50 percent rule extant in the FTA. It was clear from the position of domestic producers that eventually Canada would accept a higher rule of origin, but Canadian negotiators had another objective as well: to improve the clarity and transparency of the method of calculating rules of origin. This was a particularly vexatious problem for Honda Canada. Honda wanted a 50 percent rule but was willing to accept a higher-content rule in exchange for greater clarity. Similarly, Toyota wanted the 50 percent rule, but they were also willing to accept higher content (with a long, twelve-year transition phase) in exchange for clarity. The Canadian "Big Three" auto producers wanted a 65 to 70 percent content requirement, the parts producers wanted 70 percent, and the Canadian Auto Workers union asked for 65 percent.

The United States opened negotiations at 70 percent, which was close to the rather extreme position of the U.S. "Big Three" auto makers (who were demanding up to 80 percent[2]). However, Canadian negotiators believed that what the Big Three really wanted was 65 percent, and that would be the position that the United States would adopt eventually. The United States also asked for a four- to six-year transition period. For their part, the Mexicans were ambivalent about content requirements for autos (initially asking for the FTA 50 percent rule) but insisted on the right to preserve intact their Auto Decrees, a system of regulations governing the import and domestic content of motor vehicles in Mexico. The American negotiators were equally insistent from the outset that the Auto Decrees must go, even though they did not yet fully understand how the system operated in Mexico. Although the Americans opened with an extreme position, in fact they were willing to be flexible because they wanted to eliminate Mexico's barriers to trade in a way that would not adversely affect the competitiveness of U.S. firms operating in Mexico. In short, while they wanted the fastest possible phaseout of the Mexican Auto Decrees, they did want to give assemblers enough time to adjust.

Mexico's opening position was designed to exploit the U.S. need for a phase-in that would protect U.S. producers operating in Mexico by forcing the Americans into a debate about the Auto Decrees. This was an area where the Mexicans had an advantage because they knew their legislation inside and out. That is why, in response to the U.S. government's extreme opening position—"If you do not get rid of the Auto Decrees, we will not invest a cent in Mexico"—the Mexican negotiator responded, in an effort to ridicule the U.S. position, "Well, I'll just get rid of the Decrees tomorrow and we'll have free trade." From this initial confrontation it became clear that in order to find a compromise, it would be necessary for the U.S. and Canadian negotiators to understand the various elements of the Auto Decrees and how they fit together.

The Mexicans defined their objectives as access to the U.S. market equal to Canada's access, clear and transparent rules of origin (preferably based on the value-added method), and the fastest possible integration with the United States consistent with the preservation of the Mexican automobile industry. It would gradually become clear to the U.S. negotiators that the key element in the Mexican position was the need to defend the interests of the Mexican auto parts producers, which is the segment occupied by domestic capital in Mexico, and the largest domestic employer. To achieve these objectives, the Mexicans proposed a fifteen-year transition, during which the Auto Decrees would be phased out after ten years and then replaced for five years with Canadian-like safeguards modeled on the Auto Pact. While they were also concerned about Mexico's Auto Decrees, the Canadians were more interested in ensuring that the Canada-U.S. Auto Pact remained in place, with its guarantees of production in Canada.

## Government Procurement

In the area of procurement, the Mexicans tried to place the United States on the defensive by putting everything on the table. They began with a very aggressive opening position: "Universal coverage, disciplines on everything, everything on the table." When the United States said small business was out of bounds, the Mexicans responded, "Fine, then PEMEX and CFE [the state-owned electrical utility] are off bounds too."[3] The U.S. objective was to lock in Mexican reforms and use the procurement chapter to create internal disciplines. In this sense, the United States and Mexico were in collusion. As one negotiator put it, "After all, who are we protecting? Inefficient industries who are a drain on public finances!" Canada's main demand in procurement was to eliminate U.S. small-business set-asides.

## Services

The negotiations on services encompassed a number of areas, including transportation and telecommunications. At the outset, Canada tried to put maritime transportation on the table. The United States responded by saying, "If you bring in maritime transportation, we'll talk about culture!" To this, the Canadian negotiator replied, "Fine. You have 90 percent of our cultural industry, and we have 0 percent of your maritime industry." But the Americans insisted that they had made no changes to this sector (enshrined in legislation called the Jones Act) in the GATT, and there was no reason to include it in the NAFTA. In general, the Canadians took a rules-based approach, seeking to use the FTA as the cornerstone of the talks and finding ways to bring in Mexico. The United States took a more irritants-based approach, at least that was the Canadian view. Neither Katz nor Weekes attached great importance to the service negotiations. The Mexican negotiator was an experienced GATT negotiator, and his experience in Geneva informed his approach. According to one participant, he wanted to make the NAFTA a form of "regional GATT deal."

In the transportation working group, the negotiators agreed to break apart land, sea, and air. Once the United States had set aside maritime issues, the Canadians and Americans had little to talk about. With their open-skies agreement in place and a long-standing agreement on land transportation, there was little for Canada in the talks, except to get from Mexico whatever benefits the United States might negotiate. This left the tough negotiations to take place between Mexico and the United States. In fact, Mexico had to be "dragged kicking and screaming to the table," and once there, they insisted on giving away as little as possible and getting as much reciprocity as they could for any concession. The Mexican opening position was that the United States would have to recognize the asymmetry in the structure of the firms in the two countries; their different operational capacities; differences in enforcement of rules; and different levels of development of infrastructure, finance, and insurance. In short, according to the Americans, "Mexico acted like a typical developing country in this sector." The United States opened the negotiations with a request for access to Mexican truck and bus operations, liberalization in rail transportation, and opening in ports and civil aviation.

## Slow Progress

When the trade ministers came together again in Seattle on August 18–20, they were met by a trilateral anti-NAFTA demonstration, involving grassroot coalitions from all three countries. The ministerial meeting was able to accomplish little of substance, not as a result of the protesters, but because the working groups had not progressed sufficiently. In addition, Mexico used the ministerial meeting to assert where it would *not* go in the discussions it had agreed to on the energy sector. Serra, following direct instructions from Salinas, summarized Mexico's position in five "nos": no reduction in Mexican control over the petroleum sector, no guaranteed supplies to other countries, no change in the state monopoly over distribution, no risk contracts, and no foreign retail outlets. The Americans were bemused, Katz asking Serra, "What are the ayes?" Seated with Katz at the table, U.S. Deputy Chief Negotiator Charles "Chip" Roh produced his own visual pun, doodling a figure with five "noses / nos" and no "eyes / ayes." On the culture front, although the United States was reported to have dropped its insistence that the cultural issue be on the table (Economist Intelligence Unit 1991, 13), the change of heart, if it occurred at all, would be short-lived. To give the working groups an opportunity to progress further, the next ministerial meeting would not be held for more than two months.

During the next two months, the working groups met with increasing frequency as negotiators attempted to complete the initial brush clearing and move forward with the development of positions on the various issues. In September, an initial exchange of offers on tariffs was made, based on soundings regarding import sensitivities and export opportunities for various industries that were conducted by each government.[4] The resulting pattern of national preferences was sufficiently complex that it would not be finally resolved until nearly a year later during the end game at the Watergate Hotel. The overall U.S. objective was to get as big a package as possible, with few exceptions, and eliminate tariffs in the shortest time possible. Yet each country had its sensitive areas. Water was so sensitive to Canada that Weekes refused to allow his negotiators in the market access working group to even discuss the issue. Some of the products the United States was concerned to protect were ceramic tiles, watches, glass, corn brooms, and sneakers. Neither the United States nor Canada wanted to talk about beer because it was such a sensitive area, but Mexico insisted. Canada hoped to make significant gains in access for wood and prefabricated housing.

On October 9, 1991, Chief Negotiators Blanco, Katz, and Weekes met at a Canadian government retreat on the shores of Meech Lake, outside Ottawa, and there they tried to get a fix on the extent of progress in the negotiations in the various working groups, and the nature and size of the differences between the parties that were emerging in these discussions. As a result of this session, Jules Katz and Chip Roh concluded that the Mexicans were simply insensitive to the magnitude of the gap between Mexico's positions and where the United States wanted them to be. Incredibly, on some issues the Mexicans were acting, at least in the American view, as though they were actually on the verge of a deal, when in fact the two parties remained far apart. Perhaps, concluded Roh, if the Mexicans were to see in writing the positions of the two countries, they would get the message! It would have to be received sooner, rather than later, Katz calculated, if a negotiated deal was to be completed in time for the 1992 U.S. presidential election. In practical terms, this meant that negotiations had to be completed by the end of May 1992; after that date, it would not be possible to move the necessary legislation through Congress before the election.

For his part, John Weekes also was convinced that the task of preparing the text of a draft agreement had to begin as soon as possible if the negotiators were to complete their work in time for the U.S. election. Canada's experience in negotiating the FTA argued strongly for drafting at least the preliminary legal language of an agreement as negotiations proceeded, rather than waiting until negotiations had been completed and then turning the drafting over to the lawyers, as had been done in the FTA. This would be especially important for the NAFTA, because Congress had already indicated to Katz that it would require a text with considerably more detail than had been provided in the FTA before it would consider ratification of an agreement. Adding to the concerns of the Americans and Canadians was the fact that the NAFTA talks would shortly be placed on the back burner as negotiators turned their attentions to the Uruguay Round of multilateral trade negotiations (MTN), which were heating up once again in Geneva.

As a result of these concerns, when the trade ministers next met at Zacatecas, Mexico, on October 25–28, 1991, they agreed that the negotiators should begin the preparation of draft language for a possible agreement. Katz wanted to force the pace of the negotiations by lighting a fire under his Mexican counterparts, and a single text would demonstrate to the Mexicans how far apart the parties really were. Weekes agreed, and he pushed for a commitment to have each country construct a draft of what the treaty would look like. It was agreed: to achieve a single text, each country would prepare their version of a draft treaty for December 1991. The Canadian draft was based on the FTA, with chapters devoted to each of the working group areas, and revealed Canada's determination to use the NAFTA negotiations to achieve improvements in the FTA. The U.S. draft, reflecting the fragmentation of accountability for the various issues in the negotiations, came in bits and pieces as the various agencies responsible for each issue completed their draft chapters. Assembling a comprehensive draft text was a huge undertaking for Mexico, but they too met the deadline with a complete draft text (however, the Canadians subsequently came to doubt that the Mexicans completely understood all of the contents of their own draft). At the end of December 1991, the principal lawyers for each of the three negotiating teams met in Dallas, where they reviewed the three drafts and produced what was called the "run-on text," in which the proposals put forward by each country were simply grouped together by chapter. For many of the chapters, either Mexico or the United States failed to produce any draft language at all. The results were then distributed to the various working groups, providing each with a common base text on which to concentrate discussions.[5]

## The Going Gets Tough
### Agriculture

As 1991 came to a close, the basic configuration of the negotiation was emerging in more concrete detail on a number of key issues. Not surprisingly, negotiating agricultural provisions was shaping up to be very difficult, with the United States determined to put in place safeguards to protect its producers against a flood of low-cost Mexican products, while opening up Mexican markets for U.S. products, including grains. The United States also wanted to weaken the language in the FTA that prohibited subsidies, replacing "shall not subsidize" with "should not subsidize." Mexico, on the other hand, was looking for some escape from American import quotas and hoped to win greater reciprocity in agricultural trade. The Mexicans felt they had the disadvantages of free trade (they had taken steps toward opening their markets) without the advantages (access to the U.S. market for key agricultural products that faced a host of quotas, tariffs, and nontariff barriers). In the end, a way would be found to reconcile the two interests, but Canada would be caught in the squeeze. Canada wanted to retain the supply-management system that protected its dairy and poultry producers, and this defensive position limited its negotiation options.

## Intellectual Property Rights

On the issue of intellectual property rights, the principal lines of division were between Canada and the United States, and they mirrored a debate that was occurring simultaneously in the GATT negotiations in Geneva. There, the Americans were engaged in intense efforts to persuade the Europeans and others to accept a code of discipline on trade-related aspects of intellectual property rights (TRIPs) and to agree to provisions concerning copyright, patent, and licensing arrangements. The latter involved some particularly contentious issues between Canada and the United States, carrying over from the FTA negotiations. For several years, Canada had permitted the licensing in Canada of generic versions of pharmaceuticals patented by major American drug manufacturers, and the United States was determined that the practice should end. This Canada had refused to agree to during the FTA negotiations. In addition, Canada secured in the FTA a special exemption for cultural industries, which the Europeans, especially the French, were attempting to import to the GATT round in Geneva. In December 1991 the Draft Final Act of the Uruguay Round—known as the Dunkel Text, after Arthur Dunkel, the GATT's director general—became available. The consensus in Geneva was to prohibit compulsory generic licensing, and Michael Wilson indicated that Canada was prepared to sign on to the language in the draft. Thus, a major Canada-U.S. intellectual property issue was eliminated from the NAFTA negotiations. The Dunkel Text also included TRIPs but did not go as far as the United States wanted, so NAFTA became a second playing field on which to advance the American TRIPs agenda, over Canadian objections. Also left for NAFTA after December 1991 was the Canadian cultural exemption, symbolically a very important element of the intellectual property issue.

The Mexicans had no real intellectual property issues vis-à-vis the United States. They wanted mainly to consolidate and enhance the changes they had already undertaken with their recently reformed intellectual property legislation, and to attract greater foreign investment. There was contention over differences in legal frameworks—the Mexican system, for example, gave greater weight to the rights of authors than to producers. Among the specific demands made by the United States were the extension of patent protection, especially in the area of plant breeder rights (where breeders' support for Bush's Republican Party made this a pressing issue), and an end to the use of modified decoder chips to receive free satellite signals.

### Financial Services

Substantive proposals on financial services were also put forward in December 1991. This sector was slow off the mark because Mexico initially did not agree that financial services were on the table, and because the Mexicans were not well prepared.[6] The issue was handled by Treasury Department officials for the United States and Finance Department officials for Canada. For Mexico, officials from the Secretariat of Trade and Industrial Development, the Secretariat of Finance and Public Credit, and the Bank of Mexico sat on the working group, but the lead negotiator was a trade official. The difference was fundamental: in the United States and Canada, financial issues were not entrusted to "mere" trade negotiators, a point that was not lost on Mexican finance officials. A key U.S. objective in its negotiations with Mexico was national treatment, and while the principle had been placed on the table in October 1991, it had not been agreed to. The United States also wanted to open up the Mexican financial service market for American firms, securing for them the right to establish wholly owned subsidiaries and to market services across the border. Still to be negotiated, however, was the length of the transition period for opening, plus a ceiling or cap on foreign participation. Mexico initially proposed a permanent cap, which the United States said was "not serious." The Americans then proposed a temporary cap of 25 percent, to be phased out, which the Mexicans ridiculed, saying, "Why not 82 percent?" To bolster their position, the Mexicans deliberately exaggerated the weakness of their banking system—noting that they had just reprivatized their banks—and the threat of U.S. competition. Privately, Mexican negotiators would confide that they were willing to take liberalization measures unilaterally, but the NAFTA made it easier to sell change domestically.

As for Canada, the United States wanted to put some rules in place to strengthen the financial service provisions of the FTA, and to secure the right for U.S. banks to establish branches in Canada. For their part, the Canadians also wanted to secure access to the Mexican market, as well as the right for its financial institutions to establish subsidiary operations. With regard to the United States, as had been the case in the FTA negotiations, Canada wanted the Americans to permit Canada to establish branches in the United States, which would require reforms to U.S. regulations, specifically the Glass-Steagall Act, which separates investment and commercial banking and deters ties between banks and securities firms, and the McFadden Act, which restricts interstate banking. In the FTA negotiations, U.S. Treasury Secretary James Baker had promised Michael Wilson that the United States would proceed with Glass-Steagall reform. However, President Reagan did not follow through on this commitment. As a result, the Canadian industry believed that it had opened up in response to the FTA, while the United States had not reciprocated. Therefore, Canada would not give anything else on the issue without U.S. movement to open its system further. Canada also wanted improvements beyond the FTA, which did not include national treatment or a dispute settlement provision. In December, and throughout the NAFTA negotiations, the financial service working group operated somewhat independently of the other working groups dealing with trade issues.

## Accession

At the ministerial meeting in Zacatecas, Michael Wilson proposed to include an accession clause in any draft agreement, because Canada wanted to avoid going through a major renegotiation of Canadian access to the U.S. market each time another country wanted to join the NAFTA. The Mexicans were "horrified," according to a senior Canadian negotiator. That others might be permitted to join the club bothered them enough, but the thought that they might get in without enduring the same agony Mexico was currently undergoing in these negotiations was too much to accept. Jules Katz, focussing on one negotiation at a time, was not much interested in the idea. Nevertheless, Wilson persisted, arguing that such a clause was necessary. Based on the language of GATT Article XXXIII on accession, Jonathan Fried, the Canadian team's chief lawyer, wrote an accession clause into Canada's December version of a draft treaty. The U.S. reaction was immediately negative. They insisted on putting the clause aside, Katz warning, according to a Canadian source, "If you are going to make trouble like this, we will do a bilateral deal with Mexico." In the end, though, the Canadians would be able to convince Katz that the clause was necessary.

Following the distribution of the run-on text at the end of December, the working groups assembled in January 6–10, 1992, at Georgetown University, in the fashionable enclave of Washington, D.C. During a week-long meeting, the groups identified the elements of the run-on text where positions of the three countries were similar and more importantly, the numerous issues on which they differed. In international negotiations, the differing positions of parties for issues on which there is disagreement are isolated in square brackets in the text, to indicate the need for further work. At the Georgetown meeting, the negotiating teams worked with the lawyers to construct a single, composite draft with differences in the various chapters highlighted in bracketed text. This had the effect of focusing attention on the many significant differences that separated the three countries. This was especially important for the Mexicans, who talked at times as though they believed there were not major differences between the parties and an agreement was within striking distance, while at the same time they seemed not to understand the scale of concessions that the Americans and Canadians were insisting would be necessary if agreement was to be reached. As indicated previously, the composite text was partly intended to deliver a wake-up call to Mexico.

## Investment

In mid-January and again in early February, Blanco, Katz, and Weekes met to assess progress on the bracketed areas of the composite text. Each time, the same tough issues were brought to the chief negotiators' table by the working groups: automobiles, energy, investment, agriculture, and rules of origin.[7] The investment issue posed particularly difficult problems for all three countries. The United States wanted the provisions of the NAFTA investment chapter to conform to those contained in the maximalist bilateral investment treaties (BITs) that it normally negotiated to protect American investors. Canada, on the other hand, preferred the more limited obligations that were contained in the FTA. Each attempted to persuade Mexico to support the adoption of their approach. In addition to the BITs versus FTA question, there were three basic issues at stake regarding investment. The first concerned compensation in cases of expropriation. A typical American BIT stipulates that compensation must be "prompt, adequate, and effective," but this was unacceptable to Mexico because this was the language used by the United States against Mexico when President Cardenas expropriated U.S. oil companies operating in Mexico in 1938. Second, the United States insisted that the chapter include provisions for arbitration proceedings between the investor and the state, and again the Mexicans objected, because of the Calvo clause in Mexico's constitution.[8] Finally, the FTA provided the right to review (screen) foreign investments above a defined level, and Canada wanted to preserve this right in the NAFTA chapter. The United States, however, had accepted the screening provisions of the FTA only reluctantly and now attempted to persuade the Mexicans that they should not be a part of the NAFTA. Another contentious issue early in the negotiations was the definition of investment. The United States wanted a maximalist treaty, one that would define investment very broadly.

The opening positions in the investment negotiations were not without irony because of the conflicted positions of the United States and Mexico. A major reason for Mexico's interest in NAFTA was the desire for increased levels of American foreign direct investment, and this would be achieved, in part, by putting in place liberalized investment rules. In the negotiations, however, the strategic posture of the Mexicans was to resist the liberalization measures being urged on them by the United States. For their part, the Americans knew that a major domestic vulnerability of the negotiations was the prospect of an outflow of investment dollars to Mexico—Ross Perot's "giant sucking sound." In a sense, then, the more successful the U.S. negotiators were in their efforts to open the Mexican investment market, the more vulnerable would be the agreement to domestic critics fearful of a diversion of American investment dollars to Mexico. As the dilemma was expressed by a senior U.S. negotiator, "The better it [the agreement] is, the worse it looks."

Over time, the U.S. and Mexican positions would come closer together. Whereas both Mexico and the United States wanted strong disciplines (i.e., limitations on the regulation of foreign investment), there would always be a gap between the United States and Canada due to Canadian ambivalence about the level of U.S. direct investment it received. Canadian objectives were to maintain Canada's attractiveness as a place for foreign investment, to gain access to the Mexican market, and to build on and improve the FTA. According to a Mexican negotiator, "Mexico was closer to the US than Canada. We wanted more discipline than Canada. Canada based its position on the Canada-US FTA, which for us had little substance. Canada was more afraid of foreign investment. What Mexican wanted was more foreign investment and, while the constitution created limits, Mexico was open to strong disciplines." The Mexicans quickly detected what they called Canada's "double role": "Canada invests in Mexico and receives investment from the US. Canada was open to disciplines with developing countries [wanted to discipline their behavior], but not with the US [did not want the US to discipline Canada's behavior]. Canada had a clear strategy vis-à-vis the US, but not Mexico."

## Understanding the Negotiation

The opening rounds were often characterized by the negotiators as the "getting to know you" period of the negotiations. They provided the negotiators with a sense of the sensitivities and concerns of their counterparts and enabled them to begin to think of strategies and solutions that might lead to an agreement. Table 5.2 provides a summary assessment of the application

Table 5.2 Hypotheses: Opening Rounds

| Hypothesis | Canada | Mexico | United States |
|---|---|---|---|
| Asymmetry: weaker states are more responsive to powerful states relative to domestic pressures; powerful states are more responsive to domestic pressures relative to weaker states. | Is initially reluctant to join, and does so less due to domestic lobbying than for strategic reasons—to offset a hub-and-spoke regionalism.<br><br>Main concern is initially with the U.S. Canadian negotiators come to see opportunities in the Mexican market, but their main fears lie in U.S. efforts to undo or weaken the FTA.<br><br>Proposes accession clause to dilute U.S. power. | Is the *demandeur*. As a developing country, wants access to the U.S. market and to attract FDI.<br><br>Has already made major concessions prior to the negotiations (e.g., in IPRs, privatization).<br><br>Opening position reflects profound transformation in Mexico since the GATT negotiations in 1979–80 and 1985–86. | Is initially more concerned with the GATT; uses NAFTA as an attractive nonagreement alternative to MTN.<br><br>Seeks to push Mexico toward broader market reforms and disciplines.<br><br>Wants to set a precedent for market reforms using Mexico as a model for other LDCs and transitional economies. |
| Patterns of delayed mutual responsiveness: the lower the subjective utility assigned to the nonagreement alternative, the more concessions will be offered. | Although a weak player, has a strong nonagreement alternative in the FTA and GATT.<br><br>Seeks improvements and expansion of the FTA, which represents a domestic consensus. | A weak player, is forced to accept the FTA as a framework. Is not dogmatic about consistency between NAFTA and GATT or FTA.<br><br>Has cognitive advantage in superior knowledge of its own system. Attempts to use this to frame the debate.<br><br>Assembles best-possible team of qualified technocrats. | Pushes for the broadest possible agenda; carves out its own exceptions (maritime transportation, banking regulations).<br><br>Controls the clock (sets deadlines, shows no visible signs of impatience). |

| | Canada | Mexico | United States |
|---|---|---|---|
| Institutions: centralized, vertical institutions are a bargaining liability, while divided government is an asset. | Power is centralized in the executive branch of government. Members of parliament have little input into the negotiations. The decision to negotiate is taken by cabinet. | The system is highly centralized and authoritarian. The NAFTA initiative comes directly from the president. | Power is divided between executive and legislative branches. The Congress asserts its interest in NAFTA with the fast-track debate. |
| | The negotiating team is decentralized in structure (having learned from the FTA experience) and composed overwhelmingly of career civil servants. | The team is vertical and disciplined, "like a machine." | The U.S. negotiating team is highly decentralized. It draws heavily on political appointees with strong ties to the private sector. |
| | Well-institutionalized mechanisms are in place for consulting industry interests. | COECE, a new institution, is created for consulting with industry lobbies. Its head is appointed by the president of the republic. | U.S. producer groups shape the opening position in many areas. U.S. negotiators define their interests in terms of winning sufficient private-sector support to carry the deal on Capitol Hill. |
| | | The insulation of Mexico's technocrats gives them wide scope for implementing sweeping reforms. They are more weakly constrained by domestic lobbies. | Negotiators show acute sensitivity to domestic opposition. |

FDI = Foreign Direct Investment; IPRs = intellectual property rights; MTN = multilateral trade negotiations; COECE = Coordinadora de Organismos Empresariales de Comercio Exterior; LDC = less-developed country.

of the principal hypotheses to the negotiation process as it unfolded during the opening rounds. From the outset it was clear that Mexico, as the *demandeur*, would be playing the most difficult hand. To Mexico would fall the task of coming to an agreement with the United States, and Canada, that would secure access to the American market and create the conditions for larger flows of foreign investment, and this structural fact—that Mexico was the *demandeur*, applying for admission into the club—meant that the other two countries were in a position to set the entry fee. Canada played an obvious strategy that compensated for the fact that it was, in a sense, the onlooker during much of the negotiations: it would insist that, wherever possible, the FTA would serve as a basis for discussion. Moreover, the FTA provided the Canadians with a highly valued nonagreement alternative to the trilateral negotiations. The Canadians were in an ambiguous position: on the one hand, they wanted access to Mexican markets and to benefit from any access to the U.S. market that Mexico might secure; on the other hand, they feared U.S. encroachments that might erode the benefits of the FTA (culture and trade rules were two areas where the FTA was being challenged). As long as the outcome remained close to the FTA, NAFTA would be sold in Canada as merely an extension or improvement of an existing deal. As a result, the Mexicans immediately detected what they felt was a lack of creativity on the Canadian side. For example, the Mexican proposal to replace antidumping rules with competition policy was a creative and reasonable one, yet Canada, though supportive, did little to help the Mexicans sell the idea to the United States because they already had been unsuccessful in doing so themselves. Similarly, Canada tended to be reluctant to depart from GATT provisions, as in the area of intellectual property rights, where Canada insisted on adhering to the emerging GATT TRIPs deal rather than negotiating something different in NAFTA.

The United States, true to form, played hard to get, conveying a general disinterest in securing an agreement at the outset of the negotiations. In many different ways, U.S. negotiators sent the message to their Mexican counterparts that NAFTA was not at the top of the American agenda, that it played "second fiddle" to the MTN. As a result, they made it clear, Mexico would have to be prepared to set precedents in its efforts at reform before the United States would seriously consider providing it with preferential access to the largest single market in the world. This greater indifference is what gave the United States control over the clock. Another element of strength in the U.S. position was the obvious influence of major producer groups. In many areas, such as autos and financial services, the U.S. opening position was little more than a statement of what these groups wanted from Mexico. At the same time, the fast-track debate had demonstrated how sensitive the deal with Mexico was going to be, and thus the U.S. negotiators often had to walk a fine line between what business wanted and public fears about a loss of jobs and investment to Mexico.

The Mexicans started off with positions that were characteristic of a less-developed country (LDC). They asked for and were denied special consideration as an LDC; they suggested that certain issues, like energy and financial services, should not be on the table at all; and they insisted that the United States and Canada would have to understand the perilous weakness of their current institutions (a recently reprivatized banking system, a notoriously inefficient agricultural economy, a tenuously integrated automobile sector, and uncompetitive firms in many sectors). Mexico's efforts to frame the debate around these arguments met with only limited success, however, as the United States countered by arguing that Mexico was exaggerating its weakness and that the United States was not interested in a deal falling short of comprehensive liberalization. The Mexicans were easily convinced: their negotiators saw themselves as free traders, and they found these arguments persuasive. Soon, most of Mexico's opening positions would be abandoned.

The composite text had been constructed to demonstrate to the Mexicans how far they were from an agreement and to force significant movement from them on the tough issues. However, the Mexicans behaved as though they were engaged in a process of simple reciprocity, and appeared content to continue down an incrementalist path of exchanging small concessions on a tit-for-tat basis. They needed a graphic demonstration of how far they would need to move to get an agreement. To deliver this message, the Americans suggested that what was needed was a comprehensive negotiating session, one that would bring all of the working groups together and provide more orchestration to the pace of their progress. The prospect of providing space and ancillary services to hundreds of negotiators was a welcome one for recession-weary local economies, and U.S. cities were competing actively as negotiating sites. None competed more aggressively than Dallas, Texas, and it was chosen as the location for the first of the marathon NAFTA negotiating sessions, dubbed a "jamboree" by the U.S. hosts. As events would unfold in Dallas, the etymology of jamboree would prove instructive: a combination of the word *jam*, in the sense of being packed together, and a corruption of *bourée*, the French dance. Had the Mexicans investigated the meaning further, however, they might have uncovered a portent of events that would unfold in Dallas; in the card game of euchre, a "jamboree" occurs when one of the players holds the five highest trump cards. The Dallas jamboree would prove to be a turning point for the NAFTA negotiations, one from which the Mexicans could never look back.

## CHAPTER 6

# The Dallas Jamboree

**T**hroughout the autumn of 1991, the irascible Jules Katz had grown increasingly frustrated by the slow pace of the NAFTA negotiations. Unlike Carla Hills, Katz liked the idea of setting deadlines. Like any experienced negotiator, he was keenly aware of the importance of time: "common objectives and a fixed amount of time" was his formula for reaching a deal. He initially had set the overly ambitious date of December 1991 for completion of an agreement, and now that deadline could not possibly be met. The inexperience of the Mexicans and their initial lack of self-confidence may have delayed the negotiations. More importantly, however, much of the attention of the staff of the Office of the U.S. Trade Representative (USTR) had been deflected first by the fast-track debate and then by the Uruguay Round of multilateral trade negotiations (MTN). As a result, the opportunity to use the "prenegotiation" period to exchange information and prepare the ground for negotiations had been lost. Finally, in December 1991, a new impetus was given to the negotiations: Presidents Bush and Salinas met privately at Camp David and subsequently ordered negotiators to complete the controversial accord as soon as possible. A preparatory meeting was held before Dallas at Chantilly, Virginia, on February 9–10, 1992.

At the Chantilly meeting the ministers discussed and rejected a Canadian proposal for an expanded version of the Canada-U.S. Auto Pact, a managed trade arrangement that included investment guarantees by the "Big Three" auto manufacturers. The essence of this proposal was "a North American autos framework that would be like the Auto Pact, but trilateral." It would also involve cleaning up the rules of origin and raising the value requirement. Canada would offer to lower its external tariffs, and Mexico would have to reform its Auto Decrees to open the Mexican market. The Mexicans were somewhat interested, but the United States rejected the proposal, saying flatly, "We're free traders." The Canadians responded, "You can't say you are free traders only when you are the dominant player, but when you negotiate with Japan you create frameworks that are all distorting to investment and sourcing using other instruments."

The dispute went up to the level of the ministers, where Wilson made the case for the proposal. In the end, Carla Hills said, "This is interesting, but we are free traders," and the issue was dropped. The real reason for U.S. objections, spelled out in an internal memorandum, was that the proposal "retains drawbacks and creates incentive to bring non-North American parts into Canada for assembly and export to US."[1] The Continental Auto Pact proposal attracted considerable interest in the trade union movement in the United States and Canada, but after it was rejected, the Canadian Auto Workers (CAW) union lost interest in the negotiation process.

Prior to Dallas, in a meeting of the economic cabinet in Mexico City, President Salinas instructed Jaime Serra to wrap up the negotiations as soon as possible. The Mexicans were concerned about whether they would be able to complete the negotiations in time for NAFTA to be ratified and implemented by the end of 1992, prior to any change in government in the United States. As noted previously, the deadline for this to happen was the end of May, after which the Congress required ninety days from the initialing and signing of the accord before it could vote, plus another ninety legislative days for the implementing legislation. Serra repeatedly asked Hills, "How much time do we have?" He insisted, "We've got to be done by spring." Katz's reaction to Mexican concerns to get a deal was straightforward: "Fine," he said, "if you want an agreement, you have to move."

It fell to Herminio Blanco to give the message to his team of negotiators, and his instructions were clear. According to one Mexican negotiator, Blanco wrote a memorandum saying that Mexico would conclude the negotiations in February: "Show your cards, get to the bottom, there is no tomorrow," was the gist of the memo. As a result of Blanco's instructions, Mexico would make concessions in Dallas that according to a number of participants, left the mouths of Canadian and U.S. negotiators agape. Key concessions were made in agriculture, investment, and financial services. There was also progress in other working groups, but it was less significant.

## A Premature Crunch

The facilities for the Dallas meeting, which was held from February 17 to 21, 1992, were symbolic of Tex-Mex culture: a huge barn with partitioned

Table 6.1 Major Changes in Positions at Dallas Jamboree

| Issue | Canada | Mexico | United States | Observations |
|---|---|---|---|---|
| Trade Rules | On the sidelines. | Continues to insist on changes to U.S. trade remedy system. | Refuses to negotiate. | Meeting lasted only 90 minutes. |
| Energy | Continues to press Mexico for an energy chapter similar to the FTA. Says NAFTA is a "seamless web." Argues for national treatment of utilities. Implies that if Mexico does not offer supply guarantees, Canada may renege on this FTA provision. | Begins to hint that an energy chapter is possible. Insists on no violation of Mexico's constitution. | Accepts that the Mexican constitution has to be respected but seeks ways to circumvent it. Argues for national treatment of utilities. Argues that exclusion of energy is inconsistent with Salinas's project. | No composite energy text presented at Dallas. |
| Rules of Origin | Raises "Honda problem" and insists on clearer rules and customs procedures. Argues for cost-based equation. | Disagrees with Canada and argues for the transaction cost method of calculation. | Remains ambivalent but finally settles with the net-cost method. | By Dallas the three parties agreed to a net-cost method. Many of the differences between them were driven by the auto sector. All agreed on substantial transformation. |
| Textiles | Argues that Mexico should not constrain its competitiveness. | Listens to Canadian views and continues to seek deal with the U.S. | In private, U.S. encourages Mexico to swap a yarn-forward rule for elimination of quotas. | Little progress in this working group. The meeting in Dallas was not a key point in the negotiations. |
| Autos | Promotes expansion of Auto Pact. After this is rejected, keeps a low profile. Perceives Mexican movement. | Begins to soften its position on retaining the Auto Decrees, but does little to help U.S. understand them. Attempts to confuse and exhaust U.S. negotiators. | Not clear about the purpose and meaning of the Auto Decrees, the U.S. argues that they have to go. No Canadian-type safeguards are possible. | |

| | | | | |
|---|---|---|---|---|
| Agriculture | Insists on protecting its dairy and poultry supply management system and becomes isolated. | Places corn on the table as part of a proposal for across-the-board liberalization. Demands access to U.S. sugar, fruit, and vegetable markets. | Accepts the Mexican proposal. Pushes Canada to open its supply management system. | Fearing that Canada might withdraw, the U.S. and Mexico discuss matching the Canadian carve-out (exemption) somewhere else. |
| Financial Services | Continues to insist on changes to the U.S. regulatory system (Glass-Steagall). | Accepts the principle of national treatment. Abandons fight for permanent caps. | Resists Canadian demands. Continues to press Mexico for more access. | |
| Investment | Resists elimination of investment screening. Disputes legal language in investor-state arbitration. | Improves its offer on market shares and transition periods. Accepts the concept of an investor-state dispute mechanism. Agrees on the issue of expropriation. | Seeks to reduce the scope for foreign investment review in the Canada-U.S. FTA. Searches for expropriation language to satisfy Mexico. | |
| Procurement | Demands changes to the Buy America program. | Agrees to move quickly, on the understanding that the U.S. would move too. | Resists elimination of small-business set-asides and Buy America program. Gets a text structured and on the table. | There was a logjam in this working group prior to Dallas. In Dallas, the U.S. put its text on the table and Canada refused to accept it. After Dallas, the U.S. backed off from the position it had put on the table. |

walls served as a bazaar for 85 Canadian, 150 Mexican, and 120 U.S. negotiators, organized into nineteen working groups. The city, which saw itself as an emerging commercial hub of hemispheric trade, offered discount airfare and hotels—the only quid pro quo was a formal banquet that the chief negotiators had to attend with local notables. The jamboree format proved to be a big success from the U.S. negotiators' perspective—and a major turning point in the negotiations. For the first time, the three chiefs sat around a table and called in the heads of each of the working groups to ask them, "Where are you? What are the problems? Explain what is holding you up." The chiefs would then give their instructions and send the heads of the working groups back to work out the details. Table 6.1 presents a summary of the major changes in the positions of the three countries that occurred in Dallas.

**Agriculture**

It was in Dallas that the negotiations on agriculture really got underway. Mexico advanced its first draft text, which enabled negotiators to put together a bracketed, consolidated text at the beginning of the meeting. This provided a framework for discussion, outlining the scope and nature of the agreement. The United States saw the negotiations as an opportunity to "lock in gains internally" in Mexico and to "force change." Their position had been in favor of comprehensive liberalization across the board, including all products.

The Mexicans understood that they would have to pay for any exceptions. They were sensitive to the political consequences of liberalizing maize (and basic grains generally, including beans), dairy (especially powdered milk), sugar, and pork. Mexico had been told by the United States that unless they liberalized across the board, they would lose access to the markets they wanted for their winter vegetables and fruit—key export products with powerful producer interests in Mexico. The trade-offs were never explicitly spelled out, but it was the sense of the Mexican team that unless they placed corn on the table there would be no access to lucrative U.S. markets for their sugar and orange juice producers and no hope of shortening U.S. safeguard provisions.

Blanco opened in Dallas by upping the ante. He said that Mexico would remove impediments across the board if the United States would do so as well. Katz said, "We accept." Indeed, this had been the U.S. position all along. Opening agriculture across the board was probably the single most important concession made by Mexico in Dallas, because it meant placing maize on the agenda for the first time. This was a decision that would affect the lives of millions of Mexican peasants and consumers.

The background to the shift in the Mexican position at Dallas was the same as in other working groups. The Mexican president—in conjunction with the economic cabinet and in the presence of the chief negotiator—personally took the decision to place corn on the table and pursue comprehensive liberalization of agricultural products. Mexican negotiator Israel Gutiérrez, an official of the Secretariat of Trade and Industrial Development (SECOFI) whose genius lay in his knowledge of how to throw his counterparts off track and to delay the progress of negotiations in philosophical and technical discussions, was pulled from the agriculture working group and replaced by Luiz Téllez Kuenzler, a powerful subsecretary from the Ministry of Agriculture (SARH). This implied a clear shift in negotiating authority from SECOFI to SARH. Téllez was the architect of the reform of Article 27 of the constitution of 1917, which established the *ejido* system of communal land tenure. He oversaw the drafting of a constitutional amendment that lifted the prohibition on the sale or rent of *ejido* lands, thus opening the way for a process of privatization and commercialization of agriculture.

The replacement of Gutiérrez by Téllez signaled the high priority assigned to agriculture in the Dallas meeting by the Mexican negotiators—Téllez was a subsecretary, a full rank above Gutiérrez, who was a director general. It is also one of the key moments in which SECOFI saw its authority eclipsed by another ministry. To understand this frictionless shuffle, it is necessary to refer to Mexico's *camarilla* system, described in Chapter 1. Although the secretary of SARH was Carlos Hank Gonzales (who had no particular interest in the NAFTA negotiations), both Téllez and Gutiérrez had been promoted and were protected by Minister of Finance Pedro Aspe. As members of the same *camarilla*, it was impossible for Gutiérrez to say no to Téllez or to take him off the working group. So he did not try to preserve his fiefdom in agriculture. Nevertheless, SECOFI maintained a role in the negotiations through the presence of Eduardo Solís Sánchez, the trade official responsible for agricultural negotiations.

In contrast to the immediate acceptance by the U.S. team, Canada's reaction to Blanco's proposal was shock. The Canadians had expected that Mexico would refuse to place corn on the table, just as Canada had refused to negotiate culture. Now their position in favor of supply management left the Canadians isolated. Canada's unwillingness to match the Mexican commitment and liberalize across the board created a serious rupture in the negotiations, one that would not be resolved. The main problem was the Canadian supply management system, in which domestic production is regulated and imports are limited by quotas. Blanco and Katz believed that unless Canada was prepared to abandon supply management, then (1) Canada would have to withdraw from the talks, which nobody wanted; (2) there would be no agriculture chapter in NAFTA; or (3) the United States and Mexico would match a Canadian carve-out (exemption) on agriculture somewhere else in the agreement. Canada was truly caught in a very awkward position due to the unexpected change in Mexico's position.

## Investment

Dallas was also a breakthrough meeting for the working group on investment. Mexican investment negotiators acknowledged, in retrospect, that at Dallas they did not have a clear idea of the time frame for the negotiations, and that despite Blanco's instructions, it was unrealistic to try to wrap up a deal at that point. A Canadian negotiator, who sensed the Mexicans' impatience, said to them informally, "What is the hurry? Wait for the GATT [General Agreement on Tariffs and Trade]." The Mexican perception that the Canadians were in no hurry to wrap up the investment chapter was a development that enhanced Canada's bargaining leverage.

At Dallas, Mexico signaled a willingness to make concessions in the investment area. The Mexican team accepted the idea of a provision in the chapter on investment that would allow arbitration to occur between investors and national states, and they agreed to rules on expropriation. The major issue left was investment screening. The United States was seeking to reduce the scope for foreign investment review allowed by the Canada-U.S. Free Trade Agreement (FTA). Specifically, the FTA sanctioned the Investment Canada Act, which allowed the Canadian government to review direct acquisitions over Can$150 million. Canada resisted this, and the fight continued until the very end of the negotiations.

In the area of expropriation, the negotiators at Dallas sought to find a way of addressing U.S. concerns without violating either the Mexican constitution or the country's historical sensibilities. Mexico's constitution affirmed the right of the state to expropriate foreign firms in a manner consistent with the national interest. The United States wanted to ensure that any expropriated firm would receive "prompt, adequate, and effective" compensation. Language had to be found to address U.S. concerns without setting off alarm bells in Mexico's Secretariat of External Relations. A negotiator said: "The trade-off in Dallas was crafting a law that does not violate the Mexican constitution. We had to craft the expropriation language not using the words 'prompt, adequate and effective.' There are three paragraphs, and if you read them, you find that what they say is exactly those three words, but in substitute language." The compromise rested on the more palatable, to Mexican tastes, concept of "fair market value."

Mexico's willingness to make concessions on investment in Dallas once again left Canada in an awkward position. Canada was less willing to accept the tough disciplines that Mexico was willing to agree to in the investment areas, because the Canadian negotiators were more ambivalent about promoting foreign investment in an already heavily transnationalized economy. Mexico, on the other hand, was hungry for capital and willing to take whatever steps were necessary to ensure an inflow of foreign investment into Mexico. "We wanted more discipline than Canada," said a Mexican investment negotiator. "Canada was more afraid of foreign investment. We wanted more investment; the Constitution was our limit. But we were open to strong disciplines." The basic elements of a deal on investment were put in place in Dallas. Much work remained to be done to eliminate the extensive bracketing in the text on certain substantive areas, but broad acceptance of many of the principles was reached during the Dallas jamboree.

## Financial Services

From a Mexican perspective, the most painful negotiations occurred in the area of financial services. When the Mexicans were organizing their team, Secretary of Finance Pedro Aspe made a bid for control over the financial service negotiations and was rebuffed by Salinas. After Aspe's bid failed, the working group was headed up by a team that included members of SECOFI, the Bank of Mexico, and the Secretariat of Finance and Public Credit. SECOFI, specifically Raúl Ramos Tercero, was placed in charge. For the United States, the negotiations were led by Olin Weddington from the Treasury Department, and in Canada the lead negotiator was Frank Swedlove, from the Department of Finance. Authorities in the Secretariat of Finance and Public Credit and the Bank of Mexico noted that Department of Finance and Treasury Department officials were in charge in the other two countries, and were annoyed by SECOFI's efforts to meddle in their area. This led to a constant tug-of-war among officials from the various branches of government. After Dallas, that tug-of-war was resolved in favor of the Secretariat of Finance and Public Credit and the Bank of Mexico, but only after a major miscalculation by Serra and Blanco at Dallas had weakened the Mexican negotiating position.

After the cabinet decision to seek to wrap up the negotiations at Dallas, two senior finance officials stepped in for what they believed would be the end game. José Angel Gurría was one of Mexico's most experienced debt negotiators, responsible for negotiating a debt reduction agreement with the commercial banks under the auspices of the so-called Brady Plan. Guillermo Ortiz had been the architect of the reprivatization of the Mexican banks, and he was a powerful member of José María Cordoba's *camarilla* (Cordoba was Salinas's chief advisor). They followed Blanco's instructions to "show your cards, get to the bottom," to the letter. When the stratagem backfired, they concluded that he had made a miscalculation, and they blamed the problem on SECOFI's inability to competently manage the negotiations.[2]

In Dallas, Ortiz and Gurría accepted the principle of national treatment for financial service providers and abandoned the fight for permanent caps on foreign investment in the banking sector (the fight over caps in the insurance sector persisted after Dallas). This concession was made "stupidly" according to a Mexican negotiator, because it was not exchanged for a concession from the United States. American and Canadian officials were surprised by the Mexican action. As one Canadian put it, "I was puzzled. I thought they would have held out longer. Obviously, I was delighted." He went on to speculate that perhaps the Mexicans thought that making concessions in Dallas would move the deal forward, and that finance officials might have been responsible, while officials at SECOFI were unhappy with the result. From that point on, when there were difficulties in the negotiations, Canadian and U.S. negotiators would joke with the Mexicans, indicating that they would prefer to deal with early closers by saying, "Where are Gurría and Ortiz?" However, it was not really Gurría or Ortiz who were responsible for the concessions: they were simply acting on Blanco's instructions and did not have a sufficiently firm grasp of the negotiations to understand the implications of their action.

Officials at Finance and Public Credit and the Bank of Mexico were very unhappy with the results of the Dallas jamboree on financial services. They were furious that SECOFI had given them marching orders that they felt made no sense. The Mexicans learned the hard lesson that rather than accelerating the negotiations, the concessions made the U.S. negotiators hungry for more. U.S. officials had no incentive to wrap up as long as Mexico was giving them gifts: "They were giving things away; so I am going to keep asking until they stop giving," one said. The U.S. negotiators played hardball with Mexico, insisting that there would be no NAFTA unless every U.S. financial intermediary who wanted access to the Mexican market got it. Canada tended to support the U.S. position, although with arguments based more on persuasion than power.

The U.S. tactic was to repeatedly say, "This isn't good enough, our industry won't accept it, you will have to do better." The U.S. negotiator for financial services was in tune with Hills's strategy of not being in a hurry to get a deal: his strategy was to "keep demanding, and be patient." U.S. negotiators knew that Mexico was anxious for a deal, partly because it needed to attract massive amounts of foreign capital to sustain economic recovery. One consequence of this strategy was an overvaluation of the currency. Under such circumstances, any delay in negotiating the NAFTA could produce instability in financial markets. As one official put it, the U.S. negotiator "was prepared to sit and wait, and when the market on the Mexican peso turned a bit dicey, to push the Mexicans again."

The U.S. view of what happened to the Mexicans in the financial service negotiations was that SECOFI was eager to get a deal as soon as possible, and that the Mexican secretary of finance wanted to wrap up quickly and gave the Mexican negotiators a mandate to get an agreement. The Canadians also noted that after Dallas, the SECOFI person was there to handle the file for Blanco, but the finance people were in charge most of the time. However, both the U.S. and Canadian negotiators were surprised that the Mexicans caved in at Dallas. One interpreted the result, correctly in part, as evidence of SECOFI's willingness to "gamble with someone else's toys." In this case, the "toys" belonged to the Secretariat of Finance, and after Dallas, "Finance came in and beat SECOFI down," as one negotiator put it with blunt accuracy.

## Energy

Energy was one of the most contentious issues at the Dallas jamboree. Indeed, energy remained one of the areas where there was no bracketed text going into Dallas—the composite text prepared for the jamboree contained no provisions on energy. The three countries were still too far apart to be able to agree on even a composite draft. Nevertheless, the fact that the Mexicans had produced a proposal on energy represented significant progress from their initial refusal to even consider an energy chapter.

The United States and Canada had pressed Mexico for national treatment of utilities interested in investing in Mexico during the ministerial meeting in Chantilly, a week before the Dallas jamboree. Both Canada and the United States were pushing Mexico to accept a chapter on energy like that contained in the FTA. For more than six months, the Mexicans had refused to even accept that there would be an energy working group and a chapter on energy in the NAFTA. In Chantilly and Dallas, the Mexicans began to make references to an energy chapter and to explore its content while still being very restrictive in terms of what they would discuss. The U.S. team's insistence that energy was on the table in spite of the Mexican constitution was a source of frustration for the Mexicans. At Dallas, U.S. negotiators sought to find ways of circumventing the Mexican constitutional provision—dating back to the expropriation of American oil firms in the 1930s—that gave ownership of all hydrocarbon resources to the "Mexican people" while accepting that the Mexican constitution could not be formally violated.

It was widely understood in Canada and the United States that the decision to open the energy sector ultimately would have to be made by the Mexican president himself. The SECOFI officials in charge of the energy negotiations, Jesús Flores Ayala and deputy Carlos Villa, were not well regarded, even by other members of the Mexican team. One Mexican negotiator observed that they had difficulty booking their airline tickets properly!

José Alberro, on the other hand, was a key person: he was the representative of PEMEX in the negotiations. These negotiators stuck closely to the script that energy would be one place where Mexico would not "give away the shop."

The Mexican negotiators followed simple instructions from their president: the constitution could not be violated. But the constitution was vague on what could or could not be done. The legislation supporting the constitution was more precise, as were the government regulations supporting the oil industry. Thus, the U.S. negotiators demanded to know, did "the constitution" mean simply Article 27 of the Mexican constitution—which specifically prohibits foreign ownership in the petroleum industry—or all the rules and regulations associated with this article? Canada sought to impose on Mexico the same restrictions that it agreed to in the FTA, including Article 904 of the energy chapter, which provides guarantees of supply to the United States in times of crisis. Under this provision of the FTA, Canada agreed that in periods of supply shortage it would not reduce the proportion of energy available to the other country (based on the most recent three-year period), change historical channels of supply or mixes of products, or impose a higher price on exports than the domestic price. Mexico categorically refused to include such a provision.

Since Canada could not get out of the provisions of the FTA, they tried to convince Mexico that it was in Mexico's interest to agree to them as well. This made it impossible for Canada and Mexico to unite against the United States on energy, since it was clear to the Mexicans that Canada had accepted obligations in the FTA energy chapter that Mexico would never accept in NAFTA. Thus, having failed to convince the Mexicans that it was in their interest to open the energy sector, Canada insisted that NAFTA was a "seamless web" in which a country could not open in one area but remain closed in another. The Canadians drew on arguments from the GATT negotiations to support this position. The U.S. team accepted the Canadian view. Finally, the Canadians insisted that if Mexico prevailed on its refusal to guarantee supplies, then Canada would seek to change the FTA provisions on this issue.

Jesús Flores understood that Blanco wanted to wrap up the deal at Dallas, but he had to tell the chief negotiator that it would not be possible. Thus, in Dallas, the only agreement reached was that there would be an energy chapter, based on acceptance of the Mexican constitution as an inviolable basis for discussion. Little of substance was agreed. A host of complex issues, including state-owned enterprises, regulatory frameworks, petrochemicals, and legal issues, were left unresolved. According to a Mexican official, "If the US and Canada wanted 'a,' Mexico argued for 'not a.'" Mexico remained close to its five "nos" position, presented originally in Seattle in August 1991, and indeed remained there until the end of the negotiations.

## Deadlock on Other Issues
### Rules of Origin

The dispute over rules of origin was intensified at Dallas by the U.S. customs audit of Canadian-made Honda cars, which questioned their eligibility for duty-free entry into the U.S. market. This dispute highlighted the necessity of clearer rules for determining regional content. Canada wanted the calculation based on a cost-based equation. Mexico preferred the transaction cost method. The United States went back and forth, prepared to be persuaded by either method. U.S. ambivalence was also the result of an internal debate over the merits of the alternatives. Of course, the differences in this debate were driven by the auto sector. By Dallas, the three had agreed on the net-cost method.

### Chapter Nineteen: Dispute Settlement Provisions

In Dallas, the meeting on trade remedies lasted only a matter of minutes (one negotiator said ten minutes, another ninety). The United States simply refused to negotiate the changes Mexico was demanding, which involved modifications to U.S. trade remedy laws. Mexico insisted on its November 1991 "high ground" proposal (to replace antidumping with competition policy), which had been drafted by Blanco, with Espinoza (head of the textile working group) and Aguilar (the chief lawyer), both of whom were members of Blanco's *camarilla*. At this point, according to a senior Mexican negotiator, Mexico was acting strategically, seeking to secure access to the dispute resolution provisions of Chapter Nineteen. However, the Canadians were convinced that Mexico thought it could truly gain the high ground, and at this point, did not fully understand the benefits of FTA Chapter Nineteen provisions.

### Automobiles

Katz identified automobiles as one of the most difficult areas in the negotiations at Dallas. Little progress was made in this working group, according to Mexican negotiators, because "the US did not understand the Mexican Auto Decrees." The United States continued to demand the elimination of the decrees and argued that no safeguards on production, like those in the Auto Pact, would be permissible under NAFTA. At the same time, Canadian negotiators perceived, for the first time, a willingness on the part of the Mexicans to give up on the Auto Decrees.

### Procurement

There was a logjam in the procurement negotiations leading up to Dallas. Canada pushed for an exchange of small-business set-asides for offsets—an

Table 6.2 Hypotheses: Dallas Jamboree

| Hypothesis | Canada | Mexico | United States |
|---|---|---|---|
| Asymmetry: weaker states are more responsive to powerful states relative to domestic pressures; powerful states are more responsive to domestic pressures relative to the weaker states. | Increasingly caught in a pinch as Mexico makes concessions. | Need for a deal leads Mexico to agree to U.S. demands in a wide range of issues. | Surprised by Mexican concessions, the U.S. continues to energetically press for further concessions. |
| | | Mexican negotiators' decision-making power proves to be a liability. In response to pressures from the president, the Mexican team executes a serious blunder in conceding too early. | Also under pressure from the executive to show progress, the U.S. negotiators nevertheless make few concessions. |
| Patterns of delayed mutual responsiveness: the lower the subjective utility assigned to the nonagreement alternative, the more concessions will be offered. | Remains patient. | Concern about U.S. domestic timetable and volatility of peso make Salinas and Serra impatient. | Remains patient; retains control of the clock. |
| | Experience with FTA an asset; Canada makes no strategic miscalculations at Dallas. | Change in position reflects neoliberal ideology of technocrats who have "difficulty making protectionist arguments." | Uses NAFTA as alternative to GATT. |
| | Supply management system comes under attack. The FTA does not work as a focal point. | | |

| | | |
|---|---|---|
| Institutions: centralized, vertical institutions are a bargaining liability, while divided government is an asset. | The structure of the negotiating team—more flexible and less hierarchical than in the FTA—proves to be an asset. Few collective action problems arise. | U.S. team highly decentralized but tightly controlled by chief negotiator who "runs his shop by terror." |
| | The nature of Mexico's trade policy institutions and processes—especially the hierarchy and concentration of power in the presidency—facilitates the Mexican teams' shift from being slow to move, to folding prematurely. | Unable to make changes to its domestic rules and regulations due to domestic constraints. |
| | Mexican team suffers from intense internal conflicts (especially between trade and finance officials) and blockage in information flows associated with informal institutions (*camarillas*). | Regular consultations with industry groups, members of Congress, and staffers. |
| | Mexico's business coordinating group (COECE) proves to be "more ornamental" than a real constraint. | |

approach that did not win favor. The United States also refused to accept Canadian demands for changes to the Buy America program. In Dallas, the United States placed its text on the table and Canada refused to accept it. Mexico pushed for progress, on the understanding that the United States would move too. In retrospect, the Mexican negotiators realized that Mexico was in too much of a hurry. The U.S. refusal to move on small-business set-asides in the Buy America program created problems. The United States got a text structured at Dallas but then backed off after the Dallas meeting was completed.

## Textiles

Little progress was made in the negotiation over textiles at Dallas. Canada continued to insist on low rules of origin, arguing to the Mexicans that they should not accept higher rules that would constrain their competitiveness. The Mexicans listened to the views of the Canadians but continued to focus their efforts on securing a deal with the United States. Although the formal negotiations did not appear to be making much progress, informal contacts between the U.S. and Mexican negotiators began to lay the foundations for the deal that would emerge after Dallas in which the Mexicans would move toward higher rules of origin in exchange for the elimination of U.S. quotas on Mexican textiles.

## Understanding the Negotiation

The Dallas jamboree dramatically illustrated how asymmetries of power, different institutions, and risk orientation shaped the process of the NAFTA negotiations and the substance of the final agreement. Table 6.2 provides a summary assessment of the application of the principal hypotheses to the negotiation process that unfolded in Dallas. Mexico's impatience for a deal and its inexperience resulted in a serious miscalculation regarding the timing of concessions. The Mexicans also made the mistake of placing too much value on the fact of an agreement rather than its terms. The United States was able to exploit Mexico's impatience and to press for further concessions. The U.S. negotiators hung tough at Dallas, in part because they understood that the negotiations had not yet reached the final crunch. As one negotiator put it, "You have to wait until the end so that domestic interests will be satisfied that you have struck a tough deal. Carla Hills deliberately let the negotiation drag out."

Mexico's impatience reflected domestic imperatives in both Mexico and the United States. Serra was acutely aware of the U.S. electoral timetable and had hoped to wrap up the deal in time for ratification of NAFTA under the Bush administration. The peso was also under pressure, and every time the markets sniffed a delay in the negotiations the stock market in Mexico would register the jitters. Salinas also may have hoped to announce the conclusion of the negotiations in his March 1992 state of the union address. The Mexican negotiators' impatience also reflected institutional design. At Camp David, both Salinas and Bush decided to push their negotiators to pick up the pace of the negotiations. Mexico's centralized and top-down decision-making process translated the impatience of the Mexican president into a major miscalculation. Although details of the negotiations were left to the chief negotiator, key political decisions—such as placing maize on the table—were made by the president from his office in Los Pinos, the presidential residence in Chapultepec Park in Mexico City. Thus, one should not overemphasize the "inexperience" of the negotiators. In fact, the negotiators in each working group had little sense of the state of play in negotiations in other working groups. Since only the chief negotiator, his deputy, and the chief lawyer were privy to all the files, they alone, and the economic cabinet from which they took their orders, were responsible for the overall strategic direction of the negotiations. The negotiators in each working group had little overall vision of the negotiations outside their area. Not surprisingly, senior members of the Mexican team insisted that they "had no illusions about wrapping up in Dallas," but negotiators in a number of working groups contradicted this version. They insisted that they were trying to wrap up, though in retrospect it was clear that this was impossible.

Some Canadian and U.S. negotiators said that they believed that Mexico was trying to secure agreement on key issues at Dallas, while others said they were unaware of this. All agreed that it was premature to hope that a deal could be concluded at Dallas, given the gulf between the negotiators on such issues as autos and energy (which did not yet even have preliminary text). A number observed that the Mexican team started off with tough positions and then caved in quickly in an effort to wrap up early. Canadian negotiators chided the Mexicans for their impatience to reach agreement, saying, "The files were insufficiently mature to permit a deal."

Domestic institutions shaped the negotiation process in a number of ways. Two-level game theory suggests that the fact that an agreement has to be ratified domestically may be a powerful domestic constraint on a nation's win-set. The fact that Mexico could make major concessions without worrying about the need to ratify the deal domestically made it harder to resist U.S. pressures, and tempting to concede in an effort to wrap up early. But domestic institutions can also shape negotiations in other ways. The authoritarian structure of the Mexican team eliminated checks and balances among agencies and departments. The Mexicans modeled their trade negotiating team after the Canadian experience in the FTA, as well as their own experience in the debt negotiations in the 1980s. However, the Canadians had moved away from the sort of hierarchical structure that they adopted in the FTA, toward a more flexible model, precisely to avoid the kind of hazards to which the Mexicans fell prey—centralized decision making beyond the control of the departments responsible for particular issues.

A distinctive feature of the Mexican policy-making style was the intense loyalty that binds the members in rival *camarillas*. This could be a source of both internal cooperation and conflict. In the case of agriculture, good relations among the chiefs allowed for a smooth transition in the management of the working group because of personal connections. However, in the case of financial services, intense suspicion and conflict arose owing to lack of information, competing lines of authority and loyalty, and jealousy over turf. The highly centralized and authoritarian structure of the negotiation team meant that bad orders from above were implemented blindly, and in spite of the consequences for the country's negotiating position. The lack of information and flexibility on the Mexican team meant that personal relations— between the chief and his working group leaders, as well as between the working group leaders and their staffs—were often despotic and chaotic. When mistakes were made, a sense of betrayal and suspicion could easily arise. Moreover, there were few domestic constraints on what the president and his economic cabinet could do. For example, in the case of financial services, the banks had just been reprivatized the year before and thus were largely disorganized and unprepared for the negotiations.

In short, the nature of Mexico's domestic political system—especially the hierarchy and concentration of power in the presidency—turned out to be a liability for the Mexican government during the negotiations. The bargaining at Dallas demonstrated that decisions made at the apex of the Mexican government could scarcely be resisted at lower levels, in spite of the fact that lower levels of government were doing the hands-on bargaining and may have had a better idea of what concessions to make and when in their respective working groups. The concentration of power and rigid hierarchy were used to avoid the breakdown of discipline and chaos that some feared would result from the lack of a strong hand guiding the negotiations from above.

From a U.S. perspective, the Dallas jamboree was a huge success. This was partly because the jamboree format exposed the impracticality of Mexico's effort to place a single person in charge of many working groups. It forced the pace of the negotiations and cleared the decks so that the chief negotiators could get out of the minutiae and onto the larger issues. As a senior U.S. negotiator put it, tremendous progress was made "getting rid of junk." Although the final crunch and the most difficult decisions had not yet come, negotiators could begin to see the outlines of the deal taking shape before them, and they developed a basic understanding of the exchanges that would have to take place. They would nod to one another at appropriate moments, implicitly communicating the message that "I will eventually give you this, but you know I will need these other areas in return." At Dallas the United States was more engaged, partly because the conclusion of the Dunkel Text meant that the results of the Uruguay Round were taking shape, and now U.S. attention would shift to getting the draft text accepted. Pushing forward the NAFTA could signal the existence of an attractive nonagreement alternative to the GATT and thus enhance pressure on other countries to accept the results of the Uruguay Round. For that reason, greater political attention was finally given to the NAFTA after the very slow start during 1991.

No major alliances on issues emerged between Mexico and Canada, despite the expectation on the part of the Mexicans—and to some extent the Americans—that such a coalition might occur. It did not occur because of the defensiveness and wariness of the Canadian negotiators in their dealings with their negotiating partners, an orientation that clashed with the enthusiasm of the Mexicans.

Another reason for Mexico's willingness to make concessions was a desire to implement a radical agenda of economic restructuring within Mexico. NAFTA was the cornerstone of this policy, and many of the measures that Mexico was called on to take in the NAFTA were ones that Mexican leaders had already decided to undertake anyway. One advisor to the Mexican team said they were more committed to trade liberalization than either the United States or Canada; whereas the Americans and Canadians talked about free trade, the Mexicans actually believed it. Such contrasting beliefs and information played a major role in the negotiation. A senior U.S. negotiator suggested that the Mexicans "got caught up in their own story of trade liberalization. They believed they were more liberal than they were and as a result they accepted a more comprehensive negotiation than they understood or could manage." Salinas had hoped that having an elite cadre of technocrats trained with advanced degrees in economics and committed to free markets would play to Mexico's advantage in the negotiations; in fact, the Mexican commitment to free trade may have been a liability. As one Mexican negotiator admitted: "Mexico lacked a negotiation strategy. We had people with Ph.D.s from Stanford who knew the issues, but had little experience. Although one believes in free trade, one has to know the protectionist arguments. There were many economists on our team who could not give the protectionist arguments." The American negotiators studied at less prestigious universities but had no difficulty coming up with pragmatic (if intellectually unsatisfying) arguments for protection.

Finally, asymmetries of structural power were evident in the tone and substance of the negotiation at Dallas. The most important asymmetry lay in the fact that Mexico needed the United States so much more than the United States needed Mexico. The Mexicans had examined the alternatives and had already decided that they preferred NAFTA to anything else available to them. As a result, they focused on the gains that were offered by a prospective agreement, and were risk averse to achieve them. The negotiation result was the substantial concessions that Mexico was willing to make to get an agreement and win access to the U.S. market, albeit concessions that it might have made unilaterally to send a signal to the international community, and especially foreign investors, that Mexico was open for business. By contrast, the United States was unable to make changes to its domestic rules and regulations, which its negotiators agreed were inefficient and costly, simply because no member of Congress and no regulatory agency was going to accept such changes in order to secure a trade deal with Mexico. Thus, reasonable proposals made by Mexico and Canada were excluded regardless of their merit in principle. For example, the United States was simply unwilling to change its trade remedy rules. Mexico learned the same hard lesson that Canada had learned in the FTA negotiations. However, as soon as the discussion shifted to the inclusion of Chapter Nineteen dispute settlement provisions in NAFTA, Mexico was forced to consider wide-ranging changes to its domestic legal system. Similarly, the United States refused to consider changes to its regulations in banking and insurance merely to win Canadian support for NAFTA.

The negotiations were often adversarial and tough, but there was little explicit horse trading at Dallas. Much of what occurred there was movement toward the acceptance of a set of general principles and norms. However, there was less philosophical discussion of principles in NAFTA than in the FTA negotiations, primarily because of time constraints. Thus, in many ways, Dallas marked an important watershed in which sets of general principles were hammered out in a variety of arenas—whether expropriation in investment, or national treatment in transportation. This enabled the negotiators to move to the next stage, involving specific sectors and carve-outs, or exemptions. Where they were unable to agree on common principles, in agriculture, for example, crises threatened the negotiation process. Part of the utility of agreeing on general principles before examining specific products or issues was that this could serve to deflect domestic criticism. Once the general approach is agreed on, then what is left to negotiate are the specific timetables, terms, and trade-offs. This is where a wide range of domestic interests come into play. However, while domestic producers can press specific demands, it becomes harder for them to ask for things that go against the grain of the agreed-on principles and norms.

The NAFTA negotiations provided Mexico, Canada, and the United States with the opportunity to use an international negotiation to agree on and make a set of highly controversial reforms in the law. The use of a trade agreement to achieve such objectives allowed policy makers to present the reforms as systemic imperatives and to demonstrate that they were being implemented in exchange for reciprocity. The policies enacted were, however, policies that could have been undertaken anyway, if not under the NAFTA, then under the auspices of the GATT, or even in some cases unilaterally. In some ways, NAFTA was simply the culmination of a process of dramatic economic and social restructuring that had occurred, or was occurring, to a greater or lesser degree in each country.

# Heavy Slogging after Dallas

**T**he period between the Dallas jamboree and the end game at the Watergate Hotel in Washington, D.C., marks an important and, by and large, productive phase in the negotiation process. Progress was uneven, however, and as the agreement began to take shape, it became clear which issues were going to require the most difficult political decisions and therefore would be decided at the very end of the negotiations. Significant progress was made in a number of relatively less important working groups; for example, end game negotiations in the transportation working group occurred in Toronto in April 1992, and the deal was wrapped up in May. The auto working group, on the other hand, went into the final phase of negotiations in August at the Watergate without even having the text of a draft agreement in hand. Regardless of how much progress was achieved, for many of the negotiators the months between March and June were a period of "heavy slogging." A summary of the major changes that occurred in positions between the Dallas jamboree and the Watergate end game is presented in Table 7.1.

After Dallas, Mexican negotiators realized that the three countries were still far from reaching a deal, but they continued to hope that an agreement could be achieved by May to ensure that the Bush administration could see it through the ratification process in 1992, for implementation on January 1, 1993. As it gradually became apparent that this was impossible, each side hunkered down for protracted negotiations. Following Dallas, in late February, Bush and Salinas met, accompanied by Hills and Serra, during a "drug summit" in San Antonio, Texas. Shortly afterward, the Dallas composite text, used as a basis of negotiation in many of the working groups at the jam-

Table 7.1 Major Changes in Positions after Dallas

| Issue | Canada | Mexico | United States | Observations |
|---|---|---|---|---|
| Trade Rules | Wants to protect Chapter 19 of the Canada-U.S. FTA.<br><br>Fears the introduction of Mexico will open the door for the U.S. to push for changes to Chapter 19. | Reaches an agreement to negotiate inclusion in Chapter 19. | Agrees to discuss inclusion of Mexico in Chapter 19. | After Dallas, the most difficult negotiations revolved around Canadian resistance to changing Chapter 19 of the FTA. |
| Market Access | Negotiations for Canada stopped, pending progress in other working groups. | At loggerheads with the U.S. on a number of tariff items. | At loggerheads with Mexico on a number of tariff items. | |
| Rules of Origin | Joins into Mexico's duty drawback demands. | Argues for a partial duty drawback.<br><br>Proposes "general fallback provision." | Concerned about double taxation.<br><br>Rejects "general fallback position." | |
| Textiles | Rejects yarn-forward rule.<br><br>Proposes there would be no common rules of origin in textiles (Canada would stick with the FTA, and Mexico and the U.S. could do what they want). | Argues for elimination of quotas.<br><br>Accepts yarn-forward rule.<br><br>Accuses Canada of being "hypocritical." | Proposes yarn-forward rule.<br><br>Identifies Canada as main antagonist. U.S. negotiator says to Canadians: "Fine, we're sick of hearing from you guys." | Chief negotiators and ministers, fearing the unraveling of the deal, reject what they called an à la carte approach, instructing negotiators to find a solution to the Canadian objections. |
| Autos | Maintains low profile, seeking to avoid any public perception of change to the Auto Pact. | Seeks protection for its auto parts sector.<br><br>Becomes more flexible on rules of origin. | Breakthrough occurs when the U.S. team comes to understand the way the Auto Decrees work to support the Mexican auto parts industry. | |

Table 7.1 Major Changes in Positions after Dallas (*continued*)

| Issue | Canada | Mexico | United States | Observations |
|---|---|---|---|---|
| | Concerned about whether adding Mexico to the mix would result in elimination of safeguards from the Auto Pact. | | Offers to help ease the transition for Mexican parts producers. | |
| | Frustrated over Mexico's position on rules of origin. | | | |
| Energy | Continues to press Mexico to open up. | Agrees to negotiate chapter on energy. | Continues to press Mexico to open up. | Text exchanged but little progress toward an agreement. |
| Agriculture | Agrees Mexico and the U.S. will carve out comparable exemptions to punish Canada for supply management system. | A U.S.-Mexico package put together at Crystal City falls apart. | Agrees to move forward on bilateral basis with Mexico. | In Montreal, ministers agreed that there would be two separate bilateral deals on agriculture. |
| Financial Services | Insists on no branching in Canada until Canada receives an equal right in the U.S. (which would require a reform of Glass-Steagall). | Indicates that the U.S. would have to establish subsidiaries in Mexico in order to establish branches or banks, and Canada supports this position. | Treasury Department indicates that reform of Glass-Steagall would require bringing NAFTA before House committees chaired by Dingle and Gonzalez, both of whom oppose NAFTA. | |

| | Canada | Mexico | United States |
|---|---|---|---|
| | Opposed a number of U.S. concessions to Mexico because Canada did not receive comparable concessions in the FTA. | Mexico backs Canada's demand for Glass-Steagall reform. | Pushes for broad definition of the scope of operations. Demands "meaningful" national treatment and a relatively fast transition period. |
| Intellectual Property Rights | Insists on cultural exemption. Wants TRIPs from MTN. | Objects to neglect of the rights of the author in U.S. intellectual property rights system. Wants TRIPs from MTN. | Rejects a cultural exemption for Canada. Wants TRIPs-plus. |
| Transportation | Not a major issue for Canada. | Insists on an asymmetrical deal that reflects Mexico's lower level of development. | Agrees to generous phase-in schedules and does not insist on access to Mexican domestic trucking or investment in trucking. |

The deal is wrapped up in May.

boree, was leaked to the press and circulated rapidly across North America. Negotiators insisted that the text was outdated, and they were certainly right given the significant progress that had been made at Dallas. In spite of that, the Dallas text provided NAFTA's opponents with a glimpse of what was at stake in the negotiations, and this increased the intensity of the political debate. The U.S. presidential primaries began in the winter of 1992, and in the more sensitive political climate typical of this period, there was considerable Mexican concern about the possibility of NAFTA getting caught up in domestic U.S. politics. A summit conference call was held between the three North American leaders on March 16, partly to address such concerns.

Throughout the spring of 1992, the intense rhythm of meetings was maintained, including plenary sessions and chief negotiators' meetings in Washington on March 4–5 and March 23–27, a ministerial meeting in Montreal in the first week of April, another jamboree in Mexico City at the end of April, and meetings in Toronto on May 13–15 and in Crystal City, Virginia, on June 1–5, 1992. In addition to these meetings, many of the working groups met independently, and if the chief negotiators wanted to talk, they could always do so on the phone, as they did frequently, so that the negotiation process essentially was uninterrupted throughout this period.

## Reorganization of the Mexican Team

The painful experience of the Dallas jamboree made it clear to the Mexicans that it was impossible for a small number of negotiators to be responsible for large numbers of groups, and highlighted the problems of communication and information flows among Mexican negotiators. In response, new negotiators had to be brought in, and greater de facto autonomy was achieved in a number of the working groups, like energy and financial services. This loosened somewhat the hold of Blanco's professional and political network, or *camarilla*, on the negotiation process.

As we saw in the previous chapter, the Mexican team was both rigidly hierarchical and riddled with informal networks. In his efforts to maintain total control over the negotiations, Blanco had placed members of his *camarilla* in key positions on the negotiation team. Blanco's problem was that he only had a limited number of close confidants at the level of director general.[1] Thus, he assigned to them responsibility for multiple working groups. Blanco feared that unless he had a director general in every working group, director generals from other agencies might be able to outrank his people and wrestle control away from the Secretariat of Trade and Industrial Development (SECOFI). The idea was to avoid bureaucratic infighting, and it partially succeeded. After Dallas, however, it was clear that chief lawyer Aguilar could not manage all the groups he was given, which included intellectual property, investment, and dispute settlement, so he concentrated his attention on dispute settlement and managing the Mexican team of lawyers. Aguilar, along with Blanco's deputy, Jaime Zabludovsky, was a key member of Blanco's *camarilla*. And, as the chief lawyer, he was privy to information on all of the other working groups.

A key issue that was raised repeatedly by the Mexican negotiators in our interviews was the lack of information flows on the Mexican team. Only a handful of negotiators, in particular, the chief negotiator and his deputy and the chief lawyer, had complete knowledge of what was happening across the negotiations. Other negotiators often complained that they did not know what was going on in other working groups, and this led them to speculate about their own country's negotiating strategy. Information flowed through rumors. Negotiators complained about having to make concessions without knowing what they were getting in return. The perception of being forced to make concessions in one arena without knowing whether reciprocity was being achieved in another arena led to much speculation among Mexican negotiators about the chief negotiator and his strategies.

U.S. and Canadian negotiators found it easier to work with the Mexicans after their recognition that lead negotiators could not be given multiple responsibilities. The most contentious issues in the negotiation, involving the most difficult trade-offs necessary to secure a deal, were left for the final phase at the Watergate Hotel and were dealt with at the ministerial level. This chapter addresses the progress of the negotiations as each working group sought to clear the groundwork for the final deal by eliminating issues that could be resolved at the level of the working groups. In most working groups this required leaving only the most intractable problems for the ministers to resolve in assembling the final package.

Canadian negotiators, whose experience in the Free Trade Agreement (FTA) gave them a better sense for the rhythm and pace of negotiations, repeatedly urged the Mexicans to slow down and be more patient. In this respect, Canada was motivated in part by a preference to negotiate certain issues in the multilateral trade negotiations (MTN) rather than NAFTA, to avoid the impression in Canada that major concessions were being made to the United States in the trilateral negotiations.

## Controversial Issues in the Spring of 1992

Two issues were especially difficult in the ministerial meeting in Montreal at the beginning of April: autos and textiles. The auto working group dragged out the negotiations during this period before a breakthrough occurred in the meeting at the Four Seasons Hotel in Toronto in mid-May. Textiles proved to be an equally difficult working group in the Montreal ministerial meeting. However, elements of the agreement were in place by the end of May, and many of the outstanding issues concerned how to placate the Canadian negotiators, who were unhappy with the emerging agreement.

### Confuse and Exhaust: Mexico's Strategy on Autos

One of the most engaging stories in the NAFTA negotiations concerned the Mexican government's attempts to resist pressures for immediate liberalization in the auto sector. U.S. negotiators complained bitterly about the Mexican lead negotiator in autos, Israel Gutiérrez. The Americans felt that Gutiérrez, while he was charming and bright—he had a doctorate from MIT—was really "a pain in the ass," to quote a U.S. negotiator. According to American officials, he had "limited negotiating experience, and had trouble focusing on the general goals of the negotiation. Instead, he focused on the details of the negotiation, which he saw in 'win or lose' terms." Gutiérrez was a loud and emotional man who was clearly irritating to deal with. He was despotic with those below him in the hierarchy and servile toward those above. But he was also clever and effective.

The Mexican team was privately proud of Gutiérrez's performance, although they publicly expressed sympathy with the U.S. and Canadian negotiators for having to deal with him. Often, the Mexicans, led by Gutiérrez, would show up late to meetings or simply cancel them altogether. As one Mexican said:

> We were very tough in the negotiations, and we had a good strategy. Israel Gutiérrez is well known for his strategies. It confused them. He had them asking for things that were counter to their own interests. Then, he would give them something, and the US industries would be furious, asking [the American negotiators]: "How could you ask for something like that!" His strategy was to go from the particular to the general. Instead of starting with the general principles and later explaining the details, he would begin with the algebraic formulas. Many days were spent discussing technical details and the most important stuff would not even be commented upon. It was done, deliberately, to gradually wear them out. Katz would say: "I understand everything, except the automotive industry." He was very frustrated; the most technical stuff would be sent to the chiefs. It was funny. It was a brilliant strategy by Gutiérrez.

A Canadian negotiator confirmed that this was Gutiérrez's strategy: "The Mexicans tried to stall and got everyone mad, frustrated. They would focus on details, and that would set you off in a different direction from what you wanted. We caught on after a while!"

The delays in the negotiations on autos were due to the unwillingness of the Mexican negotiators to help the U.S. and Canadian negotiators to understand the Auto Decrees, the main legislative policy instruments by which Mexico, through a strategy of import-substitution industrialization, had built up a local automobile industry over a thirty-year period. The Auto Decrees combined performance requirements, including local content rules and trade balancing measures, with government regulations and incentives to encourage an integrated automobile industry.

Gutiérrez was one of the authors of the 1989 decrees that aimed to shift auto production toward a more export-oriented pattern of development. The Mexicans were pleased with the success of the Auto Decrees in terms of generating auto production, exports, and new investments. In their view, and in the view of the Mexican auto parts industry, the Auto Decrees were good legislation, and they wanted to keep them in place as long as possible—indeed, the initial Mexican proposal was simply to retain the decrees.

The U.S. industry wanted to phase out the decrees, immediately eliminate vehicle and parts tariffs, reduce performance requirements, and establish a rule of origin. The "Big Three" auto makers also wanted to create two tiers of auto producers: those major assemblers established in Mexico as of January 1, 1991, and those that established operations subsequently. The first tier of companies would enjoy the benefits of liberalization more quickly than the second tier. U.S. negotiators found the two-tier approach unattractive because it was outrageously protectionist, but this also helped the U.S. negotiators because it made them look more reasonable. According to a memo from Ann Hughes, the lead U.S. negotiator on autos, the Big Three's proposal demonstrated "the pressure the US is under from such a powerful industry. Its existence may help us move the Mexicans toward a more moderate approach that will still meet the needs of the Big Three."[2]

The Auto Decrees contained two major performance requirements: trade balancing and local content. The trade balancing requirement stipulated that for every dollar of auto exports, auto firms could import one dollar of autos; in other words, for balance of payment reasons, auto producers were entitled to import autos only to the extent that they also exported them. The local content requirement effectively reserved the auto parts industry for Mexicans, according to a rule that stipulated that auto parts firms had to be 60 percent Mexican-owned. Moreover, terminal auto producers were expected to purchase one-third of the content of the automobiles produced in Mexico locally. These requirements ensured a large local auto parts industry that was a major employer and source of income for Mexicans.

The U.S. team felt that it had begun to understand the Auto Decrees fully only toward the end of the negotiations. A breakthrough occurred at a meeting at the Four Seasons Hotel in Toronto on May 13–15: when the U.S. team finally realized that the purpose of the Auto Decrees was to promote a Mexican auto parts industry, they understood that the key to an agreement would be to find a way to satisfy the U.S. auto industry while meeting the Mexican need to help their parts producers. A Mexican negotiator said, "The gringos understood the importance of the auto parts industry because it is *the* industry of Mexican capital and our biggest employer. It is important because of its contribution to the GNP [gross national product] and its multiplier effects. The terminal [final assembly] industry is foreign owned. From the first meeting we insisted on the importance of the auto parts industry." The United States also understood that the auto parts industry had close ties to the ruling Institutional Revolutionary Party (PRI).

Mexico's position on rules of origin also became more flexible over time. Initially, the Mexicans had wanted to structure the rules in such a way as to preserve their ability to attract Asian assemblers to Mexico. However, as the negotiations progressed, they modified their position, becoming more flexible on rules of origin but insisting on protection for the parts industry. U.S. negotiators believed, correctly, this was due to changes in the preferences of the Mexican domestic industry. At the same time, the Mexicans also found themselves representing the Big Three auto companies—Ford, General Motors, and Chrysler—all of which had operations in Mexico. As one negotiator put it, "We had the Big Three behind the three countries around the bargaining table. They were inside [in Mexico's 'side room' where the private sector was represented] and they were outside [represented by the other two countries]. The U.S. defended the interests of the Big Three, and the auto parts industry was not a priority. They are experts on international negotiations; they had the Auto Pact, and the FTA with Israel." This accounts for much of Mexico's sensitivity in the auto negotiations. They perceived the United States to be "the industry's representative," and Mexico had to look out for the interests of its domestic industry.

Not only did Mexico have to look after the interests of its parts industry, but also it had to be concerned for the interests of the other foreign auto producers in Mexico. The auto sector is also an interesting one from the perspective of the domestic politics of producer groups, because the positions of Volkswagen (VW) and Nissan changed during the negotiations, causing a perceptible shift in Mexico's bargaining strategy that ultimately resulted in higher rules of origin in the NAFTA than might otherwise have been accepted. VW initially wanted low rules of origin. Its Mexican plant was the only VW production center in North America. Although at one point VW toyed with the idea of using its Mexican production facilities to export Golf and Jetta models into the United States, ultimately VW decided to concentrate on the Mexican market. Nissan also had a plant in Mexico, which was a part of its strategy to expand exports southward into Latin America. With NAFTA, Nissan planned to rationalize its production, centering production of its Sentra model in Mexico and producing the Altima model in the United States.

Over time, the position of the two firms shifted. They decided that higher rules of origin would not hurt them. Although high rules of origin would create a barrier to selling into the U.S. market, this did not present a problem because they did not export a lot of their production. Moreover, higher rules of origin might provide protection against new entrants, particularly Japanese firms that would be attracted by low rules of origin to use Mexico to gain access to the U.S. market. The Mexican government also initially preferred low rules that would encourage new entrants into the market, but after VW and Nissan changed their position there were no domestic interests pushing for lower rules of origin. This opened a gap between the Mexican negotiating position and the domestic industries.

Mexico's emerging position on rules of origin, then, was "neither too strong nor too weak." The key was to find a level that would attract investment to Mexico. If the rules of origin were too high, then investment would be discouraged; if they were too low, then not enough value added would occur in Mexico. In automobiles, Mexico began with the view that a 50 percent rule, the level that Canada had negotiated in the FTA and continued to defend in the NAFTA, would be best. The parts industry wanted rules of origin that would encourage the terminal auto industry to source within the region, hoping that it would be able to get a piece of the expanding auto production pie in North America, as well as protection from abrupt liberalization.

The basis for a compromise between the United States and Mexico began to emerge at the plenary meeting at the Four Seasons Hotel in Toronto in May 1992. The U.S. negotiators began to think of ways in which they could satisfy Mexican auto parts producers. They hit on the idea of easing the transition for parts producers by guaranteeing that as trade expanded, some of the new business would be channeled to Mexican parts producers. Using 1992 as a reference level, established auto producers would continue to use the same level of domestic content for five years, and lower domestic content rules would be applied to any additional growth in car production. As a result, parts producers are guaranteed a declining share of any growth achieved in the auto parts market during the transition period. In this way, Mexico would achieve liberalization while remaining integrated in the continental automobile industry. Mexico accepted higher rules of origin to assuage the U.S. concern that it would not become an export platform for fourth-country manufacturers.

Some members of the Mexican team in the auto working group rejected the notion that NAFTA could serve as an export platform to attract Asian investment in autos, and they flatly denied any concern for promoting Asian investment in particular: "This theme was not discussed," said one negotiator. "What we wanted was foreign investment, not necessarily from Japan." However, other negotiators in the same working group stressed the importance of attracting new entrants into the Mexican market as a critical and unchanging objective. Part of the explanation for the discrepancy may lie in the fact that the auto working group did not negotiate content requirements, which instead were negotiated in the rules of origin working group. Negotiators in that group were unequivocal about the issue of Asian investment. As one said, "Toyota will not come to Mexico except to sell to the United States. Rules of origin at 85 percent are not good for them."

The Canadians were puzzled by the Mexican position on rules of origin in the auto working group, especially their apparent lack of interest in attracting Japanese investors. "We kept making the point that the Japanese are here. The U.S. kept trying to structure the phaseout of Mexican rules to keep out the Japanese—eliminating regulations for U.S. firms but keeping them in place for new investors." Mexico's position makes more sense in light of the fact that higher rules of origin were part of the deal that began to emerge at the Four Seasons: the Mexicans had to accept rules that were discriminatory on behalf of the U.S. industry in order to secure protection for their auto parts producers. In short, Mexico's position on the rules of origin changed because the Mexican strategy changed: "Instead of protecting through the Auto Decrees, we protect with rules of origin."

Canada's strategy during much of the negotiation was to keep its head down to avoid any threat of changes to the Auto Pact. Its failure to gain acceptance of its Continental Auto Pact proposal at Chantilly left Canada somewhat marginalized from the core discussion, which revolved around the Mexican auto industry and its integration with the U.S. market. Canada helped move the American position along by generally supporting the United States on the need to open Mexico's auto industry, because as a U.S. negotiator put it, "the U.S. auto industry was the Canadian auto industry." At the same time, however, the fact that Canada refused to eliminate the Auto Pact encouraged the Mexicans to think that they might be able to keep the Auto Decrees. This left Canada in an awkward position, because it did not want the Auto Pact on the bargaining table.

### Weaving Free Trade from Protectionist Threads

Another major fight in the post-Dallas period was over textiles and apparel. Textiles were a major bone of contention from early 1992 onward. Little was done in the textile working group during the slow start leading up to 1992, and Dallas was not a watershed meeting for this issue. Although the essence of the deal on textiles was cut fairly early in the negotiations, it took a long time to sort out the details.

The results of the textile negotiations in NAFTA paralleled those of the auto working group. As with autos, textiles were a crucial sector for Mexico; rules of origin were a key issue, and high rules became a critical element of the compromise reached between the United States and Mexico; and Canada found itself marginalized, forced to fight both the United States and Mexico on rules of origin. U.S. negotiators considered the textile chapter the most protectionist—one used the term "Neanderthal"—part of the deal. The protectionist core of the deal emerged from private conversations between U.S. negotiator Ron Sorini, an old hand in textile negotiations with experience in the General Agreement on Tariffs and Trade (GATT), and Mexican negotiator Enrique Espinoza, who despite being a banker on secondment from the Banco Nacional de México (Banamex) and a self-proclaimed neophyte on textile negotiations, turned out to be a very able negotiator.

"Agreements are reached in restaurants, not at the negotiating table," said a textile negotiator. "At the table you have to play to your own benches." Thus, in one-on-one conversations, the Mexicans were given the impression that the United States might be flexible on the issue of quotas. In confidence, Sorini said to Espinoza, "We should think of eliminating quotas and an accelerated phaseout period. You can't have an FTA with quotas!" Following the cue, Espinoza argued forcefully in the formal negotiations for an end to quotas, saying "textiles are practically a 'show-stopper,'" and that Mexico could not sell NAFTA to the public and industry without the elimination of quotas.

The reason Sorini was so confident that quotas could be eliminated was that the industry had already identified its price: the creation of highly restrictive rules of origin. This trade-off was repugnant to the NAFTA negotiators in the rules of origin working group, but the textile negotiators—unlike those working on autos—had won the right to negotiate their own rules of origin. The role of industry was crucial in this textile deal. In informal conversations between the Mexican textile and apparel industry and their U.S. counterparts, the idea of restrictive rules of origin was discussed as a price for eliminating quotas. The Mexican textile industry resented the restrictive quotas it faced in the U.S. market, quotas that were a fraction of those on goods from China or Japan. The Mexicans argued to their U.S. counterparts that Mexico's first preference was, in fact, the lessor of two evils for the United States: it was better to lose textile jobs to a country like Mexico that imported from the United States than to low-wage Asian countries that import less from the United States.

The Mexican view, however sound on economic grounds, was destined to fail without industry support in the United States, so the Mexican negotiators asked their industry to contact its U.S. counterparts to ask under what conditions they might accept the elimination of quotas. The word came back that the U.S. industry would accept the elimination of quotas only under the condition that the products entering the U.S. market were 100 percent made in North America. The vertically integrated U.S. firms had captive yarn producers, and they wanted to prevent other producers from sourcing outside the region. They knew they would have to accept lower tariffs and quotas under NAFTA and decided it was best to fight for the most restrictive rules of origin possible. Some U.S. firms were already moving into *maquiladora* operations. In this way, the trade-off between the elimination of quotas and high rules of origin was engineered.

In practical terms, "100 percent made in North America" meant that under NAFTA rules of origin, products would be considered North American only if they were made in North America from components—from yarn forward—produced within the region. Mexico's opening position was a fabric-forward rule, meaning that any product made of regionally produced fabric—even if the fabric is made from yarn produced outside North America—and transformed into a garment is eligible for duty-free access to the North American market. Since Mexico had a successful, export-oriented fabric industry, such a rule was convenient. Earlier Canada had received with relief the news that this was Mexico's position, since many of Canada's most competitive producers sourced outside the region.

When Sorini proposed the yarn-forward rule, Espinoza accepted it, saying, "I don't like it, but it is the trade-off we need to eliminate quotas." Canada, on the other hand, was dismayed by the emerging consensus around restrictive rules of origin. According to a Mexican source, the Canadian negotiator Tom MacDonald said, "We've been railroaded." MacDonald resented the way that Mexico and the United States were waltzing together, treating Canada as a wallflower in the negotiations. The Canadians had been reluctant to agree to a separate working group on textiles in the first place because they felt the issue could be handled as part of the more general market access negotiations, as in the GATT. Now, they faced a deal that was clearly antithetical to Canada's interests because it would create major new barriers against Canadian exports.

In a meeting in Crystal City, Maryland, in June, Canada made its last stand against NAFTA's rules of origin in textiles. The Canadians proposed that Canadian apparel should be exempted from NAFTA, and Canada would remain with the FTA. Sorini said, "Fine, we're sick of hearing from you guys." But he also reminded the Canadians that the tariff rate quotas (TRQs)[3] in the FTA were scheduled to expire at the end of 1992. Said Sorini, "If you stick with the FTA, you get the whole FTA." In short, Canada would be unable to renegotiate the FTA to extend its TRQs. The issue was bumped up to the ministerial level. Here, Hills and Serra rejected what they called Canada's "à la carte" approach to the negotiations (taking a little of this, leaving a little of that) and insisted that Canada would have to accept the deal struck between the United States and Mexico. Serra accused Canada of being hypocritical and treating Mexico like a second-class citizen.

Rebuffed by the U.S. and Mexican ministers, the Canadians had to find another strategy. From that point onward, they concentrated on winning enough exemptions to ensure that access to the United States under NAFTA was at least as good for Canada as under the FTA. Although the Canadians would have preferred a less protectionist regime in textiles, they settled for a deal that at least did not worsen their position relative to the FTA. The key mechanism for achieving this was to secure the inclusion of TRQs in the NAFTA arrangement and use them to get around high rules of origin.

Basically, the Canadians did everything possible to undermine the effectiveness of high rules of origin where they affected Canada's textile and apparel exports. TRQs were the main "escape valve," and they had to be expanded dramatically under NAFTA to satisfy Canada's demands. At the same time, TRQs had to be introduced in such a way as not to be so visible to U.S. producers that it would be clear what the United States was giving away. A clear illustration of how the TRQs were used is provided by the treatment of Canadian wool suits. Under the FTA, Canada massively increased its export of wool suits. Shipped to the United States under a special quota for wool apparel in the FTA, exports of Canadian-made wool suits jumped from fifty thousand in 1988 to almost four hundred thousand in 1991, with one company, Quebec-based Peerless Clothing, accounting for 80 percent of those exports. Canada became the number one supplier of wool suits in the United States, taking a sizable part of the market. All these suits were made from offshore fabrics. The competitive edge of Peerless was that it used cheaper and higher-quality fabrics than those used by U.S. producers—and U.S. producers faced 30 to 40 percent tariffs if they imported the same wool.

It was Peerless Clothing that was pressing the Canadians to secure FTA rules of origin in the NAFTA, because the yarn-forward rule would pose a serious threat to the competitive edge that Peerless enjoyed in the U.S. market. This was exactly the intention of U.S. wool pants producers, one of the strongest textile lobbies. U.S. negotiators pushed for a specific limitation on the import of wool suits, directed at this single firm. Thus, even as late as the June jamboree in Crystal City, Canada was still resisting the inclusion of apparel in NAFTA, and the United States was still sick of hearing about it. This issue would carry on to the very end of the negotiations.

## The Easier Issues

In a number of working groups there was significant progress in the period between the Dallas jamboree and the Watergate end game. Agreement on intellectual property issues was largely a matter of importing the emerging MTN text into the NAFTA. More interesting analytically was the successful and early wrap-up of the transportation negotiations—and on terms highly favorable to Mexico.

### Intellectual Property: Importing the Multilateral Trade Negotiations

The NAFTA negotiators were concerned to reconcile the new principles, rules, norms, and decision-making procedures for the North American region with existing institutional arrangements, particularly the GATT. Such reconciliation efforts have been called "nesting" (Aggarwal 1996), and the main vehicle of nesting NAFTA in the GATT is Article XXIV. Article XXIV allows for the creation of discriminatory trade agreements (i.e., trade agreements that are not negotiated on a most-favored-nation basis) only as long as they are comprehensive (they liberalize "substantially all" trade between the members) and do not raise barriers to trade with third countries. Although NAFTA's high rules of origin in certain industries may be inconsistent with the GATT, most NAFTA provisions tend to be very similar to those in the GATT, and in some areas, such as intellectual property rights, the NAFTA text was imported directly from the Dunkel Text of the Uruguay Round. Indeed, the NAFTA negotiators often awaited developments in the MTN before drafting the North American rules.

Canadian negotiators argued that they wanted the same intellectual property provisions that were negotiated in the GATT (the so-called trade-related aspects of intellectual property rights [TRIPs]); Mexico, according to the Canadians, wanted less than what TRIPs provided and the United States wanted more. The Mexicans disagreed with this perception, arguing that they fully accepted TRIPs. However, they agreed that the United States was pushing for more. Much of the pressure to go beyond TRIPs came from domestic industries in the United States. In particular, the firms that comprised the Intellectual Property Committee[4] wrote to the U.S. trade representative urging the administration to strengthen intellectual property protection in Canada and Mexico above and beyond the disciplines laid out in the Dunkel Text, and cautioned U.S. negotiators against granting any special concessions to the NAFTA partners.

Patent and licensing laws provide an example of an extremely controversial public policy area that was negotiated simultaneously in the two arenas, the MTN and NAFTA. Canadian negotiators insisted on addressing these issues in Geneva, but they also were pushed very aggressively by the United States and U.S.-based private corporations in the NAFTA negotiations. The agreement to eliminate Canada's protection of its generic drug industry was imported into NAFTA from the Dunkel Text. "NAFTA was blamed, but the deal was done in Geneva," said a Canadian negotiator. Canada wanted to go ahead with the GATT deal and attract foreign investment to the pharmaceutical industry. Canadian regulations had created a generic drug industry that did very little of its own research and development. The global industry was restructuring, and Canadian officials decided that the Dunkel Text was "where the world was heading," and it would be necessary to jump on board if Canada hoped to attract these high-technology investments.

The view of the U.S. negotiators was slightly different. They argued that the changes were "bought" by the U.S. industry in exchange for promises of billions of dollars of new investments in Canada. The industry had been pushing for this change for years, but Canadian policy makers only decided that the benefits outweighed the costs by the early 1990s. The crucial point is that Canada could have made this concession in the MTN or NAFTA and chose to do it in the MTN for obvious reasons: it was more palatable politically to present the withdrawal of protection for the generic drug industry (and consequently the higher price of drugs in Canada) as the result of pressures from the international trading system rather than from U.S. pressures. This was a key reason why Canada did not want the NAFTA negotiations to get out ahead of the MTN, and a crucial factor in Canada's greater patience in the negotiations relative to Mexico.

Once the Dunkel Text was negotiated in Geneva in December 1991, the NAFTA chapter on intellectual property could proceed expeditiously. Most of the action in this working group took place between January and August 1992. Negotiations were facilitated in March 1992 when the Mexicans brought in Roberto Villareal Gonda, who had served as Mexico's commissioner of patents. Villareal replaced Guillermo Aguilar Alvarez, who SECOFI had also assigned to handle the investment and dispute resolution files. Villareal had played a key role in rewriting Mexican intellectual property law in 1991. He objected to U.S. neglect of the rights of the authors of intellectual property in favor of producers and stressed Mexico's desire for a different type of intellectual property system.

Although the United States and Mexico had differences of opinion, talks were facilitated by a history of negotiation in this area. Officials from the two countries had been engaged in discussions on these issues leading up to the 1990 reform of Mexico's intellectual property rights system. The U.S. negotiators knew Mexico wanted to modernize its intellectual property laws. "Reform was part of Salinas's original plan" said one Mexican negotiator. "We had to have intellectual property legislation more in line with an open economy. Otherwise, we would be like a car with a new motor and a flat tire." The Dunkel Text also helped.

The Dunkel Text constituted the basis for 95 percent of the intellectual property rights chapter in NAFTA. Agreeing on the remaining "4.5 percent was a struggle," and this included U.S. efforts to achieve what it failed to get in the MTN. A key issue for the United States was pipeline protection[5] for pharmaceutical patents and satellite encryption. The Mexicans believed that the United States was trying to regain lost patents and to use intellectual property rights legislation to compensate for the declining competitiveness of their pharmaceutical industry. The final 0.5 percent of the chapter, and the toughest issue for Canada, was the cultural exemption, and it went unresolved right to the end at Watergate.

The Canadian cultural exemption refers to Article 2005 of the FTA, which exempts specific cultural industries—printed publications, film and videos, musical recordings, and radio and television broadcasting—from FTA obligations. However, the agreement does provide for retaliation by the parties to the agreement against the use of the cultural exemption by taking actions of "equivalent commercial effect." The clash between Canada and the United States on this issue caused some very ugly fights in the intellectual property working group. The United States pushed relentlessly, arguing that the underlying issues were economic, and the Canadians resisted with equally dogged determination, arguing that cultural sovereignty was at stake. Canada had entered the negotiations saying that culture was not on the table, and this was the position the Canadians adhered to throughout the entire negotiation process. Nevertheless, it was impossible for the issue not to be discussed in some form, especially since the NAFTA was quite unlike the FTA in one crucial respect: the FTA covered only what was explicitly written into the deal, whereas the NAFTA was designed to cover everything save what was explicitly exempted. The problem became one of preserving an exemption under a new legal framework. In the words of a Canadian negotiator, "How do you get the status quo where the rules work differently?" Canada sought to preserve the integrity of the cultural exemption in the FTA by incorporating it into the NAFTA. However, as the intellectual property chapter took shape, it became clear that it covered a wide range of cultural issues.

American negotiators joked among themselves about the absurdity of the Canadian position. The favorite joke held that "the difference between Canada and yogurt was that yogurt has live culture." Pointing to Canadian broadcasting, they argued that culture was used as a commercial barrier and as a way of protecting jobs, since while the ownership of cable companies was exclusively Canadian, the programming was overwhelmingly American. The United States was concerned as much about the "contagion effect" of

Canada's exemption on Mexico, and more broadly on the Europeans in the MTN. Indeed, the Europeans did point to Canada's cultural exemption in their unsuccessful efforts to keep culture out of the Dunkel Text. Mexico, however, saw a market opportunity in the United States in the area of Spanish language products in the entertainment industry and dismissed the need for a cultural exemption.

### The Transportation Working Group: NAFTA's Jurassic Park

The negotiation over transportation provided a curious anomaly in the NAFTA. It is the one sector negotiated by what the Salinas technopols called "dinosaurs" that SECOFI wanted to keep out of the negotiations. And it was one of the few sectors in which Mexico, arguably, achieved an asymmetrical deal in its favor. The lead negotiator, Alejandro Peniche, personified the image of the pompous, macho, inflated, vulgar, and ostentatious bureaucrat from Mexico's corporatist and authoritarian past. He was also an exceptionally shrewd negotiator.

Peniche was not a sophisticated or well-educated member of Salinas's technocratic elite. He was close to retirement in a team whose average age was thirty-four years. Everything about Peniche clashed with the image of the "Ivy League–educated free traders" that Salinas's team projected for itself abroad. Whereas the SECOFI offices were located in a modern executive tower with a neo-Aztec interior design near Chapultepec in downtown Mexico City, or the posh, modern, glass and steel building in the bustling financial district of Insurgentes Avenue, the Secretariat of Transportation was run out of a dirty, dilapidated, nondescript cement structure swarming with truckers looking for permits or licenses, and buzzing outside with helicopters from the nearby police station. The man who negotiated transportation rose through the Mexican bureaucracy by working within the corporatist patronage system. This meant that he had a closer relationship with the trucking industry than many of his counterparts on the Mexican team had with their respective industries.

The trucking sector was peculiar in a number of respects. First, Mexico was not the *demandeur*. As far as Peniche was concerned, Mexico was making concessions in other areas and he had no intention of paying for access to the North American market at the expense of his industry. The Mexicans insisted that transportation was not a "give sector," and concessions would come only in return for as much reciprocity within the sector as possible. They would have to be dragged reluctantly into continental integration. Second, the U.S. trucking industry did not get its act together early enough, nor act sufficiently in concert, to influence the negotiations. Mexican negotiators insisted that the deal had to respect the asymmetries in the structure of firms, the carrying capacity of Mexican rigs, the different level of standards, the underdevelopment of Mexican infrastructure, and the lack of financing and insurance. They took a conventional developing country's bargaining position and argued for a liberalization timetable that would allow the Mexicans a chance to prepare for the competition.

On the U.S. side, the major firms initially were not excited by the idea of doing business in Mexico and only decided it was worthwhile after the negotiation process was underway. As a result, U.S. negotiator Nancy MacRae did not have the backing necessary to overcome Mexico's resistance to the total, immediate opening that the U.S. industry later decided it wanted. Thus, MacRae was one of the few U.S. negotiators who was subsequently singled out for criticism for not getting enough for the industry. However, Hufbauer and Schott (1994) suggested that the chapter on transportation achieved far more than the expectations they set out in their book of recommendations, and they awarded the chapter a grade of "A."

There was a history of negotiation and contact between the officials in the transportation sector, and these previous negotiations had not been harmonious. The Mexicans closed the trucking market in 1981. In the mid-1980s they began to liberalize, and Salinas accelerated this process. As a result of Mexican-U.S. talks prior to NAFTA, officials in the two governments already knew one another. Following one of the first meetings of the working group on transportation, a U.S. official complained to Blanco that there were "backward" people on the Mexican team. That official was subsequently removed from the U.S. team and replaced by MacRae for the duration of the NAFTA negotiations.

U.S. negotiators found the Mexican negotiating style "very macho" and noted that none of their negotiators were women. "The Mexicans wanted to extract their pound of flesh, and then some. They played a lot of games. Personality and personal relations were very important." This was confirmed by the Mexican negotiators, one of whom said relations with U.S. officials were friendly and personal: "I invited them to eat and drink in my house. We handled the issues with care. Our relations are not formal, that is a principle factor. We maintain correct forms, with an attitude of respect, not with God damn hard faces, with ties all done-up tight, and tense. There is no reason why we cannot be friends, and of course that does not mean I am not going to defend the interests of my country."

A U.S. official remained more skeptical. "It was easy to be sucked into the camaraderie, the back slapping, the drinking. Then in the negotiation the next day you would discover that it earned you nothing—except a hangover!"

Needless to say, the "dinosaurs" negotiating transportation and the young technocrats in SECOFI could barely conceal their mutual contempt. "I can't say we were fine-tuned enough to take advantage of that division," said a U.S.

official. "Often SECOFI was ready to give, but the [Secretariat of Communication and Transportation] would not give. We settled for less than we might have, had we been tougher. In the end, we got half a loaf, or less. We were prepared to accept that. We made the call that we were not going to get more than that. Mexico was making concessions in other areas."

A U.S. negotiator summarized the results: "We gave the Mexicans generous phase-in schedules. We broke down the liberalization process into discrete processes: first the border states, then the entire country are liberalized. Only international cargo is included. Then, in seven years, they can come back and there will be further liberalization. We didn't get access to Mexican trucking, we didn't get investment in trucking." Thus, while the agreement liberalizes cross-border access, allowing international cargo service, Mexican trucks and buses that only operate within Mexico are protected from foreign ownership. With the United States willing to make such concessions, and Mexico sticking to its tough position, the transportation deal was the first chapter of NAFTA to be completed. It was wrapped up in May 1992, three months before the complete agreement was signed in Washington. As one official aptly put it, "On transportation, the NAFTA was front-loaded."

### Financial Services: Three Enemies

As noted previously, finance officials felt deeply betrayed by SECOFI after the Dallas jamboree. They believed that the timing of the concessions in Dallas was an error, one that left them exposed to six more months of being "beaten over the head" as the negotiations continued: "We were naked, we had nothing left to cover ourselves with. It was a big error on SECOFI's part." While they blamed this error on SECOFI for not having a good sense of timing as far as concessions were concerned, they also blamed themselves for following SECOFI's orders. Interagency rancor stemmed from conflicts between *camarillas*: officials from the Secretariat of Finance and Public Credit and the Bank of Mexico, and those from SECOFI were members of rival *camarillas*, and the former were less willing to accept orders from Blanco without question.

After Dallas, profound distrust between SECOFI, the Secretariat of Finance and Public Credit, and the Bank of Mexico changed the Mexican negotiation dynamic. The Secretariat of Finance and the Bank of Mexico insisted on taking the lead in the financial service negotiations. Raúl Ramos, the main SECOFI official, was moved to the market access working group, and Salas, the other key SECOFI official, was relegated to "making notes" and "watching" the negotiations from the sidelines. In the words of a Mexican negotiator, "We had three enemies in the negotiations: the US, Canada, and SECOFI." For their part, officials at SECOFI felt that the people in the Secretariat of Finance were not sufficiently enthusiastic about the liberalization of the Mexican financial sector. Said a SECOFI official, "I doubt whether we would have opened had the Secretariat of Finance been in charge. There would have been an opening, but not at the same rate. Finance people will deny this, but NAFTA went beyond what they wanted." For finance officials, however, SECOFI had gone too far, too fast in NAFTA. Now, having conceded most of what they had available to give away, the Mexicans were forced into a dangerous defensive game, trying to deflect the intense pressure still coming from the United States for more concessions, especially in the area of branching.

Negotiations remained deadlocked over the issue of allowing U.S. banks to establish branches in Canada and Mexico. The Canadians insisted that there would be no branching of U.S. banks into Canada until Canadian banks received an equal right in the United States, which would require a reform of the Glass-Steagall law, which prevented banks and securities from being under one roof and kept the American banking system decentralized and fragmented. During a jamboree in Toronto in mid-May, and one in Crystal City in early June, the Mexicans also took the position that U.S. banks would have to create subsidiaries in Mexico in order to provide banking services or establish branches in that country. The United States derided Mexico's position as being simply "me too." The American response was to bring in officials from the Treasury Department who said that while they supported the idea of a reform initiative, if Glass-Steagall reform was undertaken through NAFTA, its legislation would have to be reviewed by House committees chaired by John Dingle and Henry Gonzalez, both of whom were opposed to NAFTA. This clearly made the initiative impossible. In the end, it was the U.S. financial service negotiator who was forced to back off, Jules Katz finally telling him, "Look, this is silly. Stop pushing for branching."

## Other Issues in the Post-Dallas Period

The period between March and July 1992 was a critical one for the negotiations on trade remedies. After the "high ground" proposal was defeated, Mexico shifted from its demand for the elimination of antidumping provisions to the pursuit of inclusion of a Chapter Nineteen dispute settlement mechanism. In April, in Montreal, Mexico secured American agreement to negotiate the inclusion of Chapter Nineteen in NAFTA and of Mexico in Chapter Nineteen, an idea that was originally resisted by the United States. According to one Mexican negotiator, this is what Mexico had wanted all along. A member of the Mexican team admitted that the Mexicans did not originally appreciate the value of Chapter Nineteen, a point made repeatedly by the Canadians. Nevertheless, by April they were arguing that Mexico had to have something to offer to its industry in terms of relief from U.S. trade remedy laws. They also noted that Mexico was at a disadvantage because whereas Canada had ninety years of experience with antidumping legislation and the United States had seventy-five years, Mexico had just introduced its antidumping rules four years earlier. By June, Mexico had abandoned all other proposals and agreed to concentrate on the feasibility of extending Chapter Nineteen to apply to Mexico.

Mexico's shift to seeking Chapter Nineteen–type protection for its exporters caused consternation in Canada. Canadian negotiators never intended to exclude Mexico from Chapter Nineteen, but they feared that opening up this issue to another party could result in a weakening of its provisions, especially given Mexico's civil law tradition and the closed and discretionary nature of the Mexican policy process. The Canadians were certainly more concerned about protecting the integrity of the existing Chapter Nineteen provisions than were the Mexicans, who simply wanted in. Indeed, the other negotiators noted that the Canadians often seemed to act as if their honor was at stake, becoming "crazy and unreasonable" when proposals were made that they did not like.

In the energy area, negotiations were able to proceed, since Mexico had finally agreed to negotiate a chapter on energy. Between March and June, texts were exchanged, but without much progress toward an agreement. At a June meeting in the Doubletree hotel in Crystal City, Virginia, a composite text was presented. However, the three countries went into the Watergate meetings without having resolved any of the basic issues in the energy sector and still disagreeing on the same points that they had been fighting over from the outset.

The market access negotiations were stuck between March and August because each country had a different list of key products that they wanted protected. The Canadian negotiators halted their talks in March because the tariff issues depended on outcomes on several other issues. The United States and Mexico also remained at loggerheads on a number of tariff items. The key issue in the agriculture sector was Canada's refusal to go along with comprehensive liberalization and eliminate their agricultural marketing boards. The fight over agriculture continued into the first week of May. Finally, in Montreal the ministers agreed that there would be two separate bilateral deals on agriculture. Furthermore, Mexico and the United States would "punish Canada" for its stubbornness by carving out their own exceptions. In the Mexican case, this meant denying Canada access to its powdered milk market. The 130 percent tariff on Canadian milk will gradually be reduced until it reaches the GATT tariff of 15 percent, and there it will remain. From Montreal forward, there were separate bilateral negotiations in the agricultural sector between Mexico and Canada, Canada and the United States, and the United States and Mexico.

## Understanding the Negotiation

The evolution of the negotiations in the period following the Dallas jamboree suggested that the United States was going to continue its strategy of withholding concessions, making only minimal changes in its negotiating positions to accommodate the demands of the other two players. Table 7.2 provides a summary assessment of the principal hypotheses as they apply to the post-Dallas bargaining stage. Mexico backed away from its "high ground" proposal on trade remedies, and Canada made no progress in its request for changes in Glass-Steagall regulations. U.S. negotiators did not disagree that such reforms were needed, only that they could not do them in the context of NAFTA without facing serious domestic repercussions. Since Mexico wanted the deal badly, it offered up concessions, moving progressively closer to the U.S. position on most issues. While the U.S. negotiators resisted change to their own regulatory system, they continued to press for the broadest possible access to the markets of the other two countries.

Canada was able to resist these pressures only by using the FTA as a nonagreement alternative. Canada refused to accept changes that would leave it worse off than the FTA. Where Mexico and the United States reached bilateral agreements that potentially hurt Canadian interests, Canada tried to walk away from the table. After Dallas, Canada separated itself from the agriculture negotiations. However, it was unable to do so in textiles, when the U.S. and Mexican negotiators rejected the "à la carte" approach to NAFTA, and Canadian negotiators had to find other ways of ensuring that Canada's interests were not left worse off under NAFTA than the FTA, in spite of highly protectionist rules of origin. Finally, Canada attempted to use its seat at the negotiation table to ensure than any concessions granted to Mexico would be extended to Canada. Take the case of duty drawbacks. These are duty remission schemes that allow companies to avoid paying duties on goods they import as long as the final product is re-exported rather than sold in the local market. Mexico's *maquiladora* program is essentially such a duty remission scheme. U.S. firms can bring parts into Mexico for assembly and then sell the final product in the U.S. market without having to pay a duty each time the product crosses the U.S.-Mexico border. Canada was supposed to eliminate duty drawbacks five years after the FTA entered into force, in 1994, but Canadian negotiators demanded and won a two-year extension. As a result, the United States granted Mexico a seven-year phase-out period so it would have as much time as Canada. The U.S. negotiator wanted to eliminate duty drawbacks altogether because they provide an incentive for U.S. firms to take production offshore, so he proposed a solution in which each country could rebate a substantial part of their duties on goods that did not meet the NAFTA rules of origin. This system was extended to Canada,

*Table 7.2* Hypotheses: After Dallas

| Hypothesis | Canada | Mexico | United States |
|---|---|---|---|
| Asymmetry: weaker states are more responsive to powerful states relative to domestic pressures; powerful states are more responsive to domestic pressures relative to the weaker states. | As Mexico shifts in response to U.S. demands, pressure increases on Canada to make concessions or remain isolated. This sets the stage for U.S.-Canada confrontations at Watergate.<br><br>Negotiators fail to induce shifts in U.S. positions.<br><br>Caught in a pinch when U.S. and Mexico cut deals.<br><br>Cannot walk away as easily as at the outset of the negotiations. | In response to U.S. demands, continues to make concessions.<br><br>In some cases, colludes with U.S. negotiators against Canada (e.g., cuts bilateral deal with U.S. to eliminate quotas for high rules of origin in textiles).<br><br>Negotiators fail to induce significant shifts in U.S. positions. | Repeatedly shoots down proposals that require major internal reforms.<br><br>Successfully presses for concessions from Mexico.<br><br>Has greater difficulty inducing Canada to move where changes imply departure from the FTA. |
| Patterns of delayed mutual responsiveness: the lower the subjective utility assigned to the nonagreement alternative, the more concessions will be offered. | Uses FTA as a nonagreement alternative.<br><br>Uses GATT text where possible.<br><br>Bandwagon on Mexico's achievement of partial duty drawback. | Seeks to confuse and exhaust negotiators in auto working group.<br><br>Uses prudential arguments (like Canada) in financial services. | Drags out the negotiation.<br><br>Rejects à la carte approach.<br><br>Repeats demands as a condition of reaching a deal. |
| Institutions: centralized, vertical domestic institutions are a bargaining liability, while divided government is an asset. | Remains unwilling to consider changes under NAFTA vis-à-vis the FTA that would require major renegotiation with domestic groups. | Remains willing to contemplate sweeping domestic reforms. | Uses domestic constraints to avoid changing positions. |

much to the irritation of the Mexicans, who noted that Canada had negotiated away all duty drawbacks in the FTA.

Mexico did not have an attractive nonagreement alternative and as a result, it needed the deal more than the other two countries. Thus, its strategies were more varied and somewhat less effective. Mexico tried to use the fact that it could implement sweeping domestic reforms to its advantage, and was thus less inclined to feel constrained by the terms of previous bilateral or multilateral agreements. The Mexicans tried to confuse and exhaust the U.S. negotiators on auto issues; cut an ambitious deal on quotas and rules of origin in textiles; get access to Chapter Nineteen provisions; prevent branching by banks, using prudential arguments developed by Canada; and finally, secure an asymmetrical deal in transportation, using a very different type of negotiator.

Finally, the United States continued to control the clock throughout this stage of the negotiation. American negotiators appeared to be in no hurry to get a deal, continuing to insist that their demands be met as a condition for getting agreement. Soon, however, George Bush would become impatient for a deal, and this fact would lead to the final, dramatic conclusion to the NAFTA negotiations in the Watergate Hotel, where the United States, for the first time, lost control over the negotiation clock.

# End Game at the Watergate

**T**he "great curvaceous hulks"[1] of the Watergate apartment, hotel, and office complex sit inelegantly on the Potomac River shore of the Foggy Bottom lowlands in Washington, D.C. Named originally for the modest band shell and restaurant that once stood on the site, the word *Watergate* had since become, and would remain, synonymous with scandals in Washington, from Irangate in the 1980s to Zippergate in the 1990s.[2] It was not scandal, but anticipation, that was in the air on the morning of Sunday, August 2, 1992, however, as Carla Hills, Jaime Serra, and Michael Wilson joined scores of negotiators from Canada, Mexico, and the United States at the Watergate complex. Here they would begin the seventh, and what was widely believed would be the final, round of negotiations to complete a North American free trade agreement.

The Americans were getting anxious. The Bush administration wanted the president to be able to sign an agreement before the presidential election in November 1992. U.S. law required the president to wait ninety days after the conclusion of negotiations before formally signing an agreement, and this meant that a deal would have to be wrapped up by August 5, at the latest, in order to meet the electoral timetable.[3] To put some heat on their negotiators, Presidents Bush and Salinas met at the Major League Baseball All-Star Game in San Diego on July 14, where the two stated that they were entering the top of the ninth inning of negotiations. In fact, the trilateral game was closer to the middle innings, with negotiators still some considerable distance apart on all but a few of the issues. Beyond the agreement on transportation that was reached in April, no major breakthroughs had been achieved. However, limited agreement had been carved out in some areas. On services, Mexico agreed to grant national treatment to American and Canadian advertising firms and to refrain from requiring that firms establish a Mexican office in order to do business in the country. Mexico also agreed not to pursue an exemption for cultural industries, although Canada would make no such commitment. Rules of origin for automobiles were clarified by defining what costs could be included in calculations of North American content, but the percentage of required content remained at issue. And although there was good news for the presidents in the agreement that had been reached earlier in July on the broad strokes of a deal on financial services that would open Mexico's banking, insurance, and securities industries to American and Canadian investors by the year 2000, outstanding issues remained even in this sector.

Nor were the Mexicans prepared to cede much ground on the energy issue, refusing to consider American investments and risk-sharing arrangements in Mexican oil production and distribution. "American companies 'can't explore, can't produce, can't refine, can't transport, can't wholesale and can't retail' Mexican oil, said a senior US trade official. 'Risk-sharing contracts are out.'"[4] The American oil industry had been lobbying hard to secure so-called risk contracts, which entitled foreign drillers to a share in any crude oil discovered, but instead they would be limited to performance contracts that simply offered bonuses, rather than equity, to drillers for discoveries. These provisions would appeal primarily to oil service companies, which would stand to benefit financially from their ability to perform better than Mexican competitors. Similarly, state-owned Petroleos Mexicanos (PEMEX) would open up its procurement process for goods and services to outside firms, although the extent of the opening remained to be determined. American officials had known that negotiations on energy were going to be difficult, but this dry hole was likely to cause the U.S. oil industry to sit out the ratification process, declining to lobby Congress in support of any agreement, and that was a matter of considerable concern to U.S. negotiators.[5]

The latest ministerial meeting, in Mexico City on July 25–26, 1992, failed to resolve outstanding differences on key issues, including automobiles, textiles, financial services, agricultural tariffs, investment, energy, and government procurement. However, the United States was successful in cutting a number of sweetheart deals that would afford protection for certain industries, thus ensuring support for an agreement among important free trade allies. At the Mexico City ministerial meeting, U.S. and Mexican negotiators reached tentative agreement on provisions that would allow the "Big Three" American auto producers to increase their exports to Mexico while reducing their obligation to produce in Mexico under Mexican trade balancing rules. In addition, the two agreed to a complex formula that would afford protection to Mexican auto parts manufacturers. At this meeting, as well, the United States finally dropped its efforts to eliminate the Canada-U.S. Auto Pact. The process was typical of Jules Katz's negotiating style: when John Weekes said to Katz, "You're not serious about getting rid of it [the Auto pact]?," Katz simply laughed and went on to other issues, signaling to Weekes that he would not push further on the Auto Pact.

American and Mexican officials also satisfied U.S. textile producers by agreeing, over Canadian objections, to extremely high-domestic-content requirements on virtually every element of the production process beyond raw fibers. The effect of the agreement was to require that clothing be sewn in North America from fabric made in North America, and the fabric would also have to be made from North American–made yarn (triple transformation), which would require Mexican and Canadian clothing manufacturers to buy yarn and fabrics from North American (primarily U.S.) textile producers in order to sell their products in the American market (the so-called yarn-forward rule of origin). The American sugar industry was taken care of, as well, with an agreement that would raise Mexico's quota for sugar exports to the United States, but only if Mexican sugar production were to exceed domestic demand.[6] Additional agreements in Mexico City between the United States and Mexico on the sensitive issues of corn and glassware meant that many of the remaining disagreements were between Canada and its trilateral negotiating partners, and with the United States in particular on autos, cultural industries, foreign investment, textiles, and trade remedies.

In the week following the Mexico City ministerial meeting, the chief negotiators, along with the various working groups from the three countries, had been hard at work at the Watergate Hotel in Washington, in an attempt to wrap up agreements on technical issues to clear the way for the ministerial decisions that would be necessary to conclude a deal. The principal trade-offs that would have to be engineered to produce a deal are summarized in Table 8.1. Following the preparatory work of the chief negotiators, the ministers arrived at the Watergate on August 2. Hopes were high that an agreement was within reach and could be achieved by the Bush administration's August 5 deadline. That prognosis would prove to be off by a week. The delay would not be for want of trying, however, as negotiators met virtually nonstop for ten days, attempting to reconcile disparate positions on extremely sensitive issues. Central among these was the rule of origin for automobiles, specifically the percentage of a vehicle's content that must be produced in North America for it to receive duty-free treatment. The United States was concerned lest Japanese and other foreign automobile producers bypass American tariffs by shipping parts to Mexico or Canada and assembling them there for sale in the United States.

*Table 8.1* Trade-offs in the End Game at Watergate

| Issue | Canada | Mexico | United States | Observations |
|---|---|---|---|---|
| Trade Rules | Opposes any initiative to open Chapter 19. Walks out and negotiations are frozen across the working groups for 2 days. The minister, under the authority of the prime minister, indicates Canada will break off talks over the issue.<br><br>Has to convince the U.S. that its counterproposal addresses U.S. concerns regarding the inclusion of Mexico. Canadian language prevails. | Is prepared to accept U.S. proposal, since Chapter 19 is less important to them. The Mexicans worry that Canada will break off the U.S. to reject Mexico's attempts to have Chapter 19 applied to Mexico. | Takes advantage of the gap that has opened between Mexico and Canada.<br><br>Sees Chapter 19 as a vehicle to reform Mexican law and ensure panel decisions would be implemented. Worries that as Mexico drops its tariffs, nontarrif barriers will become more attractive and they want to use Chapter 19 to prevent this. Specifically, proposes changes to the "extraordinary challenge" provisions of Chapter 19 (wants to create a special review mechanism).<br><br>Feels Canada can protect its core values without gutting the principles the U.S. seeks to achieve. | Once the impasse over Chapter 19 was resolved, and the U.S. backed off, "the rest of the deal clicked into place." This issue had to be solved before the remaining issues could be resolved at the Watergate. |
| Market Access | Mexico and the U.S. were at loggerheads, leaving the Canadians on the sidelines.<br><br>Agrees to increase rules of origin in autos to 62.5% and secures an extension of partial duty drawbacks (see Rules of Origin). | Accepts 15-year transition in agriculture but insists on nothing longer than 10 years on industrial products.<br><br>Pushes for more access in some sectors (e.g., glass, paper) but ultimately accepts U.S. position that it could no more. | By Watergate, U.S. negotiators had developed an acute sense of industry interests and were successful in keeping almost all potential sectors opposed to NAFTA neutralized. | Market access issues were "crunched" at Watergate: they had been narrowed down to the most sensitive sectors. The issues hammered out at Watergate include paper, telecommunications, computers, beer and wine, and textiles. |

| | | | | |
|---|---|---|---|---|
| Energy | Accepts that Mexico will not be bound by the same rules as Canada in the FTA. | Wins partial duty drawbacks. <br><br> Sensing that U.S. negotiators are under pressure to wrap up due to electoral deadlines, Mexico holds out. Tries to reserve all PEMEX contract work for Mexican companies. <br><br> Rejects proportionality clause. | Phase-out periods were agreed. They would be 0, 5, 10, and 15 years. The formula 0, 6, 12 failed, because agriculture needed a 15-year transition. <br><br> Accepts that they are not going to get investment in energy production in Mexico. <br><br> Pushes for proportionality clause, then relents. | Energy was wrapped up 1 week before the end. |
| Rules of Origin | At Watergate, the drawback issue was linked to the rule of origin on automobiles. Agreed to 62.5% rule in exchange for the partial, permanent drawbacks. The U.S. offered to go to 5 years on drawbacks in exchange for 65% on autos, and Canada refused. <br><br> Automotive rules of origin were a tough issue, and the U.S. negotiators "came close to telling Canada to take a hike." | Agrees to the partial, permanent duty drawback scheme. <br><br> Mexican negotiators felt they benefited from the fact that this working group was wrapped up at the ministerial level because of the respective capabilities of Serra and Hills. | U.S. negotiator offers a partial, permanent duty drawback scheme. <br><br> The "Big Three" were on the phone with the chief negotiators until the very end. The trade-off was 62.5% in return for a fix on the Honda issue. U.S. negotiators had trouble selling this to the Big Three executives. | |

Table 8.1 Trade-offs in the End Game at Watergate (*continued*)

| Issue | Canada | Mexico | United States | Observations |
|---|---|---|---|---|
| Textiles | The main problem in Watergate was Canada. Once the Mexicans and the U.S. reached a deal to eliminate quotas in exchange for restrictive rules of origin, it was necessary to accommodate Canada by creating a complex system of tariff rate quotas. Through these, Canada ensured that it had enough exceptions so that access to the U.S. was as good or better than under the FTA. <br><br> The biggest fight was over quotas on wool apparel. | Mexico and U.S. had agreed on the triple transformation rule, and this deal could not be undone by Canada. | Agrees to large increase in quota levels for textiles and apparel for Mexico. <br><br> Uses its concession to Canada on culture to resist further concessions in textiles. <br><br> Insists Canada limit wool suit exports. | Textiles was the last issue before the handshake on the NAFTA deal. |
| Autos | Refuses to go above 62.5% content rule. | Sides with Canada, but is prepared to go higher on rules. <br><br> Pushes for elimination of chicken tax (25% duty on light trucks). | Pushes hard for 65% rule, then relents. Business is disappointed. <br><br> Eliminates the chicken tax for Mexico. | Rules of origin in autos move to 62.5% in 2 stages over 8 years. |
| Procurement | The Canadian negotiator in this working group nearly fumbled the negotiations and had to be replaced by a more senior official. <br><br> Believed that Mexico had pulled a fast one on Canadians and had to bring the U.S. around. | Seeks to reserve 70% of PEMEX contracts for 8 years, then drops reservation to 50% immediately. <br><br> Initially there was the potential for a bilateral agreement between the U.S. and Mexico. | Demands access to PEMEX contracts. <br><br> Katz had been prepared to remove the issue from the table. | The final deal is closer to what the U.S. wanted: access to 50% of PEMEX contracts immediately, 70% in 8 years, and 100% after 10 years. |

| | Canada | Mexico | United States | Outcome |
|---|---|---|---|---|
| Agriculture | Canada-Mexico market access negotiations wrapped up late because they depended on the conclusion of Mexico–U.S. talks. | Main issues were export subsidies and phaseouts. | Main issues were export subsidies and phaseouts. | Agriculture was part of a grand solution—a package of concessions involving other sectors. |
| Financial Services | Only minor issues were dealt with at Watergate. | Tensions with U.S. in this working group had diminished after the U.S. chief negotiator told his working group head to stop pushing for branching.<br><br>Too many concessions made early in the negotiations to be able to exploit U.S. impatience in the end game. | On dispute settlement, adopts the general provisions of the larger NAFTA dispute settlement mechanism but with their own roster of financial experts to sit on panels, because the U.S. did not want trade people sitting on financial service panels.<br><br>Ended up getting more in financial services than expected, which helped sell the deal in other areas. | Restrictions on foreign shares of the Mexican market eliminated by 2000. Temporary caps on foreign investment (if total foreign share exceeds 25%) allowed between 2000 and 2007. Afterward, no market share caps allowed. Mexico's 4 largest banks are protected by a restriction that prevents foreign banks from obtaining more than 4% of the Mexican market by acquiring a Mexican bank. |
| Investment | Insists on retaining screening of foreign investment.<br><br>Mexico comes under intense pressure from high-level Canadians after it drops screening. Mexico is convinced to withdraw the agreement to forego screening. | Prepares to eliminate screening, then says it will not do so unless Canada also does.<br><br>Tells the U.S.: "Convince the Canadians." "But, you agree with us," say the Americans. "Yes, but without Canada it is not possible." | Presses hard but unsuccessfully for elimination of screening.<br><br>Hills and Katz expected Canadian movement on screening as a quid pro quo for U.S. forbearance on culture. | |

*Table 8.1* Trade-offs in the End Game at Watergate (*continued*)

| Issue | Canada | Mexico | United States | Observations |
|---|---|---|---|---|
| | Very bad feelings among the U.S. and Canadian negotiators. | Sensing U.S. impatience, the Mexicans ally with Canada. | | |
| Intellectual Property | Cultural industries the remaining intellectual property right issue as negotiations approach an end. | The major issue was between Canada and the U.S. on culture. | Hills, in consultation with President Bush, grants a culture exemption to Canada in spite of intense pressure from the U.S. entertainment lobby. | Culture is the second last ministerial issue settled prior to the handshake. |
| | Remains adamant that culture is not on the table. Continues to argue that NAFTA cannot leave Canada worse off than under the FTA, in which there is a culture exemption. | | | |

Canada and the United States had already been at loggerheads over the interpretation of content rules for cars produced by Japanese-owned companies in Canada for export to the United States under the Free Trade Agreement (FTA). For NAFTA, Canada wanted to clarify the rules of origin to reduce the scope for American interpretation and procedural harassment. For its part, the United States wanted to set the percentage of a car's value that actually had to be produced in North America at a level significantly above the 50 percent established in the FTA. Throughout the negotiations, the United States had been pressing for 70 percent (although their actual target figure was 65 percent), while Canada, supported by Mexico, insisted that the FTA level of 50 percent should be adopted. In the days before August 2, negotiators had made significant progress on clarifying the rules, and now it was left to the ministers to establish the content requirement. The issue surfaced quickly on Sunday, and the United States reduced its demand to 65 percent, while Canada and Mexico offered to move the content requirement to 60 percent. Now separated by 5 percentage points instead of 20, the two sides dug in, insisting that no further concessions were possible, and the issue remained frozen in this position for the next several days.

Canada and the United States also were divided sharply on the textile issue. In return for accepting the stringent triple transformation rule of origin for apparel and textile products, Canada sought U.S. agreement to extend and significantly increase the special quotas for these products that were established in the FTA but were due to be terminated at the end of 1992. While the Americans agreed to large increases in the quota levels for textiles and nonwool apparels, Carla Hills insisted that in return, Canada agree to limit exports of men's wool suits, holding them at roughly 1992 levels.[7] The issue, while esoteric, was politically sensitive, both in the United States, where the textile industry had considerable clout, and in Canada, where the industry was concentrated in Quebec, Canadian Prime Minister Brian Mulroney's home province.

The United States also was pressing Canada for concessions on the issue of investment. In the FTA, Canada had retained the right to review major foreign takeovers, to ensure they were in Canada's interest.[8] Canada also had secured agreement that any limitations on its right to review takeovers would not extend to the energy (oil, natural gas, and uranium) sector. U.S. Treasury Department officials had come under heavy criticism in Washington for conceding too much to the Canadians on investment in 1987, and the NAFTA Treasury Department negotiators were determined to reverse those concessions. Recall that the United States had persuaded Mexico to concede its ability to screen investments at an earlier stage of the negotiations, only to see the Mexicans renege on the deal under pressure from Canada. This episode strengthened the Americans' determination. Canada's situation was not helped by the fact that it had already dealt away a ready concession earlier in the year, when the government unilaterally relinquished the exemption it had obtained for the energy sector. With that in the bank, the Americans could concentrate on securing the elimination of investment screening.

Reports from the Watergate indicated that Hills and Katz expected Canadian movement on the screening issue as a quid pro quo for American forbearance on the issue of cultural industries,[9] although negotiation etiquette prevented the parties from drawing a direct link between the two issues. The exemption for the cultural sector that Canada had secured in the FTA was a thorn in the side of the U.S. entertainment industry, and they made certain that their pain was felt by NAFTA negotiators. The Americans had tried to keep culture on the table throughout these negotiations, but Canadian Trade Minister Wilson had insisted that the issue was nonnegotiable. If that truly was the case, and the Americans were half-convinced by Canadian intransigence that it was, then a price would have to be paid by Canada somewhere else on the agenda. In the early stages of the Watergate end game, the United States was looking for payment in the coin of investment screening. As we shall see, when payment was not forthcoming, American forbearance on culture evaporated.

Mexican and American negotiators also were divided on some key issues. The United States wanted to improve the access of American firms to procurement contracts let by governments and state-owned enterprises in Mexico, especially PEMEX. However, Mexico was not offering much access, proposing that initially 70 percent of PEMEX contracts be reserved for Mexican companies, with that share falling to 50 percent after eight years. The United States insisted that it needed access to more than 50 percent of the contracts at the end of the transition period. Access to secure supplies of energy was also an issue for the Americans. In the FTA, the U.S. negotiators secured an arrangement whereby restrictions on energy exports, for reasons of conservation, could not reduce the proportion of production that had been exported over the previous three years. This meant that in the event that Canada wanted to reduce oil and gas exports to the United States, the government would also have to reduce domestic consumption. American negotiators wanted to extend the same arrangement to Mexico, but the Mexicans would not agree. Finally, Mexico was looking for some compensation for its agreement to eliminate restrictions on automobile imports and to modify the trade balancing provisions of the Auto Decrees that required the Big Three auto makers to locate production in Mexico. Specifically, the Mexicans wanted an exemption from the 25 percent duty applied by the United States to light trucks (the so-called chicken tax). This issue was sensitive because the U.S. House of Representatives had recently passed tariff legislation that reclassified minivans and sport-utility vehicles as light trucks, making them subject to the duty. This afforded protection to a larger segment of the market and thus raised congressional sensitivities.

This was the state of play in the negotiations as of Tuesday, August 4: outstanding disagreements on the major issues of automobiles, energy, investment, procurement, and textiles, with culture soon to rear its head. In addition, a major conflict over trade remedies was about to threaten to derail the negotiations. A myriad of details also remained to be worked out on a host of other issues on which only the broad parameters of agreement had been secured. Given the distance that still separated the parties on all of these issues, it was clear that the original U.S. deadline for concluding the negotiations would not be met—President Bush would not be getting an agreement that he could sign before the presidential election on November 3.

However, an agreement could still be showcased at the upcoming Republican Party national convention, scheduled to open in Houston on August 17, so the pressure remained on the negotiators to make a deal. There was also speculation, after the failure to reach agreement on August 4, that Serra and Wilson might depart Washington, leaving the chief negotiators and their teams at the Watergate to continue their work, clearing the way for settlement of the major outstanding issues upon the ministers' return. However, hope springs eternal in the hearts and minds of negotiators who believe that they are close to a deal, and Bush's return to the capital, from a campaign swing to the West, on the evening of Thursday, August 6, established this date as a new deadline for agreement. Hills remained at the table with Serra and Wilson, and her continued presence made American anxieties over securing an agreement, and doing so quickly, more evident. U.S. industry groups were told they could expect a final copy of the agreement by Saturday, and others were promised a briefing by senior trade officials on Thursday afternoon. "Things are moving along," said Michael Wilson. "It's coming." However, another participant presented a different picture: "It's like the energizer bunny—it keeps going and going."[10] And so it would go, for almost another week.

Any hopes for concluding a deal on Thursday, August 6, were dashed when the United States and Mexico reached an impasse over the energy and procurement issues. On procurement, the Mexicans were reported to have made a new demand on Thursday night. After previously agreeing to grant improved access for American (and Canadian) companies to compete for contracts from governments and state-owned enterprises, the Mexicans now were apparently trying to reserve all PEMEX contract work for Mexican companies. According to participants, the move provoked an angry reaction from Carla Hills and led to an immediate adjournment of negotiations for the night. The Mexicans were being similarly stubborn in their continued refusal to guarantee energy export levels to the United States during times of shortage (the proportionality clause of the FTA), leading Canada to indicate that should Mexico prevail, they would seek to change the FTA provisions on this issue. Said a trade official, "If the Mexicans don't want this, the Canadians don't want to be stuck with it either."[11]

The impasse effectively suspended the trilateral discussions, as the Canadians were left to wait and see whether Mexico and the United States could find a basis for continuing to negotiate. In any case, the outstanding issues between Canada and the United States were far from resolution. The Americans were still pressing the Canadians to accept the 65 percent threshold for North American content in automobiles, but the Canadians, having moved 10 percentage points already, were sticking to 60 percent, with Mexico's support. In addition, tensions were growing between Canada and the United States over the issue of dispute settlement provisions regarding trade remedies. Recall that in the FTA negotiations, Canada had secured, in Chapter Nineteen, a binding binational panel review system that was empowered to arbitrate concerning the proper application of antidumping and countervailing duties. The subjection of American domestic trade remedy law to binational arbitration had been controversial in the United States, especially among members of Congress, and subsequent Canadian challenges to U.S. trade remedy actions that resulted in decisions against American practices produced further irritation.

The danger for Canada in the negotiations over Chapter Nineteen lay, in the first instance, in the wording of Article 1906 of the FTA: "The provisions of this chapter shall be in effect for five years pending the development of a substitute system of rules in both countries for antidumping and countervailing duties as applied to bilateral trade."[12] Although they would not voice their apprehension, lest they give the Americans an opening to act, Canadian trade officials were concerned that the wording of Article 1906 could be taken to mean (and was by many) that failure to agree on a substitute system meant that all of the provisions of Chapter Nineteen—especially the highly valued dispute settlement system—would cease to exist as of 1993. As a result, Canada initially was determined to secure the inclusion of the Chapter Nineteen provisions in a trilateral agreement, and this had been conceded by the United States at an earlier stage in the negotiations. Now, however, the Canadians were concerned about American proposals that in the Canadian view, could have the effect of diluting the binding nature of the dispute settlement provisions. Although the American negotiators denied any such intent, Canadian suspicions remained, and tensions were growing between the two sides over the issue.

The Mexican-American impasse over energy and procurement was papered over on Friday morning, and the trilateral talks resumed, although at a very slow pace. Most participants no longer believed a final deal was possible before Sunday, resigning themselves to a continuation of the negotiations through the weekend and into a second week.[13] Again, there was speculation that Serra and Wilson might depart Washington, leaving their negotiating teams to thrash out details in their absence, but the ministers once again decided to stay at the table themselves to try to hammer out a deal. The strain was beginning to show on all concerned. Officials had been locked in negotiations at the Watergate since July 29, and ministers had been there with them since August 2. By the end of the week, Canadian and Mexican negotiators were washing their underwear and socks in their hotel bathrooms, complaining that they had no time to purchase new supplies. Canadian Trade Minister Wilson was reported to have arrived in Washington on August 1 with only the suit he was wearing, plus a small overnight bag. The report was corroborated by Canadian negotiators, who participated in meetings in Wilson's room at the Watergate, with his socks and other apparel items hanging over the backs of chairs drying.[14]

As negotiators cut to the short strokes, focusing on issues that were potential deal breakers, the ministers, especially Hills, attempted to prevent information leaks that could further muddy the waters. As a result, the press had fewer details to present on the substantive issues of the negotiations and was forced to focus instead on whether negotiators would get an agreement by a certain date, with the speculative date under constant revision as one side or another put their particular spin on the process. As one reporter described it, "They have been hours away from finishing a North American free trade agreement for a week."[15] At a White House briefing for U.S. stakeholders on Friday, administration officials provided little clarification about the progress of the negotiations. Said one participant: "You can't get anyone on the phone. You can't talk to anybody who can tell you anything and there's just a deathly silence."[16] The proclivity of American officials for baseball imagery to describe the state of play in the negotiations continued, however. Another participant in the White House meeting stated, "They clearly indicated inside that it was the top of the ninth last week, it was the bottom of the ninth a few days ago—and it's in extra innings now."[17] It was only fitting then, that Carla Hills should take Serra and Wilson to a Baltimore Orioles baseball game on Friday night. One can only hope that the evening provided a pleasant social interlude for the ministers, because relations were about to deteriorate sharply as their negotiations entered a second week.

## The Watergate Pressure Cooker

On what was known among NAFTA cognoscenti as the Watergate Weekend (August 8 and 9), Bill Merkin decided there might be some entertainment value in camping out at the Watergate to watch the comings and goings of negotiators from the three countries. Deputy chief negotiator for the United States during the free trade negotiations with Canada in 1986–87, Merkin had since left the Office of the U.S. Trade Representative (USTR) to become a plugged-in Washington trade consultant. Sitting at the Crescent Bar in the Watergate Hotel, Merkin hailed those he knew from the passing parade of negotiators on the move, inviting them to sit for a spell and talk. Most of the talk centered on the prospects for completing the negotiations anytime soon and the roadblocks that stood in the way. It turned out that in American eyes, most impediments bore a made-in-Canada label, and Merkin heard some very strong disparaging language used about the Canadians. U.S. animosity was reciprocated by many of the Canadian negotiators.

Part of the problem lay with the sheer magnitude and complexity of the negotiations, and the stress that this generated. The negotiation process was organized into multiple rings. In the center was the ministers' table, where trade-offs had to be made, with advice from the chief negotiators. In the next ring, the chiefs had their own table, where they received the product of the working groups and gave orders back to group heads about how they should proceed. The heads of the now twenty-two working groups each had their own table in the next ring, where the details of the various chapters of the agreement were being thrashed out in dozens of meeting rooms. The lawyers also had their own room, where they sweated over the task of transforming negotiated language into legal text. Finally, there was a composition room, where the text of the agreement was being compiled as it emerged from the multiple rings. The NAFTA negotiators took up every room in the bottom three floors of the hotel. The chief negotiators were meeting almost constantly, with ministers brought in as necessary to hammer out the compromises that were needed to secure an overall agreement.[18] At the outset, the Watergate negotiators were dealing with approximately two hundred discrete issues, and they had been meeting regularly for fourteen to sixteen hours a day during the first week of negotiations. Each day, Carla Hills's driver picked Katz up at 7:00 A.M., they swung by Hills's house to pick her up, and Katz would brief her in the car. The ministers would meet on an agenda, then the chiefs would provide instructions to their working groups, and the next day there would be fewer issues, but more pressure. A senior U.S. negotiator described the Watergate process as "part negotiation, part bazaar, and part show business." His Canadian counterpart described it more simply as "a zoo."

In this atmosphere, it was inevitable that tempers would flare, and American tempers, in particular, were touchy because of the pressure on U.S. negotiators to get a deal. Carla Hills had said repeatedly that the negotiations would take as long as was necessary to negotiate a good agreement. She was wary of setting a deadline, and in this case she was supported by Jules Katz.

Hills's strategy all along had been to let the negotiations drag out, counting on Mexico's desire to make a deal to force it to make major concessions. As we indicated previously, Mexico wanted NAFTA very badly. Prior to Watergate, according to a senior Canadian negotiator, each time there was disagreement on an issue, the Mexicans asked themselves whether this was worth holding out for and putting the agreement in jeopardy. When the negotiators went back to their political masters for guidance, on all but a few issues the answer was, "No, don't jeopardize an agreement." In other words, the Mexicans were very risk averse, unwilling to endanger an agreement by withholding concessions. In the words of a Canadian negotiator, "The US took the position with Mexico, 'You are here to buy our market! What are you prepared to pay?'" However, the tough line taken by the Mexicans on a number of issues at the Watergate indicates that they finally appreciated the leverage they had, thanks to U.S. impatience to reach a deal.

Hills's strategy would work only as long as she was able to operate without a pressing deadline, a condition that had changed fundamentally by August, when the negotiations got caught up in the electoral timetable and the president's sagging poll numbers. According to a senior Canadian official, "In the final stages of the negotiations, the pressure on US negotiators to get a deal in time for the Republican convention was very visible." Nor would the United States relieve the pressure by allowing negotiators even a brief recess, fearful, according to one seasoned observer, "that if they left the Watergate, even for a couple of days, there would be the usual backtracking, and momentum would be lost. So the U.S. decided to force the issues." The pressure to get an agreement in a hurry must have been doubly uncomfortable for Carla Hills, who had a reputation as a negotiator who found it extremely difficult to close a deal. Even members of her U.S. negotiating team acknowledged her reluctance to leave the bargaining table while there was even one concession left to win. In her determination to make a deal, however, Hills could not forget about Congress. A senior U.S. official stated that, "American negotiators always have, in the back of their minds, questions about how Congress will react, because Congress can make life difficult."

Life could get especially difficult for Hills if she was forced to make major concessions to get a deal, and a senior Canadian official thought that concessions might be particularly difficult for the United States because of the nature of their decision process: "Since the US has to sell a deal to Congress, negotiators begin by saying to Congress, 'This is what we can get.' Then they turn to Canada and Mexico and say, 'This is what we have to get.' Only further down the road do they consider what they might have to give to get it. In Canada, the process is different. Negotiators say to ministers, 'This is what we might get, and this is what we might have to give to get it.' Emphasis is not exclusively on the 'getting' side of the equation." Now, with the pressure on

Hills to reach agreement, she had to be careful not to concede too much in her effort to make a deal that would boost the president's electoral fortunes, or she would put the agreement at risk of falling outside her level II win-set, leading to rejection by a Congress unprepared for major concessions.

As the Watergate pressure increased, American anger was directed mostly at Canada. Throughout the negotiations, the U.S. interest had been fundamentally bilateral, focused on securing an agreement with Mexico. Nor did Mexican negotiators pose any problem for senior U.S. negotiators, who saw the Mexicans as "bright and highly educated, but inexperienced. They appeared to be intimidated by the process, and were tentative and slow to react to proposals." However, by the end of the negotiations, a fairly good rapport had developed among many of the U.S. and Mexican negotiators. As for Canada, Canadian officials felt that the United States paid them scant attention, focusing only on "a few mistakes in the FTA that they would like to correct." American perceptions of Canada were not really quite so benign, however. According to a senior U.S. negotiator, "We expected Canada to be disruptive, and it seemed that these expectations were confirmed at the Watergate when the principal conflicts emerged between Canada and the US." As indicated previously, the pressure on the Americans was visible to senior Canadian negotiators, who were confident that "if they held firm on the critical issues, the US would fold because of the pressure on them to get a deal for the president." With the Canadians determined to take advantage of the American predicament, relations between the two negotiating teams would deteriorate further in the coming days.

### Final Trade-Offs

As negotiations among ministers entered their second week, the list of outstanding issues was getting shorter, but deliberations over the remaining issues were getting tougher. In the working groups, where agreements were struck on the basis of trade-offs within issues, the exchanges were reasonably explicit. As one official described it, "The negotiators would nod and indicate that eventually I may be able to give you X, but you know that I will need Y. The negotiation process was used as a vehicle for developing a basic understanding of the exchanges that would have to take place in order to get a deal." Among chief negotiators, and ministers, on the other hand, where trade-offs across issues were required, they were engineered tacitly. Senior Canadian negotiators, for example, described Watergate not as a process of making trade-offs, but as the completion of a process of coming to an understanding on basic principles that had been under way for some time. In fact, Canadian working group heads were cautioned against thinking that they were going to be making trade-offs. For senior American negotiators, trade-offs were recognized as such, but the exchange was done implicitly. Said one: "It's not like widgets for gadgets. Often, you are talking about groups of issues. At the end there is horse trading across sectors. You say, 'This is my final offer.' The other party comes back with half an offer. So you make another 'final offer.' But trade-offs happen late, and only with a few sectors. There are various negotiations going on simultaneously, so you can make links. You may see an agreement in sight on procurement, for example, but you don't close until you get something in tariffs or rules of origin. You don't want to isolate those areas where you have leverage, because then you can't use the links."

In this particular two-level end game, domestic interests were not forgotten either, and the calculation of the effect of an agreement on various interests was quite explicit. In the words of one experienced U.S. trade official, "We sit down and evaluate who will be pissed off or will support this." Sometimes, the approach is more strategic. On particularly sensitive issues, for example, U.S. negotiators wanted a package that they could take to Capitol Hill and say, "Look we have all these important sectors on board, and the sensitive sectors are quiet." Threats occasionally were employed to keep the sensitive ones quiet. In response to complaints from a particular industry, negotiators would say, "Does this mean you are going to pull out your support? Because if it does, then we are going to go and get even less in order to trade off your sector for something that we need to get the support of another industry." More often than not, this would bring the complainant into line, ensuring cooperation and support.

To make the deals that would be necessary for an overall agreement, trade-offs would have to occur, and major compromises would be required of one or more of the parties. One-sided compromise was the order of the day for wrapping up the details of an agreement on financial services, one of the major outstanding issues. In these working group negotiations, American negotiators were described by others as having "a score card mentality, measuring success in terms of gains minus losses, and their performance is so finely calibrated that they are often inflexible." As was the case in the FTA negotiations, U.S. negotiators were absolutely unwilling to contemplate any changes in the American regulatory system for financial services. If regulatory changes were going to happen, it would occur through the vehicle of banking reform. By the spring of 1992, it was clear that Congress was not going to produce any such reforms. Since officials were not going to negotiate changes in U.S. law, it meant that "the negotiation was all about Mexico," in the words of U.S. negotiators. The Americans were insisting on access to the Mexican financial service sector but were prepared to offer a suitable transition period for the opening. U.S. negotiators did not perceive themselves as inflexible. Instead, they said, "We're on the same side; we want the same thing you want. How do we both get there?" In the words of one senior negotiator, "You don't ask for the bottom line right away, you don't want positions staked out. Instead, you say, 'If you had X, what position would that leave you in?' We'd try to get them to accept various levels of access, get a sense of what is doable without putting people in a box." In fact, the United States would have accepted lower numbers on access than they got, but the Mexicans did not push them to take less, so they didn't. In the end, in the words of American negotiators, Mexico came a long way on financial services, and the United States gave nothing. On a score card, this was all gains and no losses, and the Americans admitted to playing hardball on the issue throughout the negotiations, prepared to sit and wait, and when the market on the peso dropped, to push again.

## A Deal Breaker

Negotiations on that Watergate weekend ran into a major hurdle in the form of serious conflict between Canada and the United States over the provisions of the agreement that addressed the settlement of disputes over antidumping and countervailing duties, contained in Chapter Nineteen. The conflict arose, initially, over Mexico's Law of Amparo (Protection), a provision of the constitution that allows Mexicans to challenge the decisions of authorities. According to the United States, the Amparo law opened the possibility that a Mexican firm could use the domestic courts to hold up or block entirely the implementation of a Chapter Nineteen panel decision concerning dumping or subsidies. This, said the Americans, raised the question of whether Mexico could guarantee that a panel decision would be enforced in Mexico. To deal with this problem, the Americans proposed the addition of a special review mechanism (SRM) to Chapter Nineteen, along with criteria that would govern its application. In bilateral discussions with the United States, the Mexicans indicated that they were prepared to see some changes in the chapter, and this provided the Americans with an opening to try to secure changes in the application of Chapter Nineteen.

Negotiations on Chapter Nineteen were being handled by officials from Canada's Department of Finance, and they were opposed to any initiative to open up Chapter Nineteen for discussion because of a concern that in reality "improvements" might be used to erode the efficacy of the chapter provisions. In particular, they were concerned that the SRM might weaken Chapter Nineteen as it applied to Canadian challenges to U.S. trade remedy actions. As American officials began to place on the table for consideration specific language on criteria that would trigger the application of the SRM,

Canadian fears grew. Essentially, their concerns centered on the possibility that the U.S. proposals would change the standard for review of panel decisions, thus making them more easily subject to extraordinary challenge. Again, it is necessary to refer to the FTA to understand the significance of this aspect of Chapter Nineteen.

Article 1904 of the FTA established an extraordinary challenge procedure that allowed either country to refer a binational panel decision to a special committee of judges for review to determine whether a member of the panel had behaved improperly or whether the panel had violated procedural rules or exceeded its authority. In the event that the special committee determined any of these conditions existed, it had the power to refer the decision back to the panel for appropriate action or to void the decision entirely, in which case a new panel would be established. This procedure was included in the FTA to guard against irregular action by a panel or its members. The first extraordinary challenge of a panel decision was requested by the United States, in the spring of 1991 during congressional consideration of the extension of fast-track negotiating authority. The case involved a finding by the U.S. International Trade Commission (ITC) that subsidies to Canadian pork exports caused injury to U.S. producers, and a subsequent binational panel review that overturned the ITC injury determination. It was reported in the press at the time that the U.S. pork industry persuaded the USTR to mount the challenge in exchange for congressional votes in support of the fast-track extension (Davey 1996, 276). In any case, Canada maintained that the Americans were not making appropriate use of the extraordinary challenge procedure, arguing that it was never intended as simply another avenue of appeal for binational panel decisions. The special committee that was to hear the U.S. extraordinary challenge agreed with the Canadians, noting that the procedure was "not intended to function as a routine appeal" but instead was intended as a review mechanism "for aberrant panel decisions"(Davey 1996, 227). American officials, especially those in the Department of Commerce, were not pleased with the committee's finding, and the Canadians suspected that in proposing a new SRM for NAFTA's Chapter Nineteen, the United States was simply looking to create another avenue to appeal binational panel decisions that went against them. For their part, the Americans insisted that their intentions were benign, that they were only seeking to address a potential problem with Mexico's domestic law.

By the summer of 1992, Chapter Nineteen had become a crunch issue for all three parties: Canada and the United States were demanding specific changes in Mexico's domestic legal system in exchange for extension of the Chapter Nineteen dispute settlement system to include Mexico; the United States was pushing Canada and Mexico to accept the SRM as a condition for the inclusion of Chapter Nineteen in the NAFTA; and Canada was resisting the American SRM initiative and trying to secure Mexican support for its resistance effort. Canada's problem was that Mexico was willing to accept the U.S. conditions in exchange for the inclusion of the binational panel review system in the trilateral agreement. In addition, Canadian officials believed the Mexicans were willing to agree with the Americans on this issue in order to preserve their leverage with the United States on the energy and procurement issues. In Canada's view, the United States was taking advantage of the gap that had opened between Canada and Mexico, using it as an opportunity to modify, and in the process weaken, Chapter Nineteen.

For senior officials in Canada's Department of Finance, this was a crucial issue, but they did not believe that its importance was appreciated sufficiently by Chief Negotiator Weekes and that they were becoming isolated on the issue within the Canadian negotiating team. Weekes was dealing with the Americans on a number of difficult issues and was reluctant to identify the SRM in Chapter Nineteen as a deal breaker, preferring instead to negotiate the issue with the Americans. Finance officials got their deputy minister, Fred Gorbet, to step in and insist to Weekes that the U.S. proposals were unacceptable. Convinced by Gorbet, Weekes decided to bring Len Legault, one of Canada's most seasoned trade policy officials, and one of the original authors of FTA Chapter Nineteen, directly into the negotiations prior to Watergate.[19] In the words of a senior Canadian negotiator, "Legault did a masterful job of educating the Mexicans with respect to their interests on this issue," and in the process he threw a wrench into the U.S. attempts to construct Chapter Nineteen. The Americans were not amused. They believed that Legault understood very well the real nature of American objectives, but he said that politically the issue simply would not sell in Canada. Legault set out to define Canadian conditions for the operation of the SRM, which would be specified in Article 1905 of Chapter Nineteen. He had to convince the Americans that the Canadian conditions would still allow Article 1905 to address U.S. concerns about the Mexican system, while eliminating any threat that it might pose to the operation of the binational panel review system established under Article 1904. The result was bad feelings all around—the Canadians suspecting that the Americans were seeking to undermine Chapter Nineteen, the Americans suspicious that the Canadians were planning some action that would have been curtailed by the SRM, and the Mexicans fearful that Canadian intransigence would lead the United States to reject the application of Chapter Nineteen to Mexico.

As the negotiations moved into their second week at the Watergate, Canada insisted that it was not prepared to pay the price the United States was asking on Chapter Nineteen in order to get NAFTA, and Wilson indicated that he had the prime minister's concurrence that the Canadians would break off negotiations over the issue if they had to. In fact, negotiations were suspended, informally, but it was Mexico that brought about the suspension. Serra said that the Mexicans would not participate further in the various working group negotiations until the Chapter Nineteen issue was resolved. They did so because they did not want the gains they were making on other issues to be undone by failure on the part of the United States and Canada to reach agreement on Chapter Nineteen. Mexico's action brought the negotiations to a standstill, freezing the process across the entire set of working groups. This was a major blow, so serious, according to a senior negotiator, that the impasse was never made public because the parties did not wish to further endanger the talks by revealing the significance of the problem that they faced. According to the Canadians, it took two days for the Americans to finally realize that Canada was in earnest about its objections. In the end, the Americans would get their SRM in NAFTA Article 1905, but its operations would be circumscribed according to Canadian specifications. While the Canadians were pleased that they had managed to prevail on the issue, the result embittered some very senior U.S. negotiators. The Americans insisted that their version of Chapter Nineteen would have provided a vehicle through which to reform Mexican domestic law and that it held no dangers for Canada. And they complained that the Canadians, especially "certain" ministers (there was only one Canadian minister at the table), had "found a new bible in Chapter Nineteen" and were unwilling to entertain any changes, no matter how worthwhile. Even several years after the completion of the negotiations, U.S. officials remained angry over Canadian obstinacy, still unable to believe that Canada might have had serious concerns about American intentions on Chapter Nineteen.

With agreement on this issue, the larger negotiation process started up again, under even more serious time constraints. A senior Canadian negotiator described the stress under which the negotiations were now conducted as "unbelievable," indicating that during the final two days—Monday and Tuesday—negotiations continued for forty-eight hours straight. The feeling among U.S. officials at the Watergate was that negotiations had gone on long enough, and it was time to make a deal. Ministers soon discovered they had another major problem, however, this time with procurement issues. The procurement negotiations had not been going well, and Katz had been prepared to remove the issue from the table "about six times" because the Mexicans were offering so little. When Mexico backtracked on its willingness to provide access to PEMEX contracts, the Americans were more than a little angry. However, in the aftermath of the Chapter Nineteen hiatus in negotiations, the two countries made significant progress on the issue, to the exclusion of the Canadians. Michael Wilson discovered on Monday that Canada was about to be the odd one out of a bilateral procurement agreement that had been struck between Mexico and the United States. Furious, Wilson removed responsibility for the issue from the hands of his working group head and gave it to Bob Clark, Weekes's deputy chief negotiator. Clark concluded that the Mexicans had pulled a fast one on the Canadians, and he prevailed on the Americans to cut Canada back into the deal. To mend the damage, Clark was joined in the negotiations by his Mexican and U.S. counterparts— Jaime Zabludovsky and Chip Roh—and the three of them concluded a trilateral deal in the early morning hours of Tuesday, August 11. Regarding PEMEX, the Mexicans granted access to 50 percent of the contracts immediately, with access increasing to 70 percent in eight years and 100 percent after ten years.

With the negotiations entering their final phase, and continuing pressure on the U.S. negotiators to get an agreement, Canada and Mexico decided they could hang tough on the issues of investment and energy supplies, respectively. On the investment screening issue, at one point, Wilson turned to Hills and said, "When you have as much Japanese investment in the US as we do from you, then you will understand our position." Reluctantly, the Americans agreed that Canada would retain its right to screen foreign investment, and Mexico would be granted the same right. The same reciprocity would not prevail on energy supplies, however. Mexico maintained its refusal to guarantee the proportion of its production that would go to exports, while Canada agreed to retain its commitment in the proportionality clause. With these major issues out of the way, officials were still left with some very tough negotiating nuts to crack: automobiles, textiles, and culture.

On autos, Michael Wilson was determined to protect the Japanese transplants located in Canada by clarifying the rules of origin that would define North American content and by keeping the content rule as low as possible. The Big Three American auto producers, especially Ford and Chrysler, were pressing hard for the United States to achieve a North American content requirement of 65 percent.[20] Senior U.S. officials originally had argued to the Big Three that 65 percent was too high a figure, particularly in comparison to the 50 percent requirement in the FTA, and that to insist on this would be humiliating to the Mulroney government. The two countries had been separated by 5 percentage points for more than a week now, however, and Canadian intransigence had changed American minds. In addition, during the Watergate negotiations the Mexicans had offered to accept the 65 percent figure and then backed off their offer. According to a senior U.S. negotiator, the Americans "came this close to telling the Canadians to take a hike on the issue." Finally, late on Monday, when John Weekes and Jules Katz were meeting, Weekes said, "You know Jules, there *are* numbers between 60 and 65." After Katz acknowledged this fact, it was left to the ministers to agree on Tuesday to a figure of 62.5 percent that would be phased in over eight years in two stages. Although Mexico also got its exemption from the 25 percent duty on light trucks, the 62.5 percent deal caused a number of other U.S. concessions to unravel, and Mexico was furious about this.

By late Tuesday, August 11, only the culture and textile issues remained outstanding. By now the Americans were terribly frustrated by Canada's insistence on preserving the FTA cultural exemption. The paramount U.S. interest in cultural industries was with the Europeans in the Uruguay Round of multilateral trade negotiations (MTN). U.S. negotiators were under intense pressure from domestic lobby groups, led by Jack Valenti, the president of the Motion Picture Association of America (MPAA), to avoid creating a precedent (again) with Canada. The United States was not doing well on the issue in the Uruguay Round negotiations and was concerned that a deal with Canada would embolden the Europeans. In fact, in Geneva, the Europeans did hold out on culture until the very end, pointing to the NAFTA exemption. In any case, American negotiators believed that the issue with Canada was not about culture but about protecting jobs in Canadian cultural industries. Canada denied this, insisting that it could not give up the cultural exemption because it had stated unequivocally at the outset of the negotiations that it would not go beyond the FTA. U.S. negotiators admitted that once the political decision had been made to complete a deal in time for the Republican convention, their position became impossible. "Canada could just keep saying no, no, no and the US would have to concede in order to get a deal."

Although the two sides were trying to find specific language that would limit the application of an exception for culture, in the end the United States decided that they would prefer to live with a complete exemption, as in the FTA, because it would be easier to defend against the inclusion of a similar complete exemption in the Uruguay Round negotiations. So the two agreed, the United States very reluctantly, that the FTA provisions would simply be extended to NAFTA. As one senior American negotiator put it: "How long do you hold out? We knew we were going to catch hell for the Canadian cultural exemption, and we got roasted. But Canada was simply not going to yield on it. You get to the top of the curve, where if you persist, perhaps you are going to lose. We got all that we wanted, and we were going to lose if we pushed any farther."[21] After the ministers agreed to extend the FTA provisions to NAFTA, Jules Katz suggested that there was no real need to write this down—that it could simply be left for the lawyers to include in their draft. Demonstrating the sensitivity of the cultural issue in Canada, John Weekes responded, "If anything needs to be written down, this is it!"

The final decision to accept the Canadian position on culture was made by Hills, in consultation with President Bush. The outcome infuriated American negotiators. Going into the negotiations, the United States had been determined to achieve a comprehensive chapter on intellectual property, an accomplishment they had been denied in the end game of the FTA negotiations. In the U.S. view, Canada had been a gadfly in the negotiations, simply making the job of getting agreement with the Mexicans more difficult. Although the U.S. negotiators got their chapter on intellectual property, they were able to make no headway with Canada on the cultural issue, and this soured the negotiation process. In the words of a senior American official, "In the end, it was all about fucking culture. This with a country [Canada] that has no culture!"

With the culture issue disposed of, only textiles remained. Here, the United States and Mexico had agreed earlier to the triple transformation rule as the price for the removal of American quotas, and despite Canadian unhappiness with the rule, Canada could not undo the deal. As a result, the Canadians simply had to figure out the implications of triple transformation and then find a way to live with the deal. This they had done. The issue of wool suits remained on the table, however, and as the negotiations wound down, Wilson continued to press Hills to permit an expansion of Canadian suit exports to the American market. Even with an agreement imminent, Hills was not about to accede to Canadian demands, however. She told Wilson, "I just burned Jack Valenti. You don't expect me to give up on textiles too, do you?" The quota for woolen garments would not be increased.

With that, the negotiations were concluded, and the three ministers shook hands on the agreement they achieved. It was 12:40 A.M. on Wednesday, August 12, almost exactly the same time on the clock when Canadian and U.S. officials shook over the FTA almost five years earlier. At the end, said one participant, "There was a lot of emotion, and some bad feelings." And a little gloating. Referring to the original dynamic of the negotiations wherein Mexico was the *demandeur* and the United States was in the driver's seat, a Canadian official opined as follows: "In the summer of 1992, this dynamic was totally reversed. There was a political decision in the US: it had to have NAFTA. This was anticipated, and meant that the deal that came out was much better than it could have been. It's a very good deal for Canada." Perhaps, but the Americans decided that Canada and Mexico should pay for the deal, quite literally, when they proposed that the infrastructure costs of holding the negotiations at the Watergate should be split three ways. These costs are normally borne by the host government and, properly, represent the price of having home-field advantage during a negotiation. When the Canadians were presented with a bill for $140,000, they objected to paying, and the issue was sent to be settled between Hills and Wilson. In the end, Wilson agreed to pay, but only after Hills claimed that a Canadian refusal would mean that a number of secretaries would have to be laid off at the USTR.

All that would come later, however. For the moment, there was a completed agreement to celebrate. After their handshakes, Hills, Serra, and Wilson, accompanied by Katz, Blanco, and Weekes, left their negotiation room, and as they made their way down the curving hotel corridor, members of the various working groups spilled out of their meeting rooms and offered a sustained round of applause for what had finally been accomplished.

## Understanding the Negotiation

The Watergate end game offers a graphic illustration of the powerful influence that nonagreement alternatives exercise over the negotiation process. Table 8.2 provides a summary assessment of the application of the principal hypotheses to the negotiation process that unfolded at the Watergate. Throughout the NAFTA negotiations, U.S. negotiators had followed a conventional American bargaining strategy, playing out the string on the Mexicans, getting them to make repeated concessions while making few of their own, and counting on Mexico's desire for an agreement to move the process along. This strategy was not as effective with Canada, however, because the Canadians always had the FTA to fall back on if the Americans demanded too high an admission price to NAFTA. At the Watergate, with the Republican convention approaching and the president's re-election in trouble, the tables were suddenly turned, as the utility of nonagreement declined sharply for American negotiators, and they were forced to make concessions in some critical areas in order to get a deal.

For its part, Canada, despite critical gains at the bargaining table—especially securing extension of the FTA dispute settlement provisions to NAFTA—which had the effect of reducing the utility of the Canadian FTA nonagreement alternative, was still willing to withhold concessions on its key issues, particularly culture and the Chapter Nineteen SRM. The Mexicans did not display a similar predisposition, despite their awareness of the Americans' dilemma. While they stood firm in their resolve not to give way on the energy issue, after initial resistance on other issues they continued their pattern of acceding to U.S. demands for concessions, for example, granting American requests for inclusion of the Chapter Nineteen SRM and access to PEMEX contracts.

Our analysis of the negotiation process at the Watergate makes it clear that U.S. negotiators felt the presidential pressure to get agreement, that their Mexican and Canadian counterparts were aware of it, and that negotiating strategies were amended accordingly. The result was a subtle change in the patterns of delayed mutual responsiveness that had characterized the negotiations to this stage in the process. The change was only one of degree, however, because Canada would not put an agreement at risk to secure U.S. concessions on textiles, nor would the Americans risk alienating the major textile lobby to satisfy Canadian demands. And the Mexicans simply wanted

Table 8.2 Hypotheses: Watergate End Game

| Hypothesis | Canada | Mexico | United States |
|---|---|---|---|
| Asymmetry: weaker states are more responsive to powerful states relative to domestic pressures; powerful states are more responsive to domestic pressures relative to the weaker states. | Major confrontations occur between the U.S. and Canada. Mexico's concessions leave Canada little cover. | Prepared to accept U.S. demands on Chapter 19 to get a deal. | Seeks to exploit divisions between Canada and Mexico on Chapter 19 but forced to concede. |
| | Remains willing to walk out over Chapter 19. | Drops screening; then, under pressure from Canada, says it will not accept an asymmetrical deal on investment screening; allies with Canada. | Forced to concede on screening. |
| | Stands firm on investment screening; lobbies Mexico to do the same. | Disappointed with lack of support from Canada in market access. | Forced to concede in culture (Hills "burns Jack Valenti"). |
| | Stands firm on preserving FTA culture exemption. | Stands firm on energy but concedes access to bidding on PEMEX contracts. | Forced to concede in automotive rules of origin and grants a partial, permanent duty drawback. |
| | Accepts U.S.-Mexico consensus in textiles in exchange for concessions that leave Canada no worse off than under FTA. | | |
| Patterns of delayed mutual responsiveness: the lower the subjective utility assigned to the nonagreement alternative, the more concessions will be offered. | Chief negotiator senses U.S. impatience to close and holds out in various sectors. | Chief negotiator senses U.S. impatience to close and holds out in various sectors. | Impending election and Republican convention force U.S. to wrap up. The sense of hurry on the U.S. side is visible. |
| | Canada, in the words of a U.S. negotiator, was "fortuitously able to negotiate brilliantly from a defensive position." | Unable to exploit U.S. impatience in such areas as financial services because major concessions were already made (in Dallas or afterward). | Decides to accept Canadian refusal to make concessions: "We all got what we wanted and we were going to lose if we pushed any farther." |
| | Jumps on bandwagon of Mexico's success gaining permanent, partial duty drawback; blocks bilateral U.S.-Mexico deal on procurement. | | |

| Institutions: centralized, vertical domestic institutions are a bargaining liability, while divided government is an asset. | Can claim "no erosion of FTA benefits" as a formula for maintaining domestic support. Business largely supportive. | By Watergate, has developed a clear sense of industry preferences, but the negotiators "call the shots" and are less constrained by business input. | By Watergate meeting, has acute sense of industry preferences. |
|---|---|---|---|
| | The consultations with business help repair the relationship between the government and private sector, but in practice provided few internal constraints on the negotiators. | | Big Three auto producers disappointed with rules of origin. |
| | | | Threatens to withdraw NAFTA benefits to industries that do not promise to lobby for NAFTA. U.S. negotiator says, "If you are going to withdraw support, I am going to go and get less in order to trade off your sector for something that another industry will support." |

the Canadians to stop being so stiff-necked so that the thing would be over and done with. Nevertheless, the principal trade-offs that were engineered to produce the deal reflect the important changes that occurred in the subjective utilities of the parties' nonagreement alternatives in the final stages of the negotiations.

It would still take the lawyers five long days, until August 17, to complete the translation of the negotiated text into legalese.[22] But the main elements of the deal were ready to be unveiled. The agreement was presented to the media in Washington later that day, Wednesday, August 12, by President Bush, who announced, "The cold war is over. The principal challenge now facing the United States is to compete in a rapidly changing, expanding global marketplace."[23] Predictably, the business sector was quick to endorse the deal, while labor groups were just as quick to condemn it. The media offered a scorecard of winners and losers in descriptions of the details of the agreement, and most pundits provided a forecast of a rocky road to its inevitable ratification by Congress. Fourteen months in the making, NAFTA was an improbable beast, constructed by a committee of hundreds under dubious economic conditions between unlikely partners. Now it would be delivered once more into the congressional crucible of American trade politics. But first, there was an election to be won.

# Another End Game

**U**nited States President George Bush hurried the NAFTA negotiations to a conclusion in August 1992 because he wanted to have the deal done in time for the Republican National Convention in Houston on August 17, 1992. He hoped that NAFTA could be sold as "good news" to bolster his re-election bid at a time when an economic slump made him vulnerable to the criticism that he had neglected domestic affairs, a criticism immortalized in a reminder posted in candidate Bill Clinton's campaign headquarters: "It's the economy, stupid!" In September, Bush notified the Congress of his intent to sign the deal.[1] Given the electoral timetable, this meant that while Bush could sign the accord before leaving office, thereby giving the executive branch's seal of approval, the next president would be responsible for shepherding the agreement through the legislative process.

The Bush campaign saw NAFTA as more than just economic "good news": they believed that it would divide supporters of the Democratic Party and force its leadership to take compromise positions that would make its candidate appear weak and vacillating on trade. But the trade issue was a double-edged sword. Opinion polls consistently showed that NAFTA was not popular (with public opinion divided roughly down the middle). However, the Bush team sought to raise the profile of NAFTA and make it a salient political issue, to accentuate the cleavage they thought would damage the Democratic Party. Much of the Hispanic community, for example, tended to align itself with the Democratic Party, yet significant segments supported NAFTA. In an effort to undermine Hispanic support for the Democrats, while highlighting an important achievement of his administration, Bush invited Mulroney and Salinas to San Antonio on October 7, 1992 to witness the initialing of the agreement by trade officials from the three countries.[2]

Many observers dismissed the initialing ceremony as "political theater," and as theater there were certainly dramatic moments. During the event, Carlos Salinas's brother, Raúl, leapt to his feet and cried out, "Arriba Agualeguas," the name of the hometown of the Salinas family; the gesture clearly embarrassed the Mexican president, bringing a blush to his face. While it was clear that initialing the agreement symbolized a personal triumph for Mexico's leader, it also came at a cost—the enmity of many Democrats who resented the apparent willingness of the Mexican government to embrace Bush in the middle of his re-election bid. Mexican officials countered that they consulted with the Clinton campaign before agreeing to attend the initialing in San Antonio and received a green light. However, the memory of San Antonio would come back to haunt them after Bush was defeated in November, as prominent members of the Clinton entourage retained a lingering resentment about the intimate ties between Salinas's cabinet and senior officials in the outgoing administration.

Bush's efforts to push the Democrats off balance and make Clinton appear to "waffle" on the issue of trade ("They don't serve waffles in the White House," said Bush) forced the Democratic contender into a tricky compromise position. Clinton spelled out his position on NAFTA in a speech on October 4, 1992, in Raleigh, North Carolina, saying that "the issue is not whether we should support free trade or open markets [but] whether or not we will have a national economic strategy to make sure we reap the benefits."[3] As part of such a strategy, Clinton proposed the negotiation of additional agreements on labor and the environment, as well as safeguards against import surges. Pointing to Chapter Seventeen, on intellectual property, as a model for such agreements, Clinton said NAFTA enforced investment and property rights but not labor and environmental standards.

Clinton's view was reiterated in his debate with President Bush and independent candidate Ross Perot on October 19. Bush began by accusing Clinton of trying to favor NAFTA and oppose it at the same time, to which Clinton replied, "I say on balance it does more good than harm 'if'—if we can get some protection for the environment so that the Mexicans have to follow their own environmental standards, their own labor law standards and if we have a genuine commitment to re-educate and re-train the American workers who lose their jobs and reinvest in this economy."[4]

By offering a qualified endorsement of NAFTA, Clinton sidestepped accusations of being an old-fashioned protectionist under the control of big unions; yet, by calling for side agreements on labor and the environment, he was able to capitalize on job insecurity and domestic opposition to environmental and social dumping. The intellectual basis for Clinton's position drew less on neoclassical economics or faith in free markets and more on a "neoinstitutionalist" concern for such issues as minimum wages, productivity gains, labor relations, and income disparities in the North American region. Critics of NAFTA noted that Mexican productivity increases had outpaced wage growth for thirteen years, so that as U.S. labor economist Harley Shaiken put it, "Why should companies invest in a high skill, high wage strategy in the United States when a high skill, low wage strategy is available in Mexico?"[5]

The idea of a set of parallel accords provided a sop to organized labor, an economically threatened constituency that Clinton could ill-afford to ignore completely. Said one of the U.S. side-deal negotiators, "NAFTA was frightening to Clinton's core constituency. People felt they were working longer for less. The idea was to change the symbolic meaning of NAFTA, to recast NAFTA not as a low wage strategy but as part of a high wage, high skill strategy." The Mexican government greeted such initiatives with apprehension because they placed labor relations and environmental practices in Mexico at the center of the U.S. debate.

The defeat of Bush by Clinton in November marked the beginning of the end of the extraordinarily cordial relationship that had developed between the leaders of Canada, the United States, and Mexico. Between 1988 and 1992, Mulroney, Bush, and Salinas, as well as senior members of their immediate entourages, enjoyed more than a friendly diplomatic relationship. These men went fishing together during vacations, genuinely seemed to enjoy each other's company, and communicated on a regular basis. Pundits made much of the "good chemistry" among the Texans in the United States (Bush, Mosbacher, Baker) and their Mexican counterparts; the good will was dubbed "the spirit of Houston."[6] Beneath the fraternity of personal contacts lay a common ideological bond, a shared vision of the future of the North American economy, and a political convergence of interests that served both domestic and international purposes. The initialing of the NAFTA in San Antonio was the final act of political unity among this fraternity of North American leaders, and from that point onward, after the electoral defeat of Bush, relations among leaders of the three countries would become considerably more tense and difficult.

In spite of the initial tensions between the Clinton team and Salinas's government, Clinton would ultimately use his control over the Democratic Party to deliver the NAFTA, a legislative victory that might have eluded Bush had he been elected without a Republican majority in Congress. In other words, a mixture of cooperation and conflict characterized U.S.-Mexican relations during the period between the election of Clinton and the ratification of the NAFTA. This mixture was apparent from the very first contact between the president-elect and Salinas, the day after the November 3 election. Salinas phoned Clinton to congratulate him and urge him to move ahead with the ratification of the NAFTA, without any renegotiation of its provisions.

Salinas had another reason for calling Clinton: to sooth market fears that the NAFTA process was coming unraveled. Mexican officials, brandishing copies of Clinton's campaign speech in Raleigh, put the best possible spin on the outcome of the U.S. elections. However, no amount of spin could hide the nervousness of the Mexican establishment, and these jitters gave rise to what was supposed to be a secret initiative. José Cordoba Montoya, Salinas's most trusted senior advisor, traveled to Washington in late November to meet senior members of the Clinton team to urge them to ratify NAFTA within six months of the incoming president's inauguration. At this meeting—the substance of which was reported in the media—Democratic campaigner Barry Carter said Clinton had not yet decided to sign the NAFTA. Asked when Clinton expected to send the implementing legislation to Congress, Carter replied, "It will depend on how long it takes to negotiate additional agreements on labor and the environment."[7] Cordoba stressed the importance of having NAFTA signed in December, which meant that it would be signed by Bush, and added apologetically that Bush had insisted that Salinas be present at the initialing ceremony in San Antonio.

Clinton agreed that Bush should sign the NAFTA on December 17, 1992, ninety calendar days after the notification of Congress of his intent to sign, and thereby starting the clock for congressional ratification within ninety legislative days of the signing. This meant that the vote in Congress would have to occur, at the latest, at some point in the autumn of 1993. During the early part of 1993, from Clinton's January 20 inauguration until mid-March, when supplemental agreement negotiations began, there was—especially for the Mexicans—a nerve-wracking period of indecision, political posturing, and apparent drift as the new administration started up and began to face a complex legislative agenda.

In December 1992, prior to Clinton's inauguration, Salinas proposed a North American development fund, modeled along the lines of the European social development fund; he also raised the issue of migration. The subtext of the proposals was clear: if the United States could bring new issues to the table, so could Mexico. Salinas's ideas, predictably, were rebuffed, but a signal had been sent—supplemental accords were going to be difficult to negotiate. At the same time, more quietly, the Salinas government had another message for Clinton: delays in the ratification of NAFTA would weaken the Mexican economy and disrupt the complex process of presidential succession, thereby threatening to produce the sort of political instability in Mexico for which no U.S. president would want responsibility. This second message appears to have resonated with Clinton. The Mexican government was certainly aware of reports of guerrilla activity in the southern state of Chiapas. Indeed, a cabinet shuffle in January 1993 had brought the governor of Chiapas into the Salinas cabinet as secretary of the interior. Clearly, Salinas was watching events there closely.

Salinas's message about the potential for instability in Mexico was driven home even before Clinton's inauguration. The Mexican government had requested a meeting between Salinas and Clinton, and Clinton's transition team had responded that such a meeting would have to occur on U.S. soil: Clinton could not meet with Salinas in Mexico before being sworn in. So, Salinas traveled to Austin, Texas, where the two leaders were hosted by Democratic Governor Ann Richards. Briefing papers on Mexico that were given to Clinton prior to the meeting emphasized the importance of ensuring domestic stability in Mexico. Salinas's frustration with Clinton's insistence on side-deal negotiations and his emphasis on the need to "deepen Mexican democracy" was betrayed in his frowning countenance and impatience with a translator at a press conference after the meeting.

During this second prenegotiation process, members of the Clinton administration attempted to sort out their views on NAFTA, and by February the U.S. position began to firm up. On February 3, an "interagency task force" was set up by the White House. It was composed of Lawrence Katz (the chief economist in the Labor Department, and Labor Secretary Robert Reich's right-hand man), Charles Fox from the Environmental Protection Agency (EPA), and "Chip" Roh from the Office of the U.S. Trade Representative (USTR), and was under the direction of Barry Carter, who was appointed deputy undersecretary in the Department of Commerce during the Clinton administration. Later, in May, Joaquin "Jack" Otero, the deputy undersecretary for international labor affairs, replaced Katz as Reich's assistant.

Jorge Perez-Lopez, the director of the U.S. Labor Department's international affairs office, who had participated in the NAFTA safeguard negotiations, directed the preparation of a policy alternative paper for an interagency National Economic Council (NEC) subgroup on labor issues. The paper outlined three possible "packages" that the government should consider. The first possibility was an unobtrusive commission that could only exercise "weak moral suasion." It would promote minimum standards for a narrow range of labor rights, requiring only a small staff and "three fax machines."[8] The focus would be on nonpolitical and easily defined worker rights, such as child labor, work hours, and health and safety. Enforcement mechanisms would be limited under this proposal.

The second alternative, imaginatively labeled Option B, was a commission with more independence, a larger staff, and a mandate to examine issues such as worker rights and participation, the link between wages and productivity, protection against downward harmonization of social security, and efforts to reduce inequality. Language could be drawn from the Mexican constitution, the social provisions of the Canadian Charlottetown constitutional accord, and the European Social Charter. Option B would also include "trinational labor-management dialogue on labor standards in key sectors." Option C would include all of the provisions of Option B but would add trade sanctions or similar border measures as a means of enforcement.

The various positions articulated in the NEC draft demonstrated that the United States went into the negotiations divided. The draft used language strikingly similar to a report written by the Congressional Office of Technology Assessment, entitled "United States-Mexico Trade: Pulling Together or Pulling Apart." This report was written in 1992, in an effort to influence the position of Democratic candidate Bill Clinton, and it seemed to have an impact on the candidate judging by his campaign speech in Raleigh, where he proposed the negotiation of additional agreements. The report envisaged two possible scenarios for North America: one based on competition through low wages and low productivity, which would lead to social and political problems; and another based on high wages, high productivity, and increased investment in human labor. It was the latter strategy that fit with the thinking of U.S. Labor Secretary Robert Reich.

The United States also floated the idea of a "green commission" with broad enforcement powers. When Mexican officials got wind of U.S. thinking—which they did almost immediately, thanks to a tendency for U.S. proposals to be aired publicly in the trade publication *Inside NAFTA*—they completely dismissed the notion of such a commission, calling the U.S. proposal "inadmissible." On environmental policy, Mexican policy makers such as Luis Donaldo Colosio, the head of the Mexican social development ministry (SEDESOL), argued that they had already demonstrated a strong commitment to environmental protection.

In preparing for the negotiations, Mexican policy makers adopted a defensive posture. They disliked being involved in these negotiations in the first place because they regarded them as an outcome of U.S. electoral dynamics. Indeed, they felt they had already addressed these issues in the debate on fast track, when a delegation from the United States, led by Jorge Perez-Lopez, had worked with Mexico's secretary of labor and social welfare, Arsenio Farel, to write a memorandum of understanding on labor cooperation that, at least from the Mexican perspective, was designed to show that labor problems in Mexico were not so bad. Similarly, the Salinas administration had made a number of dramatic gestures—such as closing PEMEX's Azcapotzalco refinery in Mexico City and creating a national program to plant 100 million trees—to show seriousness in the effort to improve Mexico's environmental record. As Salinas put it, "Mexico's commitment to the environment is complete, decisive."[9] Salinas and his economic cabinet (including secretaries of trade, Serra, and labor, Farel) established three guidelines: the final accords would have to respect Mexico's sovereignty, they could not re-open the NAFTA and introduce labor or environmental standards as "disguised protectionism," and they could not include traditional commercial sanctions. The Mexican position was elegant in its simplicity, reflecting their desire for the weakest possible side agreements.

Twice in February (February 8 and 17), Mickey Kantor, the new U.S. trade representative, met with Michael Wilson and Jaime Serra in preparation for a ministerial meeting in March to launch the side-deal negotiations. Working groups were set up on the two subjects, labor and the environment, and chief negotiators were named. Then, just as the negotiations were about to begin, a major scandal threatened to undo the halting steps toward the bargaining table. Representative Richard Gephardt publicized knowledge of a fund, to which a Mexican development bank (Nafinsa, a government bank) had contributed, to lure U.S. firms to Mexico. Called the "Amerimex Maquiladora Fund, L.P.," the idea was to help ailing U.S. firms relocate to recover their competitiveness by using cheaper Mexican labor. Gephardt wrote a public letter to Salinas accusing the Mexican government of "stealing jobs" from American workers. Clinton threatened to call off the NAFTA, and Kantor called Serra to demand an explanation. The Mexican government responded quickly by pulling Nafinsa out of the fund, and the scandal subsided. However, the episode confirmed the worst fears of NAFTA opponents in the United States.

The Amerimex scandal was not the only event in March that cast a cloud over NAFTA. Early that month, Brian Mulroney announced that he intended to step down as prime minister. Mulroney's announced departure made it clear that NAFTA ratification in Canada would be entrusted to a new head of government. In fact, because of the nature of the Canadian parliamentary system, NAFTA ratification was never in doubt. The NAFTA bill entered second reading in the House of Commons in late March and was passed by a vote of 112 to 94. It was then brought before the House for final reading at the end of May, passing on May 27 by a vote of 140 to 124. The Mulroney government's strategy was to get the bill through both the House and the Senate prior to the leadership race in June, and then proclaim the NAFTA law at the end of the year, after general elections.

In the spring of 1993, however, the future of NAFTA appeared very uncertain. There were those who, like former U.S. Trade Representative Carla Hills, warned of a "contentious" ratification battle and criticized Clinton for holding NAFTA up until the side deals could be negotiated. Others, like Lloyd Bentsen, now Clinton's treasury secretary, suggested that the president should postpone NAFTA until other policy initiatives—like health care reform—could be moved forward.

## Negotiating the Supplemental Accords

The NAFTA supplemental agreement negotiations began on March 17, 1993 in Washington, D.C. The opening positions of the parties and the final results of the negotiations are presented in Table 9.1. The negotiations were opened officially by Rufus Yerxa, the newly appointed deputy U.S. trade representative, and NAFTA veterans John Weekes and Herminio Blanco. Jaime Serra continued in his role as the Mexican cabinet official responsible for the negotiations. His role, like that of Blanco, was intended in part to provide a link with the previous NAFTA negotiation, as well as to reassert the Secretariat of Trade and Industrial Development's (SECOFI) control over the negotiation. However, Blanco and Serra gave plenty of scope for negotiating to Santiago Oñate, Mexico's attorney general for protection of the environment, who took charge of the negotiations on the environment, and Norma Samañego, assistant secretary for labor, who was in charge of those on labor. Israel Gutiérrez, who had negotiated auto provisions in the NAFTA, served as Blanco's eyes and ears in the side-deal negotiations. Mexican cabinet officials did not appear to have major frictions on how to manage the side-deal negotiations. Serra would play a more active role later in the negotiations, along with Kantor and Wilson (and his Canadian successor, Tom Hockin). Lawrence Katz was the key U.S. negotiator on labor, and John McKennirey represented Canada. On the environmental side was Dan MacGraw for the United States and Keith Christie for Canada.

At the outset, the labor and environmental talks were held together, so that it was possible for issues to "spill over" from one negotiation to the other. One U.S. negotiator, representing the EPA, attended both the labor and the environmental talks. He discovered that Secretary of Labor Robert Reich was very serious about giving teeth to the labor side deal, and as a result, the negotiators were placing a strong emphasis on obligations and enforcement. The USTR also wanted an environmental accord with teeth for political reasons. The EPA was initially ambivalent, however, and as a result of the push for clear obligations and enforcement in the labor talks, the EPA officials decided to demand a similar focus on enforcement of environmental regulations in order that the environmental accord would not appear to be weaker than the labor accord. In the end, the result was the reverse of EPA's fears: the labor agreement was weaker than the one on the environment.

The first meeting was a "getting to know you" session, and no concrete proposals were placed on the table. Blanco seized the opportunity to outline the guidelines that he had been given: Mexico wanted respect for sovereignty, no renegotiation of NAFTA, and no trade sanctions. However, it was not until mid-April, in a meeting in Mexico City, that the United States placed its opening positions on the table, and it became clear that the major

Table 9.1 Opening Positions and Results of Side-Deal Negotiations

| Issue | Canada | Mexico | United States | Observations |
|---|---|---|---|---|
| Opening Positions | Wants no trade sanctions, weak accords, no violations of sovereignty.<br><br>Initially rejects idea of independent secretariats.<br><br>Then supports the idea of a North American Commission on the Environment (NACE) with specific functions.<br><br>Proposes that appeals from private groups for an investigation would first have to be taken up by a NAFTA government. | Wants respect for sovereignty, no renegotiation of NAFTA, and no trade sanctions.<br><br>Rejects the idea of commissions or tribunals that might supersede Mexico's domestic laws.<br><br>Agrees with Canada that secretariats should be structured along national lines, and responsive to national governments. | Wants accords to be broad in scope, e.g., covering industrial relations and containing "teeth" (i.e., enforcement provisions).<br><br>Proposes some form of dispute settlement mechanism between the governments to address cases where a government fails to comply with the terms of the agreements "on a consistent basis." A commission would serve as a watchdog.<br><br>Position on sanctions is ambiguous at outset of the negotiations; forces the issue at the end. | Negotiations on labor and the environment initially were held together, then broken into separate groups.<br><br>Negotiators expect the labor accord to be stronger than the environmental accord. |
| Results | Instead of trade sanctions, agrees that the Federal Court has the power to fine the federal government if found by a trinational panel to have failed to enforce its own standards. | Accepts weak form of trade sanctions; ensures they are enforced only after a country has persistently violated its own laws and refused to pay fines after a dispute resolution process has assessed damages. | Drops insistence that labor accord covers industrial relations.<br><br>Panels cannot address issues other than health and safety, child labor, and minimum wages. | Environmental accord is trilateral; labor accord involves three separate national administrative offices. The environmental secretariat is not subservient to national governments. |

stumbling blocks would be what kind of obligations would be accepted and what sanctions would be used to enforce the agreements. U.S. negotiators argued that the side agreements would have to involve some form of dispute settlement mechanism between the governments to address cases where a government fails to comply with the terms of the agreements "on a consistent basis." However, the U.S. plan initially did not include any authority to issue subpoenas or enforce sanctions; rather, it allowed private groups to appeal to a commission (which would serve as an ombudsman or watchdog) with the power to carry out studies and inquiries into violations of national labor and environmental laws. Its findings would be nonbinding and would carry only moral suasion.

Canada initially opposed the idea of an independent commission or secretariat, but supported the idea of a North American Commission on the Environment (NACE) with specific functions and proposed that appeals from private groups for an investigation would first have to be taken up by a NAFTA government. Wilson suggested that NACE could promote harmonization toward higher environmental standards, limits for specific pollutants, promotion of green technology, and regional cooperation for sustainable development. Canadian officials also opposed trade sanctions because they saw them as another instrument of protectionism in the U.S. arsenal—only this time, sanctions would be cloaked in the politically correct language of labor and environmental protection, not commercial interests.

The Mexicans were extremely wary of even the most limited forms of outside intervention on these issues. They rejected out of hand the idea of creating commissions or tribunals that might try to supersede Mexico's domestic laws. Mexico's negotiators stuck to their guidelines. One described the U.S. proposal as "infamous, imperialistic, and aggressive. They wanted secretariats with powers to intervene and inspect businesses, oversee labor justice, and approve the constitutionality of labor laws. We told them to fuck off [*nosotros los mandamos a la chingada*]."

The Mexicans knew that strong side agreements could erode the benefits of NAFTA, making businesses that would otherwise be enticed to invest in Mexico more reluctant. But they also knew that the accords were dictated by domestic political necessities in the United States and that the Democrats, in particular, wanted to appease labor unions and environmentalists opposed to NAFTA. Moreover, they knew exactly what U.S. unions and nongovernmental organizations (NGOs) were pushing for. The biggest fear of the Mexican negotiators was that American unions, especially the AFL-CIO, and environmentalists would use the delays caused by the side-deal negotiations to intensify their opposition to the NAFTA.

Mexican Labor Secretary Arsenio Farel was especially concerned to preserve intact Mexico's corporatist system of labor relations, and he had solid support from official unions. As one Mexican labor specialist put it, leaders of organized labor were "going to resist any changes that threatened their monopoly of representation of the labor movement." State-sponsored unions had more or less accepted Salinas's economic program in spite of initial reservations about whether neoliberal policies would benefit workers. Under the leadership of Fidel Velásquez, organized labor threw its support behind Salinas's reforms and boycotted all opposition efforts. Within the constraints of a top-down system of labor relations, official unions had influence, or at least a veto, in the side-deal negotiations. As in the main NAFTA negotiations, a *cuarto a lado* (side room) was reserved for representatives of organized labor and business during the side-deal negotiations. As one negotiator put it, "After the negotiations had ended during the day, we would meet with the labor and business people and exchange points of view. This would be passed along to Norma Samañego who would represent them in the negotiations." Mexico's negotiators believed that the side room "provided strength to the Mexican position."

It was not hard for the United States to make the case that NAFTA would not be ratified by Congress unless side agreements that addressed the concerns of domestic constituents were reached. This was not a case of the government "tying its own hands" but rather exploiting undisputed political realities. Domestic pressure in the United States was public and vociferous. Peripatetic public advocate Ross Perot emerged as a potent critic of the administration, voicing harsh criticism of the NAFTA in Senate hearings, in televised interviews, and in his extensive, paid "infomercials." Some members of Congress loudly demanded trade sanctions, insisting that the terms of the environmental deal go beyond enforcement of domestic laws to the creation of a broader commission that would have investigative powers backed by trade sanctions. Some NGOs even demanded binding arbitration with mandatory sanctions, an idea that found little support among the government's negotiators.

At the same time, the government's win-set was narrowed by Republican hostility to side-deal negotiations. Twenty-seven Republican Senators threatened to oppose the passage of NAFTA if in their judgment, the commission was granted too much power, and business leaders warned Clinton to ratify NAFTA as soon as possible. In an effort to maximize the power of congressional Democrats, House Democrat Sander Levin urged his colleagues to avoid staking out a position on NAFTA until the supplemental agreements were negotiated. Other prominent Democrats, including Richard Gephardt, followed suit, saying that their support for NAFTA would depend on the effectiveness of the side agreements. Gephardt was kept up-to-date on the progress of the side-deal negotiations by Department of Labor negotiators.

A second round of talks was held in Mexico City in the middle of April—the labor meeting was held on April 14 and the environment meeting on April 15. During this round, the United States backed away from an ambitious proposal for a deal on import surges, submitting a more modest proposal. In early April, Mickey Kantor, during meetings with Michael Wilson in Ottawa, had broached the idea of an agreement on import surges to complement the negotiations on labor and the environment that were already underway. Wilson expressed unequivocal opposition to the idea, and it was quietly dropped. Instead, a "face-saving" deal was proposed in which an "early warning" system would be established to ensure imports are not dumped into a NAFTA country. Yerxa acknowledged this U.S. shift in Mexico City. In fact, the U.S. concern was largely about the level of understanding within domestic constituencies of how snapback provisions would work to protect the United States. Thus, the United States had to appear to be showing concern about this issue, but in the negotiations, Mexico and Canada repeatedly pointed out that this had already been negotiated within the NAFTA.

In the proposals that Yerxa presented to his Canadian and Mexican counterparts, there was still a discrepancy in the strength of enforcement provisions between the labor and environmental proposals. Moreover, the vagueness and lack of detail in the proposals reflected the lack of consensus within the executive branch, as well as the desire to negotiate principles before details. In the first two weeks of March, Mickey Kantor had appeared before the House Ways and Means Committee and the Senate Finance Committee to discuss the impending negotiations. He said at that time that the United States would not seek "supranational powers" for labor and environmental commissions. However, as the negotiations progressed, the United States ratcheted up the pressure on Mexico and Canada. Yerxa claimed that the future of NAFTA was in the balance, implying that the issue of enforcement was a deal breaker. There was an evident inconsistency in the message coming from the U.S. team. Blanco remained publicly optimistic, but the Mexican side feared that dragging out the negotiations would exacerbate a fragile situation in Mexico and give NAFTA opponents in the United States more time to organize.

One participant in the negotiations described the lack of consensus within the Clinton administration in the first months of 1993. During interagency meetings to hammer out a position:

> Each agency treated the President's NAFTA campaign speech as the bible, reading into it support for the positions that they wanted to take. Fundamental underlying disagreements about how to think about NAFTA remained submerged. For some, NAFTA remained an affirmation of the

virtues of free markets and free trade; for others, it was a way of stabilizing our largest neighbor and rewarding it for efforts to move away from statist economic policies; for some negotiators of the trade provisions, NAFTA had to go through to justify the way that they had spent the last two years. (Herzenberg n.d., 8)

The initial proposals outlined the need for independent secretariats in both areas, but "wider latitude and greater power" was given to the labor secretariat. "Not only could the secretariat, apparently of its own accord, choose to remit enforcement cases to dispute resolution, but it also would have four branches whose duties are spelled out in much greater detail than those of the environmental secretariat. The labor proposal calls for research and liaison, enforcement oversight, complaints and investigation, and dispute resolution branches of the secretariat."[10]

At this point, the U.S. proposal for a trinational public advisory committee in the labor accord followed the outlines of Options B and C in the NEC paper. It meant that labor, management, and other NGOs would participate in the work of the labor commission. The labor proposal called for commitments similar to those in the environmental proposal on the enforcement of continental labor standards but went further in calling on NAFTA governments to commit themselves to internationally recognized standards and rights on a wide range of issues, including freedom of association and collective bargaining, forced labor and child labor, work hours, wages, health and safety conditions, and discrimination. During the course of the negotiations, the imbalance between the labor and environmental accords shifted in the opposite direction, leading to a stronger environmental accord. This was due to the willingness of U.S. environmentalists to support the administration, as well as staunch Mexican opposition to anything that would expose their hierarchical system of labor relations to external scrutiny or control.

The difference in the positions of domestic constituencies in the United States concerned with the labor and environmental side deals became more clear early in May, when environmental groups offered support for NAFTA on the condition that the administration press for an independent environmental commission with "meaningful powers." The groups included some of the most important environmental organizations in the nation: the World Wildlife Fund, Environmental Defense Fund, National Wildlife Federation, Defenders of Wildlife, Nature Conservancy, National Audubon Society, and the National Resources Defense Council.

Around this time, a "radicalization" of the U.S. position was observed and clearly reflected internal pressures within the administration. On April 30, Jeff Faux, president of the Economic Policy Institute, a policy think tank linked to the Democratic Party and organized labor, sent a memorandum to the White House saying: "The deal they are negotiating now is not good enough. It has no teeth and everyone knows it." Faux went on to suggest that Clinton should "begin to extricate himself by sticking to his earlier demands that tough side agreements be negotiated with high standards and *strict* enforcement, including trade sanctions" (Faux 1993). In the meantime, the talks should be slowed down and a contingency plan should be prepared to back out of NAFTA. In fact, by now there were many in the White House who would have been happy to let NAFTA die.[11]

White House Budget Director Leon Panetta said in early May that NAFTA "is 'dead,' for now," meaning that if NAFTA were brought to a vote at that time, it would fail to garner the sufficient number of votes to pass in the House.[12] José Cordoba traveled to Washington in mid-May to stress that Mexico had no contingency plans for a ratification defeat, and he appealed to the "new mentality" in support of the redefined economic relationship that had emerged in recent years among policy makers in the three countries. Although Kantor called Serra to provide reassurances, when negotiators went into the third round of what was to be four days of talks in Ottawa, starting on May 19, the United States took a very tough position on trade sanctions, provoking a visible division among the negotiators. Vehement arguing began over dinner on the first day, as Rufus Yerxa proposed trade sanctions and an independent secretariat as the key elements of an agreement. Fighting between the chief negotiators left little for the working group negotiators to do, except work on drafting less controversial parts of the text where brackets remained (such as the preamble).

Draft texts used as a working basis for the negotiations showed clear differences. Mexico's draft proposal on labor excluded trade sanctions wielded by an independent secretariat, and in their place called for using the International Labor Organization to prepare nonbinding reports on labor conditions. The U.S. text, based on a position that was endorsed by the White House Council of Economic Advisors on May 12, provided enforcement powers to NACE, including trade sanctions for repeated and persistent violations. NACE would oversee environmental laws, accept complaints from any of the three governments, and rely on ad hoc panels of experts in reaching decisions. Unable to resolve their disagreement over the issue of sanctions and enforcement powers, the negotiations broke off early on May 21. Mexico and Canada simply refused to negotiate on the U.S. proposal, which John Weekes called "too adversarial and too prosecutorial."[13]

As the talks broke off, the negotiators were uncertain about how to approach the usual, scheduled press conference. Yerxa proposed to simply state in public the nature of the divergence of views. The Mexicans feared that this would give ammunition to NAFTA opponents, but they recognized that making the impasse public would increase the pressure on the White House to recognize that the U.S. bargaining position was not tenable. However, when Herminio Blanco acknowledged disagreements among the three teams at the press conference, it was the Mexican stock market that plunged.

A fourth round of talks, held in Washington in the first week of June, failed to resolve the deadlock between the United States, on the one hand, and Canada and Mexico, on the other. Whereas the Americans continued to propose some form of trade sanctions to be managed by an independent regional secretariat, Mexico and Canada indicated that they would only accept penalties—such as fines—as long as they were unrelated to trade. Jaime Serra said, "The Mexican position has been that we will not accept trade sanctions.... Now, to have measures on persistent behavior of not applying laws consistently, we are willing to do that—but they have to be measures that provide a remedy, not cross over to trade."[14] In effect, Mexico was ready to accept penalties for violations, but not trade sanctions. Unable to overcome this disagreement, the negotiators exchanged views, rather than texts, and no concrete progress was made. Serra was still hoping that the negotiations could be completed by the end of the month, telling business leaders that the negotiators were at the "bracket eliminating stage," but Kantor believed they would stretch into July.

Following the fourth round of side-deal negotiations, Prime Minister Brian Mulroney left office as one of the most unpopular outgoing prime ministers in recent memory, and his Progressive Conservative Party knew they faced a difficult challenge going into an election. They hoped that a new face would help restore the party's popularity. In a national convention, Kim Campbell, a strong advocate of continental and global trade liberalization, was proclaimed the new Conservative leader and prime minister. Among the members of the party most disappointed by this result was Michael Wilson, who was urged by Mulroney and leading party strategists not to run for the leadership in order to allow Campbell to win. On June 12, Campbell became prime minister. To replace Wilson, she appointed Thomas Hockin as Canada's new international trade minister. Hockin's appointment came just after the Canadian Senate passed NAFTA by 47 to 30 votes on June 23, making Canada the first country to ratify the agreement. However, the signature of the governor general,[15] necessary to make the agreement law, would wait until after a fall election.

By the end of June, it had become apparent that the United States was looking for an "exit strategy," some way to back down from the tough bargaining position they had articulated throughout the meetings in April and May. Mexican negotiators sensed a weakening of the U.S. position, but they were puzzled by the U.S. negotiators' request for time to change the position of their own government. "Aghast, we sent several messages to the White House that on our side negotiations were about to break down" (Bertrab

1997, 91). As if the side agreement negotiations were not difficult enough, NAFTA itself ran into a legal road block at the end of June. Domestic pressures in Washington, especially on the environmental side, began to intensify over the summer months. Three environmental groups—Ralph Nader's Public Citizen, Friends of the Earth, and the Sierra Club—brought a case against NAFTA on environmental grounds to a U.S. District Court. On June 30, Judge Charles Richey ordered the U.S. administration to prepare an environmental impact statement on NAFTA. In his decision, the judge ruled that such a statement would have to be prepared before the NAFTA could be submitted to Congress for approval. His decision was based on clear language to that effect in the National Environmental Policy Act. Furthermore, the judge ruled that the Bush administration had violated the Administrative Procedures Act by failing to carry out such an assessment before the agreement was negotiated.

The White House responded angrily to Judge Richey's ruling, but it did not prevent the administration from continuing to negotiate the side deals. Mickey Kantor stated, "The judge did not say we could not continue on, which we will continue to do."[16] However, the ruling did significantly raise the political costs of pressing forward in the absence of such a statement and reinforced the intense domestic pressure in the United States for a strong environmental side deal. The Clinton administration filed an appeal and proposed a schedule for filing briefs that would bring the case to a close sometime in August. Uncertainty caused by the legal debate in the United States caused fears among investors in Mexico's stock markets that Serra attempted to assuage, saying, "There will be absolutely no interruption in negotiations for the parallel accords...everything is moving forward with full rigor."[17]

The fifth round of talks, held in Cocoyoc in Mexico on July 8–10, followed a series of phone calls and meetings between ministers and chief negotiators, in an unsuccessful effort to break the deadlock over sanctions, independence of the environmental secretariat, and the scope of the negotiations. Although the United States presented no new proposals, various possible scenarios were discussed for the way a North American environmental commission might operate, in particular, what powers it might have, how it would finance environmental cleanup along the U.S.-Mexican border, and different ways of dealing with patterns of nonenforcement. Each country left its initial positions on the table, and the decision on enforcement mechanisms would await the final round of talks.

In this round of negotiations, the United States backed away from tough sanctions, and Mexico moved toward acceptance of some form of sanctions in the hope that this would facilitate NAFTA ratification. Rufus Yerxa denied that the United States had made any concessions in terms of weakening trade sanctions, saying that such a decision would have to be made at the ministerial level. Moreover, after the meetings were concluded, Mickey Kantor denied reports that such concessions had been made: "We have not changed our position at all...we want real teeth, real enforcement."[18] Canada continued to oppose any form of sanctions but remained open to the idea of fining repeat offenders.

The negotiations shifted focus from the issue of trade sanctions—to be determined later—to the structure and functioning of possible regional organizations to enforce labor and environmental standards. U.S. negotiators insisted on regional environmental and labor commissions that would be independent, including a secretariat and staff that would be appointed independently, and that would have the power to initiate inquiries into violations of labor and environmental standards based on its own criteria. Mexico and Canada insisted on secretariats structured along national lines and responsive to national governments. A compromise began to take shape as negotiators focused on the possible role of different bodies responsible for administering the agreement, including commissions, ministerial councils, national offices, and international coordinating secretariats. There was also discussion of a Canadian proposal involving fines as an alternative to trade sanctions. Officials from SECOFI stated that the negotiations had entered their final stage, and Mickey Kantor agreed, saying that they could be wrapped up by the end of the month.

The final, and most difficult, stage in the side-deal negotiations—the end game—began with the sixth round in Ottawa starting on July 19. The chief negotiators hoped that this would be the final push, and their objective was to produce a unified text with bracketed areas, to be resolved by the ministers, who were scheduled to join the talks the next week. The deal, it was believed, could be wrapped up by the end of the month. In fact, however, it was not concluded until the middle of August. The central outstanding issue remained the controversy over trade sanctions. As late as the end of July, Kantor insisted that the side deals would include sanctions that "will have bite,"[19] while Canadian trade minister Hockin continued to insist they could be avoided.

The three governments argued over the strength and scope of the agreement. Whereas the United States wanted the agreement to create a higher international standard, Canada and Mexico wanted the deal to be based on each country's existing laws. The problem for Canada was that most labor laws are under provincial jurisdiction, while Mexico was reluctant to expose its system of corporatist bargaining to international regulation. The consensus reached was that the deal would cover "mutually recognized" rather than international standards. Another issue was the scope of the agreement, and here the discussion revolved around a broad agenda including freedom of association, the right to collective bargaining, the right to strike, prohibitions on forced labor, and child labor. However, it was understood that labor standards would be treated as objectives rather than obligations. Mexican unions strongly resisted the idea of worker rights, which threatened the basis of corporatist bargaining in Mexico.

The Canadian and U.S. negotiators did not involve their domestic constituencies in the side-deal negotiations as well as they had in the NAFTA negotiations. Senator Christopher Dodd, a Connecticut Democrat, voiced the criticism that "a lot of these agreements are being negotiated without talking to people who have a deep interest in what is to be included in them."[20] There was intense frustration on the part of the U.S. business sector about not being consulted, and unions in both countries were largely opposed to the NAFTA. Thus, on the labor side, Mexican negotiators' hands were more tied than those of their counterparts. Mexico built on the tripartite multisectoral bargaining framework that had been used to negotiate a social pact on macroeconomic policy, called the PECE (Pacto de Estabilización y Crecimiento Económico). In fact, Mexico's chief labor negotiator, Norma Samañego, was a technical secretary in the labor secretariat responsible for negotiating the PECE, and she was able to draw on this mechanism to involve the major trade union confederations, as well as unions representing teachers and public sector workers.

Pointing to domestic constraints, the Mexican negotiators argued that the final deal would have to respect Mexico's labor legislation; they were unwilling to adapt or harmonize their labor standards to those of another country. They argued that every country is entitled to legislation that reflects its level and rhythm of development, and emphasized the differences in legal traditions among the three countries. They pointed out that Mexico subscribed to eighty-seven International Labor Organization conventions, whereas the United States subscribed to only nine and Canada to twenty-six. Moreover, Mexico's system was based less on written precedents.

As the negotiations proceeded, the labor and environment issues were divided into separate negotiations, in spite of the fact that the negotiators wanted the two side accords to look similar, to avoid the need to explain discrepancies. They were divided because it became clear that the labor agreement was going to be weaker, and the U.S. negotiators responsible for the environmental negotiations did not want to get the same sort of defective dispute settlement procedure that emerged in the labor side deal.[21]

At the end of July, and then again at the beginning of August, ministerial meetings were held at the Madison Hotel in Washington. The meeting that began on August 4, which was scheduled to last two days, dragged on for six and went throughout a weekend. When the ministers finally broke off this marathon, after sixteen straight hours of negotiation, the working group negotiators continued on over into the second week of August. During this time, Kantor and his officials consulted labor leaders, including the United Auto Workers and Teamsters, for suggestions on how to improve the labor accord.

U.S. waffling created confusion among the Mexican negotiators. At one point during the negotiations, Serra turned to Kantor and asked him to make up his mind—"Is it [industrial relations] in, or is it out?" he asked. Jack Otero, Secretary Reich's assistant, could see how the U.S. position was weakening, and he struggled to avoid a slippery slope of further concessions that would weaken the labor accord. Yerxa, who did not want to be known as someone who could not finish an agreement, was eager to wrap up too. He did not want to be left in the sweltering heat of August in Washington while Kantor went on vacation.

Finally, on the weekend of August 8, Mexico accepted trade sanctions and the United States dropped its demand that the deal cover industrial relations. Explained a senior U.S. negotiator, "Kantor was convinced that he could not get a deal with industrial relations in it." The United States convinced the Mexicans that trade sanctions were the "bottom-line price they have to pay to get the NAFTA through Congress." The trade-off was that Mexico would accept sanctions in exchange for an accord narrow in scope. Kantor accepted this trade-off because time was running out for the administration, and there was strong domestic pressure, as well as pressure from the Mexicans, to submit the deal to Congress in time for implementation on January 1, 1994. Moreover, Kantor knew that if he went too far linking trade with industrial relations, Republican support in Congress for the deal could be lost.

As the United States moved toward the deadline for ratification, Mexican negotiators felt that they were gaining the upper hand, since time, once again, had shifted in their favor: "We learned from the NAFTA about US negotiating behavior; we learn to move in these circles. They know how to move slowly." This negotiator pointed out that, in the Watergate end game, "Bush wanted to wrap up before the convention, they were desperate." The Mexicans learned from this experience: "We had no hurry in the side deals. And they became desperate; 'Please, Jimmy [Jaime Serra], give me something,' Kantor said at one point near the end. So we gave in on using minors and the minimum wage."

The Mexican government, which had called sanctions a deal breaker, decided to accept a mild version of trade sanctions, instead of the Canadian proposal for court challenges, because it believed that "suing Mexico in its own courts attacks the concept of sovereignty and as such is inadmissible."[22] In the end, they were convinced that trade sanctions were the price of getting a deal that could be ratified by the U.S. Congress. On August 6, Serra met with House Majority Leader Richard Gephardt, who emphasized the importance of trade sanctions. In retrospect, one negotiator felt that Gephardt's support was taken for granted, in the sense that he would ultimately come around to supporting NAFTA, while fears of Republican defections were exaggerated. Gephardt had wanted a commitment in the side deal to link wages and productivity: all he got was an agreement to monitor this link. The more the debate heated up, however, the more administration officials worried about losing Republican support.

Mexican negotiators were pleased with the weakness of the labor accord. Mexico strongly resisted the idea of international scrutiny of its domestic affairs, particularly the system of industrial relations. Nor did Mexico want the issue of independent unions to be brought up among the list of issues that could come under scrutiny at the ministerial level. Thus, the labor accord creates national labor offices—unlike the environmental accord's trinational secretariat. The U.S. negotiators knew that they could have pushed Mexico harder, but there was ambivalence within the U.S. side. In the end, however, U.S. negotiators believed that the Mexicans would not have walked away from a stronger accord on labor.

Canada put up an intense fight against trade sanctions. While Serra and Kantor waited, Tom Hockin returned to Ottawa where he met with cabinet colleagues and senior officials. Prime Minister Kim Campbell's direct intervention at this time was decisive. With an eye on the impending election, she indicated that she would not accept an agreement involving trade sanctions: "We don't support the use of trade sanctions for non-trade issues."[23]

Ministerial talks resumed in Ottawa on August 12. The United States bowed in the face of Canadian resistance to trade sanctions. In a breakthrough that was achieved late on the evening of Thursday, August 12, the United States and Mexico agreed that Canada would be exempt from trade sanctions for nonenforcement of standards. To get this deal, Hockin agreed to have Parliament approve a special clause giving the Canadian Federal Court powers to fine federal or provincial governments if they are found by a trinational panel to have failed to enforce their own standards. This clearly watered down U.S. demands for commercial sanctions, and in return, Canada's power to challenge enforcement of laws at the subfederal level in Mexico or the United States was reduced.

The Mexican negotiators were jubilant. On the evening of August 12, after late-night calls, celebrations were held in Los Pinos in Mexico City as the president received the news that the side-deal negotiations had been wrapped up. The next day, Friday, August 13, Mickey Kantor announced what he called a historic agreement on labor and environmental accords to supplement the NAFTA. A key feature of the deal was the differential treatment of Canada and Mexico in terms of enforcement, as well as the weakness of the labor accord by comparison with what was negotiated on the environment.

Canada had insisted into the final hours of the negotiations that it could not accept trade sanctions, and the United States backed down in the end. As a result, trade sanctions could be applied between Mexico and the United States in the event that one of the two countries engaged in a pattern of persistent violation of its own laws and then refused to pay fines after a dispute resolution process had assessed damages. In the Canadian case, however, the refusal to pay fines could lead to a court challenge that could result in a court order to pay the fines. Canadian officials noted that the final deal did not give Canada a free ride. In a press conference, Tom Hockin emphasized that Canadian courts offered a strong enforcement mechanism, noting that they had never failed to enforce an order in their 132 years of existence.

The final deal also produced extremely weak provisions on the issue of labor standards. Although the labor and environmental accords have the same enforcement power, they have different structures to implement the accord: the environmental accord is trilateral, whereas the labor accord involves three separate, and autonomous, national offices. Moreover, the labor accord is restricted to health and safety, child labor, and minimum wages, and complaints can only be brought to national labor offices where the issues concern goods and services traded among the NAFTA countries.

The final deal created an environmental secretariat that does not investigate but rather gathers information on how the three countries enforce their environmental laws. However, it is an independent body that is not subservient to national governments. The environmental NGOs were happy with the shape of the environmental agreement. It, therefore, served the purpose of neutralizing opposition to NAFTA from environmentalists, by splitting environmental NGOs and their political allies. By contrast, the unions and their principal ally in congress, Richard Gephardt, remained opposed to NAFTA.

The attitude of the AFL-CIO and their allies among the Democrats in Congress weakened the labor accord. As Stephen Herzenberg (n.d., 9) put it: "From the beginning, the signal sent by the AFL-CIO, and some other branches of the anti-NAFTA coalition, was that their support could not be won. For some this reflected visceral fear of NAFTA. For others, it reflected a view that the way the trade agreement hamstrung state authority, or the way NAFTA would whipsaw US against Mexican workers, could not be addressed effectively without changing the agreement or unilateral changes in Mexican labor law. Ambivalence among NAFTA opponents about bargaining with the Clinton Administration reinforced the hand of those within the Administration who felt strengthening the side agreement would cost more votes than it would garner."

A Mexican negotiator provided a pithy description of Mexico's perspective on the side deals:

Mexican officials regarded the outcome of the side deal negotiations as a bit of a joke. You know how the side deals work? There are consultations—you can complain about anything. If there is no agreement, there is a committee to evaluate complaints. The committee is composed of three experts, one from each country. The country denouncing gets to pick from a list of experts from the country it is denouncing—a nice feature. Then opinions are gathered, with a recommendation. At the second stage, what themes can be discussed? Anything except political issues—freedom to unionize, right to strike, collective negotiations. At the second stage there are arbitral panels. In the event of reiterated noncompliance, which causes unfair competition (that is, reduces costs), this can be penalized, *but only if a comparable norm exists in the other country*. The system is not worth a damn [*El sistema no sirve un carajo*]. It is a forum for complaints, and at the end of the day everyone says, "Nice to talk with you, good luck." Basically, it is to be used by the US against Mexico. But themes of unionism cannot go to the panels, only consultations. Lots of public discourse, nothing more. This is the result we wanted.

Another Mexican official involved in implementing the environmental accords was similarly happy with the weakness of the accords: "The mechanisms for sanctions are extremely long—a country has to be looking for sanctions to be imposed."

The weakness of the deal partly reflected the strength of Mexican opposition to anything that appeared to open up politically charged issues concerning Mexican industrial relations. Some U.S. negotiators felt that the Mexicans were hiding behind their industrial relations system, which was largely controlled by the state. In this sense, Mexican efforts to portray themselves as domestically constrained may be an example of how domestic constraints can be exaggerated for the purpose of "tying one's hands" in international negotiations. However, this argument should be complemented with the observation that the United States clearly did not push as hard as it could have, for its own domestic reasons.

Official labor unions in Mexico, on the other hand, were pleased with the results of the negotiation, not only because they were included in the process, but also because the final deal respected existing legislation and would not encourage challenges to their privileged position within Mexico's corporatist system. It did not go beyond such issues as safety, child labor, and nonpayment of wages to include the more sensitive problems of industrial relations, namely, collective agreements and union rights. Mexico's negotiators were satisfied that although the deal permitted trade sanctions, the process is so convoluted that it is unlikely ever to matter.

## Congressional Ratification

The side-deal negotiations were required by the Clinton administration in order to secure ratification of NAFTA in the U.S. Congress. Clinton's labor secretary, Robert Reich, made no bones about this in February 1993, when he said that the purpose of negotiating these accords was to ensure passage of the NAFTA through the legislature. The accords had to be sufficiently strong to sway domestic environmentalists, and to a lesser extent labor, in order to enable Democrats to vote for an agreement that was the creation of conservative governments, while at the same time not being so strong as to alienate core Republican supporters of NAFTA and their business allies.

These contradictory imperatives account for the often erratic behavior of U.S. Trade Representative Mickey Kantor. However, once he felt a balance had been achieved in the side-deal talks, one that could be sold to Congress, the negotiations were wrapped up. From a substantive point of view, the supplemental accords were unlikely to win enthusiastic support from either of the contending parties in the fight over NAFTA; politically, however, they represented a viable middle ground for the impending legislative debate. Even before the negotiations were over, the arduous task of "selling the deal on the Hill" began. In early July, Clinton began to consider names for a "NAFTA Czar" responsible for orchestrating the political campaign to win a majority of votes in the House of Representatives and the Senate. He finally named William Daley to the post.

Bill Daley, son of the late Richard J. Daley, legendary political fixer and former mayor of Chicago, served as the chairman of Clinton's Illinois campaign in 1992 but was passed over for a cabinet post in the spring of 1993. Kantor urged the White House to hire Daley to manage the NAFTA campaign on the Hill. When Daley began to put together his staff in September, the challenge of winning over support for NAFTA was a formidable one. As Sidney Blumenthal (1993, 89) put it, "Daley faced an electorate of four hundred and thirty-four," the total number of seats in the House of Representatives. He needed roughly 220 votes to win and, with about 120 Republicans committed to NAFTA, this meant that 100 supporters had to be found among the Democrats.

One of Daley's major jobs was to orchestrate private-sector support for NAFTA. The main business organization supporting the agreement was the USA-NAFTA Coalition, which by mid-1993 was composed of twenty-three hundred corporations and lobbies. Each state was assigned to a corporation that served as the "captain" responsible for convincing the public of the merits of NAFTA. Caterpillar and John Deere, for example, along with the Illinois Farm Bureau, the Illinois Retail Merchants Association, and other groups, banded together to form a 220-member "Illinois NAFTA Coalition" to lobby their congressional delegation in support of NAFTA.[24] AT&T was assigned seven states, IBM had five, and General Electric had the New England states. All but one of the thirty-five captains was from the five hundred largest firms (Bertrab 1997, 116). Opponents countered the USA-NAFTA Coalition by attacking the corporate behavior of member firms. A study by the Institute for Policy Studies found that the thirty-five captains had recently laid off 178,000 workers.[25]

Mexico also undertook a major public relations and lobbying effort to sell the trade pact. The Center for Public Integrity called Mexican lobbying for NAFTA the "most elaborate, expensive lobbying campaign ever conducted in Washington by a foreign interest."[26] They further noted that Mexico hired thirty-three former U.S. government officials and took forty-eight congressional staffers on expenses-paid trips to Mexico. Some observers worried that "with Mexico hiring a large number of former officials, it can look like they're trying to buy the treaty."[27] Former U.S. Trade Representative Bill Brock was paid $30,000 per month by Burson-Marsteller, which had a $323,000 per-month contract to handle Mexico's public relations. Mexico also helped set up the US Alliance for NAFTA. That lobby group was formally created in New York on October 9, 1992, at a meeting between Salinas and top U.S. and Mexican business people, with U.S. business represented by James D. Robinson of American Express and Kay R. Whitmore, chairman of Eastman Kodak.

Opposition to NAFTA had hardened during the summer of 1993, and the signing of the side deals did little to mollify labor's opposition. The labor accord was lampooned as soon as the details of its provisions were made public. Bob White, the head of the Canadian Labor Congress, called it a "toothless tiger." U.S. labor was no more charitable, asserting that the agreements fell short of Clinton's stated objectives.

On September 14, 1993, the side deals were signed in the presence of three former U.S. presidents. The event was organized by Daley, who saw it as a way of building consensus behind NAFTA. Shortly thereafter, an appeals court overthrew the ruling of Judge Ritchey, thereby clearing a legal path for NAFTA's ratification. But polls showed Americans remained ambivalent about the deal, and the vote in Congress was expected to be close. Throughout September and October, Daley worked the back rooms on Capitol Hill, firming up support and trying to keep the undecided from joining the opposition. Salinas appealed for support for the NAFTA, saying that any rejection of the agreement would represent the loss of an opportunity that presents itself only once in a generation. Salinas recognized that a unique moment of cooperation in U.S.-Mexican relations had arrived, and had already begun to pass.

Events in Canada, meanwhile, offered an unwelcome portent for U.S. lawmakers. On October 25, 1993, Jean Chrétien's Liberal Party won a commanding majority in the Canadian federal election, picking up 99 new seats to win an absolute majority of 178 in the House of Commons. The election wiped the Progressive Conservative Party off the political map, leaving them with only two representatives in the House of Commons, down from 153 seats. Chrétien had promised to renegotiate NAFTA in the event of a Liberal victory, and within days of the election he called for a reopening of the provisions of the NAFTA dealing with energy, subsidies, and dumping.[28]

Salinas bluntly rejected Chrétien's call to renegotiate NAFTA, but it was clear that Chrétien's victory was another unnerving event that would diminish "the spirit of Houston." In his annual address to the nation, Salinas, for the first time, began to play down the importance of NAFTA and called for strengthening economic relations outside of the North American region. At the end of October, the Mexicans estimated that there were 101 votes in favor of NAFTA in the U.S. House of Representatives, with 131 against, and the rest undecided (Bertrab 1997, 140).

In the months leading up to the vote, Ross Perot played an especially important role in the opposition to NAFTA, not withstanding the fact that his credentials were, to put it mildly, questionable. As a businessman, he stood to benefit from NAFTA, and his arguments lacked the sophistication and depth of research that the opponents in think tanks and advocacy groups linked to labor and the Democratic Party had. Nonetheless, he was able to use his substantial resources to buy air time on television to present a distinctly negative image of Mexico and the future of the United States under NAFTA. Perot had published a book against NAFTA, with Pat Choate, that tapped into a prevalent concern about foreign influence in U.S. politics, economic insecurity, and U.S. nationalism. Perot's critique was rebutted, point by point, in a widely circulated seventy-four-page paper issued by Mickey Kantor.

To head off (or perhaps, more cynically, to build up) the Perot challenge, U.S. Vice President Al Gore offered to debate Perot on the television talk show "Larry King Live." The debate occurred in early November, just before the vote, and Gore's reassuring performance added a sense of momentum to the pro-NAFTA camp. More than thirty members of the House endorsed NAFTA during the week following the Gore-Perot debate. Ironically, Perot's scatter-shot approach to criticizing NAFTA deflected attention away from the crucial issues of labor relations in Mexico (including freedom of association, the right to unionize and engage in collective bargaining, and the lack of links between productivity and remuneration), issues that the Clinton administration acknowledged were important and motivated the search for a side deal on labor. Instead, Perot emphasized "the giant sucking sound" of jobs going south—the theme of one of Perot's thirty-minute "infomercials" was "keeping your job in the USA." Perot's attacks had the effect of turning around Daley's efforts, undercutting opposition to the NAFTA: after the Gore-Perot debate, calls to Congress went from eight-to-one against the deal to almost eight- to-one in favor of it.[29]

In the final days before the vote, President Clinton lobbied long and hard for the agreement. He cajoled those members of Congress who would not make up their minds until the final days or hours of the debate, offering to have bridges and factories built in their constituencies. He offered side payments to producers of cucumbers, tomatoes, and frozen orange juice and promised to address trade disputes with Canada over wheat and peanut butter. Kentucky Republican Jim Bunning said, "If we tried this vote-buying in Kentucky, there'd be a grand jury looking into it."[30] In spite of intense presidential engagement, the vote was a cliff-hanger. Debate on the floor went on for eight hours (thirteen hours by the clock), with 225 members rising to speak—over half the House. A congressional staffer who was closely involved admitted that it was not clear if NAFTA would pass right up until the last day. Nevertheless, in what was widely regarded as a major victory for the president, on November 17, Clinton comfortably secured passage of NAFTA through the House by a vote of 234 to 200 in favor. The Senate approved the deal on November 20.

## Understanding the Negotiation

The results of the supplemental negotiations strongly reinforce the major arguments outlined in Chapter 2. In particular, we argued that asymmetries of power do not necessarily inhibit cooperation, as neorealists argued. Mexico, the United States, and Canada were able to negotiate formal accords on labor and the environment, even though these agreements ostensibly cut to the very heart of national concerns over sovereignty and autonomy. As we argued, asymmetries of power do not necessarily lead to asymmetrical results when the weaker player has an attractive alternative to a deal or is more patient. Asymmetrical results between Canada and Mexico illustrate the point: whereas Canada was prepared to walk away from a deal that involved trade sanctions, Mexico was not, and as a result, the deal imposes trade sanctions on Mexico but not Canada.

Why did Mexico accept this seemingly asymmetrical result? In part, because it was unwilling to risk the NAFTA. Faced with further concessions, the Mexicans swallowed the bitter pill necessary for domestic ratification in the United States. But there is another reason why Mexico accepted the side deals: the accords would only weakly constrain Mexican policy autonomy.

Here, again, we note that the most powerful state is driven by the interests of domestic constituents more than the need to reach an agreement with their Level I counterparts. The supplemental accords were dictated by the requirements of ratifying NAFTA in the United States and were aimed at placating opposition in the ranks of labor and the environmentalists, rather than constraining the policy autonomy of the member states. Table 9.2 provides a summary assessment of the application of the principal hypotheses to the negotiation process that unfolded in the supplemental negotiations on labor and the environment.

An unexpected consequence of NAFTA was the greater U.S. and Canadian scrutiny of Mexico's labor and environmental practices. This, combined with the competitive political process and distributive issues raised by NAFTA, led to the negotiation of the supplemental accords. The NAFTA supplemental negotiations on labor and the environment provide a striking example of domestic politics driving international negotiations, but they also show how seemingly domestic issues—such as wages, employment, and environmental protection—can be internationalized. In the process of globalization and regional integration, domestic constituents increasingly see their interests and values tied up with international developments.

The U.S. Congress played a key role in the side-deal negotiations, just as the Mexican corporatist system of labor relations constrained its negotiators and made Mexico sensitive to concessions in this area. However, the differences in domestic ratification procedures meant that these domestic institutions tied the hands of the negotiators in different ways. Whereas the Mexican negotiators wished to avoid disrupting Mexico's corporatist system of labor relations, the United States was constrained by its narrow Level II win-set.

The supplemental accords demonstrated the role of side payments in promoting international agreements. Mexico's concessions on labor standards and environmental protection were additional payments that had to be made to ensure the domestic ratification of NAFTA in the U.S. Congress. Having completed the negotiation of NAFTA with a Republican administration primarily concerned with opening the Mexican market, the Mexican negotiators were then compelled to negotiate with a new administration with an entirely different agenda, rooted in the promises of the Clinton campaign during the autumn of 1992. These promises were aimed at shifting attention from the overall benefits of free trade with Mexico (which was what Bush emphasized in his efforts to use NAFTA as a foreign policy success story for his administration) to the domestic distributive costs and environmental externalities of such an agreement.

The distributive issues were raised by the United States and Canada, rather than by Mexico, where income inequality is greater, because of the acute sense of threat experienced by labor unions in the north, as well as their abil-

*Table 9.2* Hypotheses: The Side Deals on Labor and the Environment

| Hypothesis | Canada | Mexico | United States |
|---|---|---|---|
| Asymmetry: weaker states are more responsive to powerful states relative to domestic pressures; powerful states are more responsive to domestic pressures relative to the weaker states. | Side deals a minor issue in Canada; however, sanctions are politically explosive. | Unable to walk away; is compelled to make further concessions to a government with a different ideological agenda. | Clinton administration often seems indifferent to fate of NAFTA.<br><br>Side deals a condition of ratification of the NAFTA. |
| Institutions: centralized, vertical domestic institutions are a bargaining liability, while divided government is an asset. | Did not mobilize domestic constituencies on behalf of side deals.<br><br>The deal would have to be ratified by the provinces: a source of internal constraint. | Unions oppose any challenge to the monopoly of representation under the corporatist labor relations system.<br><br>No major frictions among Mexican cabinet officials on the side-deal negotiations. | Domestic interests narrow negotiators' win-set: Democrats want accords "with teeth"; Republicans threaten to withdraw support for NAFTA if side deals are too tough.<br><br>Union opposition to NAFTA weakened the labor side deal. Environmentalists, because they were willing to work with the administration, obtained a stronger accord. |
| Patterns of delayed mutual responsiveness: the lower the subjective utility assigned to the nonagreement alternative, the more concessions will be offered. | Trade sanctions used to appeal to nationalism during the 1993 election. | Uses ILO conventions as focal points. Notes that Mexico has signed more conventions than Canada or the U.S.<br><br>Mexicans patient. They "learned from the NAFTA" negotiation how "to move slowly." | Calls sanctions a "deal breaker." No sanctions, no NAFTA. In fact, domestic support is mixed.<br><br>USTR runs out of time, becomes impatient for a deal. |

ILO = International Labor Organization.

ity to influence elected officials. Mexico's labor unions supported the Mexican government, and fear of upsetting the corporatist system of industrial relations provided the Mexican negotiators with a powerful incentive to resist foreign intrusions. Opposition to NAFTA emerged through noninstitutional channels, including a debtors' cartel and a rural rebellion in the southern state of Chiapas.

Paradoxically, the labor side deal turned out to be weaker than the environmental one, contrary to the initial expectations of the negotiators. The greater willingness of environmentalists to compromise and support the deal gave them more leverage in the negotiation process. The unwillingness of organized labor to work with the U.S. government undercut its leverage. The Mexicans also proved to be tough bargainers when it came to preserving their nation's system of labor relations. Finally, a strong labor-environmental coalition emerged within the United States, and environmentalists cooperated across the border, but no comparable political alliances were possible between labor groups in the United States and Canada and Mexico.

By the end of November, Mexico had finally secured the U.S. approval of the agreement it had been seeking for so long, and it would come into effect a little more than a month later, on January 1, 1994. Rather than heralding the coming of a new age of prosperity and stability for Mexico, however, the inauguration of NAFTA would usher in a tragic period in Mexican affairs.

# A Mexican Tragedy

**T**he New Year's Eve party in Los Pinos—the presidential residence in Chapultepec, Mexico City—was an occasion for celebration.[1] President Carlos Salinas de Gortari could look back on 1993 with satisfaction. He had overcome the resistance of a new Democratic administration in Washington by negotiating supplemental accords on labor and the environment, and in November 1993 the U.S. Congress had passed NAFTA and its implementing legislation. The treaty entered into force as Salinas and his guests sipped champagne in the ballroom at Los Pinos. At two o'clock in the morning Salinas was abruptly jarred from the revelry by a call from the minister of defense. Guerrillas had seized San Cristóbal de las Casas and other cities in the southern state of Chiapas.

Thus began Mexico's *annus horribilis*. The insurrection by the Zapatista Army for National Liberation was followed by the March 1994 assassination of Luis Donaldo Colosio, the candidate for the presidency Salinas had handpicked to be his successor. The presidential election in August was narrowly won by Ernesto Zedillo Ponce de León, and his administration was immediately rocked by scandal and mishap. Even before Zedillo took office, the Mexican political establishment was shocked by another assassination in the ruling party, followed by a bungled currency devaluation in December 1994 that would cause a veritable meltdown in the Mexican banking system and a sharp economic contraction in 1995.

Even the most scathing critics of President Salinas were astonished by the denouement of his term in office. Until the end of 1993 Salinas was held up by his admirers as the very model of what an Ivy League–educated, liberal-reformer could do. He had negotiated the NAFTA, applied for Mexican membership in the Organization for Economic Cooperation and Development (OECD), and was widely touted as the first leader of the newly created World Trade Organization. At the end of 1993, it looked as if Salinas was going to go down in history as one of Mexico's most successful presidents, yet by the middle of 1995 he was reviled by Mexicans for his role in the collapse of the Mexican peso, his brother was in jail facing charges of illicit enrichment and murder, and he was forced to flee to Ireland (which has no extradition treaty with Mexico), fearing arrest in connection with the assassination of his handpicked successor.

A major explanation for the unraveling of the Salinas administration in 1994 lies in Mexico's vulnerability to external shocks. Salinas relied on foreign savings to finance growth, and most of it (over 80 percent) came from portfolio investment—the acquisition of existing assets on the stock market—fueled by the prospect that NAFTA would enable Mexico to "join the First World." In 1994 alone, $10 billion flowed into Mexico (Canada Department of Finance 1995, 6), while the rate of domestic savings declined from 22 to 16 percent of the gross domestic product (GDP) under the Salinas government.[2] Worse, the GDP growth stalled at 0.4 percent in 1993, and per capita income began to fall (Pastor and Wise 1998, 45, 49). Capital, drawn back to the United States by higher interest rates, started to leave Mexico. Mexico could have countered by raising its own interest rates, but the cure would have been worse than the disease: the economy would have been driven deep into recession in an election year.

Another solution was to devalue the peso, but this was ruled out by the need to maintain credibility and confidence among investors, especially foreign investors. Salinas desperately hoped that the ratification of NAFTA would make an end-of-*sexenio* devaluation unnecessary. Thus, when major institutional investors like Fidelity Latin America began to refuse to buy peso-denominated federal treasury certificates, or Cetes, the Salinas administration made a grave error: it began to rely increasingly on U.S. dollar–denominated treasury bonds (Tesobonos).

The overreliance on Tesobonos increased the risk that the government shouldered relative to foreign investors in an effort to maintain Mexico's attractiveness as a place to invest. Whereas the value of Cetes issued by Mexico decreased from $26.1 billion in 1993 to $7.5 billion in 1994, the value of Tesobonos increased from $1.2 billion in 1993 to $17.8 billion in 1994.[3] The combination of growing Tesobono obligations and declining international reserves was a major cause of the loss of investor confidence.

The challenge of managing external shocks was greater than the complexities of defending the peso. Early in his presidency, Salinas had decided to embark on bold economic reforms designed to transform the nation's economy while leaving the political system—especially, the centralized powers of the presidency and its control over the succession process—essentially intact. Salinas had promised perestroika without glasnost, but ironically, pressures for political change undid his administration. As we shall see, the catastrophic sequence of political and economic shocks during 1994 had the unintended consequence of placing political reform back at center stage under President Zedillo.

## The Events of 1994

From the perspective of the broad sweep of history, the Mexican political system is one of the most stable and enduring systems of government in the world. Mexico's remarkable political stability is the legacy of the 1910–17 revolution. The postrevolutionary political settlement was based on a set of unwritten rules of the game[4] that were informal but highly durable and respected. At the heart of the system lay the extraordinary powers of the presidency, his control over the succession process, and the discipline of all other major actors in the political system. It is no exaggeration to say that in the twentieth century, Mexico was the country in Latin America most successful in solving the problem of political succession. Since the founding of the ruling Institutional Revolutionary Party (PRI) in the late 1920s (when it was called the Party of the Mexican Revolution, or PRM), for *sexenio* after *sexenio*, one civilian president replaced another without a shot being fired.

Authoritarianism allowed the Mexican government to negotiate NAFTA, even as the "perfect dictatorship" (as Mario Vargas Llosa described the Mexican system) began to crumble. A more democratic system, one in which a system of checks and balances constrained executive authority, probably could not have implemented such sweeping changes all at once. Indeed, NAFTA may have contributed to an acceleration of political change in Mexico, though the final outcome of this process of transition remains unclear.

It should be recalled that Salinas came to office in the midst of allegations of widespread fraud and that the elections were intensely contested due to the division of a fraction of the ruling party, which then ran in 1988 under the leadership of Cuauhtémoc Cárdenas. The crisis of succession had already begun, and it reopened in 1993 when Salinas, following customary practice, personally designated his successor by, to use the metaphor popular in Mexico, "finger-pointing" (or *dedazo*). The decision to continue with the much criticized practice of the *dedazo*, rather than, say, internal elections or some sort of primary system, reflected Salinas's cautiousness in matters of political liberalization, and contrasted with his radical approach to opening Mexico's economy and society to market forces.

Salinas boldly undercut key policies and institutions of the revolution: the *ejido* land tenure arrangements were revised through a constitutional reform so that communal land could be bought and sold on the market, the traditional wariness of Mexican foreign policy toward the United States was reversed with a policy of closer trade and investment linkages, the strategy of state-led industrialization in pursuit of national goals was abandoned, hundreds of state-owned enterprises were privatized, and a process of deregulation and administrative simplification was undertaken in spite of substantial bureaucratic resistance. Salinas also sought to bypass the corporatist institutions that had served as the basis for clientelism and political control, replacing them with a more direct link between the president (and his increasingly rich and powerful office of the presidency) and local communities. In so doing, he undermined the power of traditional party bosses (colloquially referred to as "dinosaurs"), but he did not hesitate to use traditional mechanisms of political control when they suited him, and made only tepid advances toward democratic reforms such as improving the fairness of the electoral system. When it came to choosing his successor, Salinas continued the practice of the *dedazo*.

The choice of Colosio was also controversial, not among those who saw in the candidate an exemplar of the reformist technocrat, but among a sector of the party that feared a continuation of the Salinas clan's influence. The rules of postrevolutionary politics in Mexico gave extraordinarily centralized power to the president, but then expected him to leave office and retire quietly after his term ended (enjoying the spoils, cynics would add, of six years of private enrichment at public expense). "No re-election," was a rallying cry of the Mexican revolution, and one of the few restraints on presidential power. But the way Salinas selected his successor made it clear that he expected the candidate to continue his legacy. As political scientist Jorge Castañeda (1995, 74) put it, Salinas "nominated the PRI candidate without any attempt at dissimulation; he...committed his protégé to his own policies, and then surrounded him with his own lieutenants." At the same time, Salinas made no secret of his aspiration to lead the World Trade Organization.

The catalyst for Mexico's succession crisis was the Zapatista uprising. At first the insurrection looked like a local problem, and the instinctive reaction in Los Pinos was to respond with overwhelming military force. In the heavy fighting that ensued, the Mexican army drove the rebels back into the Lacondón jungle, but the death toll and the reports of human rights abuses prompted a backlash of protest against the government both in Mexico and abroad. The Zapatistas linked their demands to the policies of the Salinas government they said would hurt the poor, especially indigenous peoples and peasants, such as the liberalization of trade with maize and beans under the NAFTA, and the modification of Article 27 of the Mexican constitution (which protects communally held *ejidal* land). NAFTA was, according to the Zapatista spokesperson Marcos, a death sentence for the indigenous people. By framing their cause in terms of opposition to Salinas's economic policies, and by calling for badly needed political reforms, the Zapatistas were able to guarantee themselves international attention and ultimately, survival.[5]

The Zapatista uprising sent shocks through the international financial community, but editorialists noted that Mexico retained a strong reserve position and could hold the line against speculative attacks on the peso. The Central Bank of Mexico did not have to use the $25 billion it held in reserves to intervene in the market. Indeed, Mexico's reserves grew to nearly $30 billion in February. On January 12, Salinas called a unilateral cease fire and appointed Manuel Camacho Solís to negotiate a peace accord with the rebels. Camacho had been the mayor of Mexico City, an unelected position at that time, and a rival for the PRI candidacy for the presidency. An ambitious and popular politician, Camacho did not hide his disappointment at being passed over to succeed Salinas, and although such public grousing was taboo in Mexican politics, Camacho had the credibility with the left necessary to negotiate with the Zapatistas. In a short space of time, Camacho eclipsed Colosio as the most visible political leader in the nation after Salinas. While Colosio seemed unable to get his electoral campaign into high gear, Camacho's role as commissioner in the peace talks captured the headlines in the nation's major newspapers. Pundits sensed that the old rivalry between Colosio and Camacho had been rekindled, and began to speculate that Camacho was preparing to declare his own independent candidacy. It was in this context that Colosio was shot while on the hustings during a rally in a Tijuana shantytown on March 23, 1994. The immediate reaction of many party loyalists was to turn on Camacho, who was neutralized for the remainder of the campaign.

Judging by a wave of capital flight in late March, the assassination of Colosio did more to spook the international financial community than the Zapatista uprising, which angered investors but did not lead to capital flight. The Central Bank intervened repeatedly in the aftermath of Colosio's death, and a full-blown financial crisis was averted only by timely and effective policy management. The crisis was managed by officials from the finance ministry, in particular José Angel Gurría, who had been involved in the NAFTA financial service negotiations. In March 1994, he was the head of Nacional Financiera, one of Mexico's most powerful development banks. In an effort to head off a speculative attack, officials at the Secretariat of Finance and Public Credit activated a $6 billion swap fund[6] that had been negotiated between the Secretariat of Finance and the U.S. Treasury Department (the leading Mexican official responsible was Guillermo Ortiz). Although negotiated "secretly" around the time of the debate between U.S. Vice President Al Gore and NAFTA-critic Ross Perot, the swap fund had been known to insiders for months.

To gain time in order to get approval from the U.S. government to activate this fund, Secretary of Finance Pedro Aspe, Guillermo Ortiz, José Angel Gurría, Miguel Mancera Aguayo (the head of the Central Bank), and other finance officials, with the agreement of the president, decided to shut down the Mexican stock market (or Bolsa de Valores) for a day. Ortiz called Lawrence Summers, undersecretary for international affairs at the U.S. Treasury Department, who activated the Exchange Swap Fund. Then, Mexican finance officials "began trying to win back investor confidence by calling everyone they could think of around the world from traders to chief executives." " 'The performance was magnificent,' according to one portfolio manager. 'Almost every investment bank and every investor in the US was on the phones from 8 to 9 in the morning and had it all laid out for them by the Mexicans.'"⁷ Salinas also played a key role, meeting with business and labor leaders to re-sign the corporatist *"pacto economico."*⁸

The crisis caused by the assassination of Colosio demonstrated Mexico's vulnerability to external shocks. Although the bargaining around the assassination forestalled a deeper crisis, it did not address Mexico's balance of payment problems, which continued to grow, nor did it reduce the government's reliance on foreign savings. After the assassination, foreign investors became increasingly assertive. One group of mutual funds sent the Mexican government a list of suggestions to bolster the currency and, to lend weight to their advice, said they were willing to pour an additional $17 billion into Mexico during 1994 if the government enacted reforms.⁹ "Who says you have to be elected to influence policy?" boasted one fund manager, "The market is saying to policymakers 'We're your watchdog.'"¹⁰ Yet few of these self-appointed watchdogs knew how to interpret the events of 1994.

Admittedly, the details of the Colosio killing were hazy. According to government prosecutors, the assassination was the act of a gunman named Mario Aburto Martínez, a *maquiladora* factory worker. Aburto Martínez confessed and was convicted, but although it seems unlikely he acted alone, government investigators bungled the inquiry so badly that the full truth may never be known. At one point the chief government prosecutor stated that a number of individuals were involved in the assassination, and then later he decided it was the act of a lone gunman. Subsequently, others were implicated in the killing, but the evidence proved insufficient for convictions.

Conspiracy theories swirled around the investigation into Colosio's death. The government prosecutor, a former president of the Chamber of Deputies, had helped Salinas to come to power in the fraudulent 1988 elections. He later served in the attorney general's office and was appointed to the Colosio case by Salinas, in spite of the fact that prosecutors in homicide cases are not generally picked by presidents. Such apparent violation of judicial independence does not prove the existence of a cover-up, but it helps explain the lack of public confidence in the results of the inquiry. An alternative hypothesis points to the role of drug traffickers, suggesting that Colosio refused to deal with drug traffickers or had fallen out with them. A third hypothesis, the one favored by Salinas, is that Colosio was killed by party bosses in the PRI seeking to stop Salinas's reformers from remaining in power.

According to the polls, most Mexicans believe that there was a conspiracy to kill Colosio, and presume Salinas himself was involved. A group within the PRI called for Salinas's expulsion from the party and an investigation into his involvement in the Colosio assassination, though such statements could be regarded as politically motivated innuendo.[11] In the absence of direct evidence or reliable testimony linking Salinas to the Colosio murder, we have to ask in what way the president could have benefited from the death of his handpicked candidate. Did something happen between Colosio and Salinas that made the president regret his choice of successor and want desperately to remove him in spite of the lack of a clear replacement? One explanation is that Salinas was angered by speeches made by Colosio that suggested he might repudiate some of Salinas's policies. Efforts by Colosio to dynamize his lackluster campaign with populist promises may have upset Salinas, but it hardly seems reason enough to shoot the candidate. Another possibility is that Colosio was involved in a dispute between the Salinas and Ruiz Massieu families, a dispute that might be connected to a second assassination later in 1994.

With Colosio dead, Salinas needed another candidate, yet the alternatives were either unpalatable or ineligible. The unpalatable alternatives were the dinosaurs or party bosses in the PRI who sought to exploit the crisis to assert a candidate with fewer ties to the Salinas coterie. Ineligible were members of the cabinet like Secretary of Finance Pedro Aspe. He would have been a good choice for Salinas, but Mexican law holds that cabinet members have to step down at least six months prior to running for office. The fact that Colosio's campaign manager, Ernesto Zedillo Ponce de León, was chosen in the middle of a major political crisis led pundits to call him the "accidental candidate." Zedillo was considered a weak choice. El Nerd, as he was nicknamed, had little political experience, and seemed to personify the dry, noncharismatic technocrat. And it reinforced the impression that Salinas preferred a weak candidate he could control from behind the scenes.

Zedillo was an uninspiring stump speaker (critics mocked his repeated mantra, "We're going to wiiiiiiiiin!"), but he was aided by the lack of a credible opposition. The candidate of the left-wing Party of the Democratic Revolution (PRD) was Cuauhtémoc Cárdenas, son of the late Lázaro Cárdenas, the popular president of Mexico who had nationalized the oil industry. However, the PRD was riven with internal factions. More damaging still was the effect of the Zapatista uprising. In the face of frightening changes, many Mexicans decided that, to use the popular refrain, the "bad you know is better than the good you don't" (*mejor es el malo conocido que el bueno por conocer*). The PRI was able to capitalize on this mood, presenting itself as the party of continuity, stability, and as the campaign slogan went, "welfare for your family." Fernandez de Cevallos, the candidate of the right-wing National Action Party, PAN, started off with an impressive performance in the televised presidential debate (pointing out that only he had been democratically selected by internal primaries, unlike both Zedillo and Cárdenas), but then he dropped out of sight and did not press his advantage, causing speculation that the PAN did not want to win the election in 1994.

The Zedillo victory in August 1994 was narrow but decisive. The electoral process was cleaner than usual, and the PRI would certainly have won without the vote buying and fraud that nevertheless occurred throughout the country, especially in rural areas. The PRI took half the votes, while the PAN won 30 percent and the PRD won 16 percent. Although the opposition parties complained bitterly, and with some reason, about the persistence of fraud in the electoral process, the Zedillo victory was a convincing one. But between the election in August and the first days of office in December, Zedillo was dealt two crippling blows, and Salinas was implicated in both.

The assassination of José Francisco Ruiz Massieu on September 28, 1994, was the third shock to the Mexican political system in 1994. The Ruiz Massieu family was an influential political clan, and more importantly, it was tied to the Salinas family by marriage and commerce. Salinas's sister Adriana was married briefly to José Francisco, and Carlos Salinas's father, Raúl, Sr., brought José Francisco into the family business. Even after Adriana and José Francisco were divorced, the two families maintained close business ties. There are also allegations that both families had connections to drug traffickers, and although the extent of these links is unclear, both Raúl Salinas, Jr., and José Francisco's brother, Mario, would later have multimillion-dollar foreign bank accounts frozen by authorities investigating drug money laundering in the United States and Switzerland.

Carlos Salinas and his brother Raúl seemingly had a falling out with José Francisco over failed real estate deals in Acapulco. One of the most credible sources of information on this dispute is the case presented by the Department of Justice in the U.S. District Court in Houston in its efforts to determine the source of over $9 million that Mario Ruiz Massieu had deposited in bank accounts in Texas. According to this source, members of both the Salinas and Ruiz Massieu families had numerous meetings with drug traffickers in which they offered protection so that drugs could be transported across Mexico to the United States. A split allegedly arose between the two families when José Francisco was caught stealing money from the Salinas clan.

It has been speculated that this led Raúl to hire an assassin to have José Francisco Ruiz Massieu killed; whether political motives were also involved is not clear. Did the Ruiz Massieu family represent a threat to the Salinas clan, and were they in collusion with Colosio? Such a case is often linked to the supposition that the Ruiz Massieu family knew something about Salinas's involvement in the assassination of Colosio. In a bizarre twist, José Francisco's brother Mario, as deputy attorney general, was named special prosecutor to investigate his brother's death. He covered up the culprits in the killing in order to prevent his own family's ties to drug trafficking from being exposed, until his resignation on November 23, when he claimed that the PRI was covering up the killing.

At the time that Ruiz Massieu was assassinated in September 1994, few people understood the whys and wherefores, but the mere fact that a very prominent member of the political establishment, and a leader of a major clan in the revolutionary family, could be killed by a hired assassin in broad daylight in the middle of downtown Mexico City suggested that there were volcanic forces at work below the crust of stability in Mexico. The hired gunman, a ranch hand by the name of Daniel Aguilar Treviño, was captured in a street near the scene of the crime, and Congressman Manuel Muñoz Rocha, a federal deputy from Tamaulipas and a friend of Raúl Salinas who is alleged to have organized the killing, disappeared the next day and is presumed dead.[12] Given the nation's vulnerability to shocks to business confidence, such events could not be taken lightly. Fearing further instability, a new wave of capital flight began as wealthy Mexicans funneled money out of the country into safer places abroad.

In spite of the growing capital flight and declining Central Bank reserves, the Salinas cabinet refused to devalue the peso. In a meeting in September, Guillermo Ortiz proposed a devaluation, and his proposal was rejected. In November, less than two weeks before the transfer of government, Ernesto Zedillo met with Carlos Salinas in the presence of Pedro Aspe to discuss a devaluation of the peso. Aspe opposed the measure, in spite of declining reserves, and Zedillo and Salinas accepted Aspe's position. On December 8, Jaime Serra, newly appointed as Mexico's secretary of finance, outlined his "Economic Criteria for 1995," in a document prepared in consultation with members of the outgoing administration (including Pedro Aspe, Carlos Salinas, and Guillermo Ortiz). Later, Serra gave an interview to the *Wall Street Journal* in which he denied the possibility of a devaluation. Shortly thereafter, the value of the peso began to slide, and the stock market fell by 4 percent. Business analysts judged Serra's document insufficient and called for a correction of the current account deficit. Finally, in an environment of impending crisis, business leaders called for a meeting with Serra.

On the night of Monday, December 19, 1994, Serra met with the country's business and financial elite in the offices of the Secretariat of Labor and Social Welfare.[13] Luis German Carcoba, head of the Business Coordinating Council, had asked for the meeting to discuss measures to correct the current account deficit, which was causing anxiety in financial markets. Serra entered the meeting at 10:00 P.M., accompanied by Mancera, of the Bank of Mexico. Mancera spoke of an alarming decline in reserves, and suggested allowing the peso to float. He was confident that the peso would not lose more than 15 percent of its value but admitted it could go lower. Since the assembled bankers and entrepreneurs opposed this measure, Serra provided an alternative: widening the band within which the peso would be allowed to slowly depreciate. This would allow the government to avoid using the word "devaluation" when it announced the measures. The assembled businessmen, all members of Mexico's "Pacto Economico," deliberated together before indicating their approval for Serra's proposal. Serra then suggested widening the band enough to allow the peso to drop in value by 15 percent. The meeting was adjourned at 4:00 A.M., while European and Asian markets were still open.

As the group dispersed, the bankers reached for their cell phones and placed orders to buy dollars. The consequences were summarized in a Canadian report on the situation:

> Naturally, this meeting [with Serra] gave the bankers a head start, since discussions were going on when European and Asian markets were already open, and many were able to make frantic calls to their brokers in the early morning hours to buy dollars before Jaime Serra's ill-fated announcement to the Mexican media.... In just a few hours, billions of dollars poured out of the country—in effect, the inexperience of the government in handling such delicate financial matters (i.e., having bankers influencing the decision to free float) led to a run on the country that to a large extent caused the current crisis.[14]

The flight of capital forced the hand of the government, which first announced a widening of the currency band and then, on December 21, 1994, was forced by lack of reserves to let the peso float. When Serra met with investors in Washington and New York after the devaluations, he was unprepared for their hostility. They complained that Serra had given his assurances that there would not be a devaluation. Having lost the confidence of domestic and foreign investors, Serra resigned and was replaced by the subsecretary of finance, Guillermo Ortiz. Thus began the financial crisis that would leave many Mexicans feeling that just at the moment that NAFTA had opened a door to the potential for First World status, they had been shoved back into the Third World. They were correct, in the sense that there was more to the crisis than the miscalculation of a cabinet official who treated a devaluation as if he were negotiating a trade agreement.

## Zedillo's Challenges

The devaluation of the Mexican peso in December 1994 triggered a panic that required massive intervention by the U.S. government and the International Monetary Fund (IMF) in an effort to prevent a full-scale collapse in emerging markets. Zedillo quickly replaced Serra with Ortiz, who had played a key role in managing the crisis caused by the Colosio assassination in March 1994, and Ortiz immediately traveled to New York in an attempt to regain investor support and to speak with the IMF. At home, Zedillo met with his cabinet, workers, employers, and rural organizations and agreed on a new austerity package that would reduce wages and impose severe fiscal and monetary measures. Further privatizations were promised, including parts of the state electrical utility, ports, airports, and telecommunications. In spite of these measures, the Zedillo government suffered from a lack of credibility among investors, and in meetings in the World Economic Forum in Davos, Switzerland, at the end of January—where the Mexicans were accustomed to being toasted by other nations—Zedillo's officials were ostentatiously snubbed by investors and roundly criticized by other Latin nations.

By the end of January 1995, President Clinton had cobbled together a package of loan guarantees in excess of $50 billion. A plan to provide $17 billion in loans to Mexico was rammed through the IMF so hastily that six European members of the IMF abstained from voting.[15] U.S. officials insisted that the speed of the markets demanded a faster response than that to which a bureaucratic agency like the IMF was accustomed. Mexico also received $20 billion in loans with up to ten-year maturities through the U.S. Treasury's Exchange Stabilization Fund, and the U.S. Federal Reserve agreed to provide short-term bridge financing of up to $6 billion. The other industrialized nations would provide, if necessary, an additional $10 billion in credit through the Bank for International Settlements (BIS).

The IMF extended $17.8 billion in credit, with $7.8 billion (300 percent of Mexico's IMF quota) made available immediately. Overall, Mexico received 688 percent of the quota for which it was eligible, the largest-ever financing package approved by the fund.[16] Since most of the hard money in the bailout package was from the United States, the Clinton administration was able to impose strict conditions on Mexico. Loan guarantees were to be backed by oil revenues held as collateral by the Federal Reserve Bank of New York. Mexico would have to buy back the pesos it had exchanged for dollars with the United States at 2.25 percent or more over treasury bill rates of varying maturities. The terms included the unusual accounting practice that every withdrawal of funds would have to be approved in advance by the U.S. Treasury, which would oversee how all the money was spent.

Negotiating with the United States was not Zedillo's only headache. In the aftermath of the crisis, a bitter dispute developed between Zedillo and Salinas in which all the unwritten rules of Mexican politics were cast aside. The feud began when the outgoing president blamed Mexico's financial collapse on what he called the "errors of December," implying that the crisis could have been avoided by a more competent team. A furious Zedillo appointed Antonio Lozano Gracia, a member of the opposition PAN, to the post of attorney general and gave him a long leash to investigate the political crimes of 1994. The first member of an opposition party to hold cabinet rank in a PRI government, Lozano lost no time investigating Raúl Salinas's involvement in the Ruiz Massieu shooting. On February 15, 1995, one of the murder suspects in the Ruiz Massieu case testified that Raúl Salinas ordered Muñoz Rocha to hire an assassin to kill José Francisco Ruiz Massieu, and on February 28, Raúl Salinas was arrested on murder charges.

In a dramatic move that symbolized the confrontation between Salinas and Zedillo, Salinas sent his bodyguards to protect his brother, and a brief standoff ensued at Raúl's home in Mexico City. Failing to prevent his brother's arrest with a show of force, Salinas went on a hunger strike that won him little sympathy and, indeed, exposed him to ridicule. Shortly thereafter, Mexico's once-powerful leader fled the country, fearing arrest in connection to the death of Colosio. Mario Ruiz Massieu also fled Mexico in March 1995, after he was questioned about his role in covering up the plot behind his brother's death, and was immediately detained in New Jersey with a suitcase containing $46,000 in undeclared cash.

In the course of his investigation, Lozano discovered that Raúl Salinas used false identities and fake documents to keep bank accounts in London and Switzerland and to acquire businesses, luxury homes, ranches, and other properties throughout Mexico. He used his fourth wife's name, Paulina Castañón, to hide a Swiss bank account containing $84 million. After Raúl was arrested by the authorities and detained in the Almoloya prison outside Mexico City, Castañón traveled to Switzerland to pick up false passports and move money to safer places; there she was briefly detained by Swiss authorities in November 1995.

The biggest challenge facing Zedillo in 1995, however, was to shore up the banking system. Mexican policy makers shared the diagnosis that the underlying problem revealed by the peso crisis was rapid financial liberalization in the absence of a strong regulatory framework in the financial sector, and they took major steps to improve domestic regulations. At a significant cost to taxpayers, the stability of the banking system was ensured. To understand the fragility of the Mexican banking system, it is important to recall that in 1991–92, the banks were reprivatized. Many were purchased by industrial conglomerates, and some were managed by entrepreneurs with little experience in banking. The new owners sought to recover their investments as quickly as possible. High profits were earned during 1992–94, in a period of credit expansion. As financial intermediation deepened, with Mexicans depositing more of their savings in banks, consumers acquired unprecedented access to credit cards, mortgages, and other loans. At the same time, the lack of a well-developed regulatory system to monitor the banks contributed to the growth of nonperforming loans. This latent problem was manifested after the collapse of the peso in 1994, which drove up domestic interest rates from 20 percent to as high as 120 percent in a few months, while the GDP in the second quarter of 1995 fell by over 10 percent. As a result, the number of nonperforming loans increased drastically.

Mexican regulators decided to guarantee deposits and prevent a run on the banks. To bring interest rates down and provide liquidity to the banks, they focused on improved regulation, attracting new sources of capital, and providing debt relief. Their programs included a temporary capitalization program, new reserve requirements for credit, a restructuring program for debtors, and a loan purchase mechanism for banks. In 1996, additional programs were put in place to help support mortgage loans; to provide credit to very small, small, and medium-sized enterprises; and to create a program for foreclosed real estate assets.

There was no run on the banks in Mexico—a number of foreign investors remained in the financial service market, or entered after 1995 to buy up banks in distress, and the system emerged with fewer institutions. The shakedown consolidated Mexico's banking system into five major domestic financial groups[17] and five banks under foreign control.[18] The new foreign investments were made possible by April 1995 rules that lifted NAFTA restrictions on foreign banks acquiring Mexican banks in distress (while still exempting the three balance of payment banks, Banamex, Bancomer, and Serfin). At the end of the process, 20 percent of the Mexican banking system was in foreign hands. The government had allowed credit to expand at a modest rate, while reducing the growth of past-due loans and improving the capitalization of the banks and enhancing their provisions for past-due loans. Gradually, due to a variety of restructuring programs, the ratio of nonperforming to total loans fell.

Mexico changed its regulatory system in the midst of the crisis, emphasizing both prudential measures and self-regulation by the banks. Self-regulatory measures include efforts to make more timely and reliable information available to the markets. This involves strengthening external auditors, rating agencies, and credit bureaus. In 1995, the National Banking and Securities Commissions were merged, and in June 1996 a new capitalization regime was created for banks and brokerage firms. Accounting procedures were modernized, and financial reporting tightened.

Zedillo did not focus all his attention on economic reform, and in this he differed from Salinas. In one of the crowning achievements of his administration, the president negotiated a National Political Agreement on Electoral Reform, which was accepted by all Mexico's political parties and passed by the Congress unanimously in July 1996. The Agreement established the Federal Electoral Institute (IFE) as an independent body free of political control, its president to be chosen by a two-thirds vote in the lower house of Congress, thereby ensuring greater transparency and honesty in electoral procedures, especially vote counting. These reforms provided the foundation for the historic 1997 midterm congressional elections and the election, for the first time, of the mayor of Mexico City. Cuauhtémoc Cárdenas won the election in Mexico City by a comfortable margin, and the PRI lost control over Congress for the first time in September 1997 when four opposition parties, which collectively controlled 261 seats in the lower house of the Congress against the PRI's 239 seats, appointed PRD leader Porfirio Muñoz Ledo as their president.

The loss of the PRI's majority in Congress meant that the ruling party could no longer assume the Congress would rubber-stamp executive initiatives. More than this, questions about the integrity and honesty or malfeasance by those in power could be raised by the opposition parties, and new issues could be placed on the legislative agenda even if the opposition parties did not have the votes to win passage of its legislation. One of the strongest debates between the president and the Congress occurred in 1998 when the government asked Congress to recognize FOBAPROA (Bank Fund for Saving Support) liabilities as public debt. FOBAPROA was the bank fund, administered by the Central Bank, that acquired nonperforming loans in order to guarantee deposits and prevent a run on the banks. The total cost of this rescue package, which came to 552 billion pesos, or U.S. $65 billion dollars, dwarfed the international bailout of Mexico orchestrated by the United States in 1995.

Given the shift in the lower chamber of Congress, the cost of bailing out Mexico's banks generated a debate that could not be suppressed. FOBAPROA covered 440,000 bad loans, most of which were quite substantial (330,000 were in excess of 50 million pesos each), and many were made by Mexico's largest banks.[19] The legislative debate over FOBAPROA revolved around the wisdom of providing near-universal liability protection for bad loans. One concern raised by the opposition was the problem of moral hazard that results from an incentive structure that only lightly penalizes bad banking practices. But a more politically explosive issue was whether FOBAPROA provided insurance for "crony capitalism." Newspapers were rife with stories of bankers lending money to cronies in other banks, to family members, to their own firms, and to drug traffickers. Owing to secrecy laws protecting bank transactions from public scrutiny, such information was available only in the cases of banks that had fallen, with bankers that were fugitives from the laws.[20] The fact that FOBAPROA covered such bad loans left a stain of illegitimacy on the rescue package. If this were not bad enough, the debate on FOBAPROA coincided with a sting operation by the U.S. Drug Enforcement Agency that implicated many of Mexico's banks in the laundering of narcotics monies and revealed the pervasiveness of corruption and the weakness of regulation in the banking system.

The fight between the executive and the legislature involved contrasting views of transparency and political responsibility. On the one hand, FOBAPROA's defenders argued that the fund had saved the banking system and that it was a system of protection for depositors, not the bankers, and that any obstruction of the program would have catastrophic implications for the nation's economic security—perhaps provoking a crisis similar to the one in 1994–95. Moreover, auditing of the program in violation of the nation's secrecy laws would result in a collapse in confidence in the system. On the other hand, opponents of FOBAPROA argued that Mexican taxpayers could not be expected to pick up the tab for a massive bailout program without a full accounting by the executive, with assurances that any wrongdoing covered by FOBAPROA would be punished.

Saddled with FOBAPROA liabilities, Zedillo needed to show he was prepared to be tough on corruption. The most conspicuous symbol of corruption under the Salinas government was Raúl Salinas, who was known by the epithet "Mr. Ten Percent" for the amount that he allegedly creamed off of business deals that required the approval of his brother.[21] Investigations into his illicit enrichment revealed that corruption under the Salinas government happened on an unprecedented scale. It was discovered, for example, that Carlos Peralta wired $50 million to Raúl Salinas while he was closing a deal with Bell Atlantic to win his cell phone franchise. Raúl also had a personal banker at Citibank in Mexico, Vice President Amy Elliot, who helped him transfer huge sums of money out of Mexico.

The trial of Raúl Salinas lasted until January 1999, when he was convicted and sentenced to fifty years in prison for his role in the murder of José Francisco Ruiz Massieu. In the twenty-four bound volumes that summarize the material introduced in court, there was neither direct evidence nor a confession of guilt; only circumstantial evidence was brought forward. Moreover, the trial was a tragicomic affair that Carlos Salinas easily cast as evidence of political persecution rather than due process of law.[22] For example, the second special prosecutor for the case, Pablo Chapa Bezanilla, the man who replaced Mario Ruiz Massieu, hired a clairvoyant to help find the remains of Muñoz Rocha, the fugitive who had hired Ruiz Massieu's killer. She led the investigators to a ranch used by Raúl Salinas. When a human skeleton was dug up on the ranch, it turned out that the remains belonged to a relative of the psychic! Chapa Bezanilla was fired and arrested for fabricating evidence.

However, Raúl Salinas's conviction was widely seen as a vindication for President Zedillo, who had staked his reputation and credibility on the ability of his government to bring at least Raúl, if not Carlos, Salinas to justice. But was the decision motivated by a desire to avoid dealing a blow to Zedillo and provoking a major public outcry? Critics noted that the prosecution failed to establish a clear motive for the killing of Ruiz Massieu, and the claims that he "threatened the Salinas project" amounted to little more than speculation.[23]

Zedillo's biggest achievement, however, is that he, as he liked to say, had cut off his own finger. In November 1999, the ruling PRI held primary elections to select its candidate for the presidential race of 2000. Francisco Labastida Ochoa won by a wide margin. The use of primary elections, in which an estimated ten million people voted, to decide the future candidate, instead of the customary *dedazo* (finger-pointing), was hailed as a progress in Mexico's process of democratization.

## Conclusion

The lamentable events that befell Mexico during 1994 and led to the disgrace and exile of President Salinas cast the NAFTA negotiations in a new light. Throughout the negotiation process, the Mexican government demonstrated its risk aversion, and consequently its willingness to make concessions in an effort to get a deal as early as possible. Only with the knowledge provided by hindsight is it possible for us to appreciate the complexities of the tasks facing Salinas as he neared the end of his mandate.

Mexico was a country in crisis and Salinas knew it. Contrary to the image of Mexico that Salinas projected abroad, which was one of a nation exuding confidence and optimism, Mexico faced a difficult succession struggle, a simmering insurrection, and a fragile economic recovery based on an overvalued currency and reliance on short-term "hot money." It is hardly surprising, then, that Salinas was reluctant to put NAFTA, the cornerstone of his administration and its plans for economic recovery, at risk when disagreements arose among the three countries.

Salinas moved boldly to reform Mexico's economy, and he used the nation's centralized and vertical political system to achieve changes that would have been impossible under democratic conditions. He feared the Russian experience—which he attributed to the attempt to pursue political and economic change simultaneously—and instead sought first to get the country's economic reforms on track. Yet, pressures for political change contributed to the unraveling of the Salinas presidency. Zedillo has struggled to preserve the economic changes implemented by Salinas, while also undertaking necessary political and economic reforms to create more openness in the Mexican political system.

## CHAPTER II

# Conclusions

We began our investigation by inquiring into the conditions that shaped the NAFTA negotiations. Why would countries as unequal in power and wealth as Mexico, the United States, and Canada agree to negotiate a formal accord? What role did domestic and international institutions play in shaping the NAFTA negotiations? What patterns of delayed mutual responsiveness were exhibited by the negotiators in the bargaining process, and how were these patterns related to their alternatives to an agreement?

U.S. negotiators repeatedly told the Mexicans, "You're here to buy our market—what are you prepared to pay?" Such a question exposes the asymmetries between the two countries: Mexico gains access to a massive market of 265 million people with an average per capita income of $27,000; in return the United States gets access to Mexico's smaller market of slightly over 90 million people with a per capita income of less than $7,000.[1] Clearly, Mexico would have to do something to make the deal worthwhile for the United States. "You need us more than we need you," the Americans would remind the Mexicans. "The US was brutal. Their positions were based on force more than reasoning," said one exasperated Mexican negotiator. "You ask 'why?' on logical grounds and there is no answer.... There was an asymmetry."

The Mexicans were told there was no prospect of a NAFTA without liberalization of financial services, and that "access for every last American financial intermediary who wanted to do business in the Mexican market" was the U.S. price for Mexico's access to its market. Similarly, in autos, the U.S. negotiators made it clear that any future U.S. investment in Mexico's automobile industry depended on elimination of the restrictive Auto Decrees. New investment rules would be required, including investor-state arbitration and dispute settlement mechanisms that overturned long-standing Mexican policies. In agriculture, the Americans said: "We wanted an agreement that would be comprehensive, with no exceptions, one that would go beyond the Uruguay Round. Mexico was told that they were getting access to the US market, but there was no NAFTA without agriculture." These were the kinds of concessions that would be necessary for Mexico to get access to the U.S. market.

Contrary to neorealism, however, asymmetries of power did not inhibit formal cooperation between the United States and Mexico, as anticipated by Krasner (see Table 2.1). Rather than eschewing formal accords out of a preference for unilateralism, the United States sought to negotiate a deal with Mexico that would set high standards, important, according to a U.S. negotiator, "because of the precedential effect." They rejected any special consideration for Mexico as a less-developed country (LDC) and argued that the deal would have to break new ground in order to set a precedent for other negotiations, including the Uruguay Round of multilateral trade negotiations (MTN). Asymmetry meant the United States could use its bilateral leverage to open a developing country market in ways that would be impossible in multilateral negotiations dealing with large coalitions of LDCs.

In NAFTA, the weak state entered into bilateral negotiations with a stronger state in spite of the long-run risk of increasing its vulnerability, because vulnerability, like anarchy, is "what states make of it" (Wendt 1992). Mexico's negotiators repeatedly stressed that NAFTA was part of a package of necessary economic reforms that were initiated in the 1980s. The reforms were made necessary by the exhaustion of the previous import-substitution industrialization (ISI) model of development, which was already apparent in the 1970s, and became more obvious with the rise of global interest rates and the decline in oil prices in 1982 and 1986 that resulted in Mexico's inability to meet its international debt obligations. Thus, the negotiators repeatedly stressed, Mexico was prepared to open its economy, unilaterally if necessary.

Indeed, as a lead Mexican negotiator said, "Mexico had opened its economy unilaterally after 1986, only to find (as Salinas discovered in Davos) that the rest of the world was also changing and Mexico was unlikely to win any reciprocity for its reforms." No longer able to rely on petroleum exports, Mexico needed access to the U.S. market to sustain export-led growth to generate foreign exchange. Mexican policy makers perceived, especially after the Canada-U.S. Free Trade Agreement (FTA) was negotiated, that the United States was seeking to complement multilateral negotiations with bilateral agreements, using the latter to place "new issues" on the agenda. Mexico could help the United States with these new issues in return for preferential access to its market.

Thus, Mexico was willing to enter into an accord with a more powerful state because it redefined vulnerability in a manner consistent with the new economic model. According to David Mares (1987, 803), the new economic model implied a different understanding of the trade-off between development and independence. Mexico's newly ascendant technocrats believed that autonomy is achieved by adjusting to outside forces. This demands restructuring and making the economy efficient, and using direct foreign investment to gain technology and international markets. The state would attempt to do less in the economy but still guide it. By maintaining this management role, the state would be able to negotiate for better terms in its acceptance of interdependence. Salinas's NAFTA initiative was the culmination of this strategy. The error of neorealism was not that it assumed that asymmetry implies vulnerability, but rather that it assumed that the only appropriate response to vulnerability was to avoid interactions with more powerful states. Just as self-help does not follow from anarchy, so autarchy, Third Worldism, or a preference for authoritative allocation over markets does not necessarily follow from vulnerability.

Concern for how the accord would be implemented did not inhibit the negotiation of NAFTA. In fact, Mexico followed Canada in seeking terms that would protect it from the contingent protection of U.S. trade remedy actions. One of the most intense debates during the negotiations was over whether Mexico would get Chapter Nineteen protection from U.S. trade remedies. Mexico, in spite of its weak bargaining position, prevailed in this effort in spite of serious reservations by Canada and the United States about differences in the legal systems. Mexican negotiators felt NAFTA would protect them from the threat of the use of instruments of aggressive unilateralism, such as antidumping and countervailing duties.

Mexico was not deterred from negotiating NAFTA by a concern that greater interaction with the larger state would result in costly alterations in the distribution of human and material resources within the state: on the contrary, that was one of the objectives of NAFTA, to root out opposition to the new economic model in the remaining pockets of resistance left in the federal bureaucracy. A special "Office of Deregulation"[2] with extraordinary powers was established within the Secretariat of Trade and Industrial Development (SECOFI) and given a mandate to bring other government agencies—such as agriculture, fisheries, health, and transportation—into line with NAFTA. None of these government agencies wanted to be stripped of their regulatory powers, and some of them offered stiff resistance. However, the Office of Deregulation had two advantages: it was perceived to have a privileged relationship to the NAFTA negotiating team ("People supposed we knew what was going on in the negotiations," said one official) and it had the full backing of the president. A call from the president's office ensured access to any government official.

In a similar way, negotiations over standards resulted in a change in how the Mexican government regulated industry. In the past, government regulations were made without consultations with business. Herminio Blanco, in consultation with the economic cabinet, decided to move toward a new system, in which regulations must be published ninety days before coming into effect, business is given an opportunity to react to the proposal, and government has to respond. Said one former SECOFI official: "As a Mexican I was happy, but as a government official I was worried." After all, this change significantly reduced the government's discretionary power.

Culture was an issue between Canada and the United States, but was not an obstacle to NAFTA. Canada retained the exemption it had negotiated in the FTA, and Mexico was not concerned about the issue. Although the Americans fought hard to eliminate the exemption, in the end they were unsuccessful, and the negotiations revolved around assuring Canada comparable protection in the NAFTA, in spite of the fact that its rules operated differently. As a Canadian negotiator put it,

> NAFTA was different from the FTA. The cultural exemption in the FTA says the US cannot retaliate on cultural issues. Of course, they can retaliate anytime they want. But there is no basis for it in the FTA. In the NAFTA, everything is covered, and exceptions have to be specified. So the question is, how do you get the status quo where the rules work differently? We got a deal that supports a cultural exemption across the board. Where NAFTA does not address an issue under culture, the FTA applies.

Culture was not a major issue for the Mexicans. One of the leading U.S. negotiators said, "We told them the U.S. culture industry gave us a lot of trouble with the Canadian cultural exemption: we would not put up with a cultural exemption for Mexico."

Mexico did not find multilateralism more attractive than bilateral negotiations, in spite of the opportunities for coalition building with other developing countries. However, the benefits of multilateral coalition building may be less significant in an era of regionalism and competitive liberalization. Mexico clearly was concerned about getting credit for its reforms in spite of the fact that many other countries—both in the developing world and in the former Soviet Union—were undertaking similar policy changes. Thus, Mexico reformed its intellectual property rules in advance of the NAFTA negotiations on the grounds that there would be advantages to being one of the first countries in the developing world to adopt such rules, above all in terms of attracting new investments. Many developing and transitional countries would be embracing market reforms in the 1990s, but only Mexico would have a preferential relationship with the United States.

We do not presume that asymmetries of power lead inevitably to asymmetrical outcomes in all negotiations. We have found, however, that the overwhelming asymmetries of power between Canada, the United States, and Mexico played a major role in shaping the outcome of the negotiations, neoliberal institutionalist cautions notwithstanding. Asymmetry played a role that admitted a wide variety of interpretations, including neoliberal institutionalist and neorealist ones. For example, Keohane's argument that the costs of exclusion in a world of competitive trading blocks could make small countries willing to give up independence rather than risk being left out aptly captures part of the logic of Mexico's NAFTA initiative. However, this is not a distinctively neoliberal argument; the same point is made more emphatically by Krasner.

The results of our research provide little support—at least insofar as the NAFTA negotiations are concerned—for Keohane's hypothesis that a unified and committed small state can bear greater costs and fight more intensely for its goals, thereby prevailing in negotiations with a stronger power. Of the three countries, Mexico was more centralized, hierarchical, and authoritarian. The United States was highly decentralized and loosely structured and operated within a system of checks and balances. Canada was in between these extremes: less centralized than in the FTA negotiations (which was Mexico's organizational model) but more cohesive than the United States. Mexico's centralism and authoritarianism were not assets in the negotiations, and U.S. fragmentation was not a liability. Mexico's intense commitment to NAFTA compelled it to make repeated concessions in an effort to facilitate ratification in the United States.

The United States had a smaller win-set because of domestic pluralism and the nature of Level II institutions. Putnam (1993, 444) argued that large, more self-sufficient countries "should make fewer international agreements and drive harder bargains." This argument holds for the NAFTA negotiation. The separation of powers, and a complex set of jurisdictional boundaries dividing government offices and agencies, provided an enormous source of bargaining strength to the United States. In accordance with Putnam's observation that "the stronger a state is in terms of autonomy from domestic pressures, the weaker its relative bargaining position," the United States was clearly the state least autonomous from domestic pressures and the toughest negotiator, whereas Mexico was the most autonomous from domestic pressures and the weakest in the negotiations. The low level of autonomy of U.S. negotiators forced them to balance a wide range of interests. A U.S. official involved in the investment negotiations said that a strong agreement would deliver benefits for business but risked alienating constituencies that feared greater U.S. investment in Mexico rather than at home. Recall his ironic judgment that "the better we did, the worse it looked."

Mexican and Canadian negotiators often expressed frustration with their U.S. counterparts, who seemed to act like agents of the private sector and were often political appointees eager to prove their mettle: "They come in, shoot ten people in the head, and move on," said a Mexican negotiator. U.S. negotiators called concessions from their counterparts "trophies" that they could show Congress or the private sector. The importance of the latter two is further indicated by the estimate by a senior U.S. official that over the course of the fast-track proceedings and the actual NAFTA negotiations, the American negotiating team held more than four hundred meetings with members of Congress and staffers, and between twelve thousand and sixteen thousand meetings with the private sector.

U.S. domestic constraints contrasted with the Mexican leadership's wider scope for action. The ratification debate was milder in Mexico, owing to its larger Level I win-set, Level II institutions, as well as the opportunities for synergistic linkages and Level I strategies. The fact that Mexico, at the time of the negotiations, did not have a properly functioning system of checks and balances, and indeed used corporatist-authoritarian institutions to promote the economic opening, undermined the negotiating team's bargaining leverage. One Mexican negotiator said, "In the case of Mexico, it is not credible to say that Congress will not accept." As a substitute, Mexico built up its private-sector consultative organization, the Coordinadora de Organismos Empresariales de Comercio (COECE), so that negotiators could more credibly say, "I can't: the industry would hang me!" The other domestic constraint used by Mexico was its constitution, which served it particularly well in resisting U.S. encroachments in energy. The president outlined the five Mexican "nos," and the message was delivered in a firm and consistent manner: Mexico would not change its constitution to accommodate NAFTA.

A number of Mexican negotiators stressed that their decision-making power was both an asset and a liability. In the words of one, "Our greatest strength was also our greatest weakness: we could decide a lot. But we could not say 'Congress won't like this,' or even 'the industry won't accept this.'" The procurement issue offers an example of the way in which such power could be an asset. Mexico wanted access to the massive U.S. procurement market, so its negotiators adopted an aggressive strategy: "Everything is on the table," they said. This forced the U.S. negotiators to defend their small-business set-asides. In response, Mexico took PEMEX and the CFE (Comisión Federal de Electricidad, the state electrical utility) off the table: a sacred cow had been saved. More often, Salinas's power was a liability. Another Mexican negotiator observed that in the United States "there is a separation of powers and strong lobbies that strengthen the executive. They would say 'I can't do that, the Congress will never approve it.' [My counter-part] said to me, 'All Salinas has to do is pick up the phone and he gets what he wants.' This gave them leverage."

The Mexicans clearly believed that a highly sophisticated, disciplined, and unified bargaining structure that reported directly to the president and the economic cabinet would be an asset in the negotiations. As one negotiator said: "The Mexican team functioned like a machine. It had much flexibility and much cohesion, but it lacked information." This vertical structure had advantages, but it also had severe drawbacks, such as when the chief negotia-tor gave marching orders that forced working groups to make concessions at inopportune moments. A U.S. negotiator noticed that the Mexican chief ne-gotiator and his deputy expected to exercise considerable control over all the working groups: "If a Mexican negotiator proposed something without au-thorization, he would say 'Wait, I didn't say that. I have to talk to my boss. Don't even say that I said that.' "

Too much centralization in a negotiation can cause divisions. Said one ne-gotiator from another government agency, "We needed SECOFI to provide a mechanism for sharing information, participation, and coordination. But SECOFI was jealous and immature. The problem was institutional: the coor-dinator can't say 'this comma goes here, that one there.' Each working group has to define these things. We had a leader in charge of a number of working groups, and he couldn't manage." He complained that unlike in the United States, where a cabinet official will fight for his turf, in Mexico other cabinet officials deferred to Serra who had been given the mandate to negotiate NAFTA by Salinas. As a result, lower-level officials had trouble preventing SECOFI's negotiators from making mistakes in areas outside their compe-tence. Recall the devastating judgment by a senior Mexican negotiator: "We had three enemies in the negotiations: Canada, the US, and SECOFI."

Formal institutions, including a constitution that provided for the separa-tion of powers, provide little guidance in understanding the behavior of Mexican negotiators. In practical terms, extraordinary powers were concen-trated in the hands of the president of Mexico, including the power of ap-pointments and control over the cabinet, the bureaucracy, and the party ap-paratus. These powers rested on informal networks of loyalty that pervaded the Mexican bureaucracy, the *camarillas*. "Rising stars have coteries of fol-lowers that move with them from one position to another," noted a trade lawyer on the Mexican team. By the time leaders reach top positions in the government, their vast *camarillas* may extend throughout the bureaucracy and the political system.

The *camarilla* system played an important role in Mexican negotiating be-havior. Herminio Blanco sought to have members of his *camarilla* in every working group, which is why some working group heads were responsible for multiple teams. A Canadian negotiator observed that "Serra and Blanco had decided that people in the ministries were not adequate or trusted for the job of negotiating an agreement, so they brought in a cadre of lead negotiators who were personally interconnected." Blanco's desire to centralize all information and control the entire Mexican team became an obstacle to progress in the negotiations, at least until the February "jamboree" in Dallas. When all the working groups were brought together under a single roof, it became impossible to have a single person in charge of multiple working groups. Moreover, top-down instructions on when to make concessions led to serious tactical errors that could have been avoided had certain working groups (especially those outside the competence of trade officials, like financial services) been given greater autonomy.

Whereas Mexico's formal institutional arrangements provided few constraints on the president or his negotiating team, synergistic linkages served Mexico well, as did Level I strategies. Salinas was able push forward with a host of domestic reforms that would have been sabotaged by the bureaucracy and opposed by the public had they not been seen as crucial to securing NAFTA, the central goal of the Salinas presidency. Whether it was a more cooperative foreign relationship with Washington, a change in domestic regulations, a new system of intellectual property rules, or a reform of Mexico's traditional land-tenure system, the level of domestic opposition was sharply reduced by the perception that all of these reforms were necessary and beneficial within the larger context of the inclusion of Mexico in the First World via the negotiation of NAFTA.

NAFTA was not just an agreement to create more efficient international institutions; it also had the effect of restructuring basic property rules and state-society relations in each of the three countries, but especially in Mexico. It was also an effort to "lock in" the reforms the Salinas government had already undertaken or was planning, and it was a way of providing investors with the same risks and guarantees in their operations throughout North America that they enjoyed in the United States and Canada.

In their efforts to restructure Mexico's domestic society and economy, the Mexican reformers received enthusiastic support from U.S. policy makers, both within the context of the negotiations and more broadly. The "good chemistry" among the chief executives was emphasized for public relation purposes, and the implication was that there were benefits for everyone from the closer and more mature relationship among the leaders of the three countries. Transnational alliances improved Mexico's bargaining position and the terms of the agreement in certain areas. At one point the Mexicans used information provided by the U.S. aluminum industry—courtesy of connections provided by Mexico's industry—to refute claims made by the U.S. negotiators. For the most part, however, such alliances were promoted in an effort to help ratification in the United States. Mexico spent considerable sums on advisors and domestic lobbies to promote NAFTA within the United States. However, one former U.S. trade negotiator questioned whether such expenditures were wise, because Mexico was forced to make further concessions even after the negotiations were ostensibly wrapped up: "Mexico was taken to the cleaners. They were given bad advice: 'Give this, and that, and the other, because senator so-and-so needs it.'"

Canada has a more unified system, although it adopted a more decentralized negotiation structure for the NAFTA after finding that a highly centralized team in the FTA was a mistake.[3] Yet its bargaining position was enviably simple: at minimum, to preserve the benefits of the FTA, and, at maximum, to enhance them and secure for Canada comparable benefits for any additional advantages that Mexico might negotiate. Said a Canadian official:

> In Canada, the party in power can always get it through: the party in power is in charge of the legislature. The US is different. It is more complicated. There is a double set of negotiations going on. First, the negotiations that ended in August 1992. Then, a second set of negotiations in November 1993. The US will also try to put into the implementing legislation things that they did not get in the negotiations, in order to satisfy domestic constituents. You can say, 'This is not in the agreement,' and they will say, 'How can you satisfy this congressman?' and if you can't you are back to the bargaining table.[4]

Thus, divided government enhanced the U.S.'s bargaining power.

More important than the degree of unity or decentralization of government is whether negotiators have attractive nonagreement alternatives. More than anything else, this determines whether asymmetries in power capabilities will translate into asymmetrical outcomes. In the NAFTA negotiations (1) the United States did not need an agreement with Mexico to achieve its trade policy goals, since this could be done largely through the the General Agreement on Tariffs and Trade (GATT); (2) Mexico did not cultivate any nonagreement alternatives, placing all its hopes on NAFTA; and (3) Canada had the FTA as an attractive alternative to the NAFTA. Thus, the United States was in a strong bargaining position not only because of its market size, but also because from the outset of the negotiations in 1991, domestic constituencies in the United States constrained its Level II win-set and reduced the number of its acceptable Level I agreements, ensuring that American negotiators would assign relatively high subjective utility to their nonagreement alternatives to NAFTA. When this subjective utility decreased toward the end of the negotiations, as a result of President Bush's need for a deal in time for the Republican convention, American risk aversion increased, and negotiators became more willing to make concessions to secure an agreement. As one frustrated U.S. negotiator put it, "Once the political decision had been made by Hills and Bush that a deal had to be done before the Republican convention, and the U.S. was pressing for an agreement, then Canada could say, 'No, no, no,' and the U.S. had to concede in order to get a deal." Although American impatience was exploited more by the Canadians than the Mexicans, nevertheless U.S. haste in August was one factor that contributed to Mexico's ability to avoid concessions in energy, even at the very end of the negotiations.

Mexico's willingness to make concessions makes sense only in light of the fact that its leaders believed they had few attractive alternatives to NAFTA. Salinas believed that Mexico had three choices, given the rise of regionalism in the world economy: remain closed, open the economy unilaterally, or develop a strategy of negotiated liberalization. Although Mexico had joined the GATT in 1986, its efforts to liberalize on a multilateral basis provided no assurance that it would not be left behind as the world moved toward regional trading blocks centered on Washington, Bonn, or Tokyo. Once Salinas opted for NAFTA, he made little effort to cultivate alternatives. The rationalization for this strategy was that many of the concessions Mexican negotiators would make within the negotiations involved policy changes that would have been undertaken anyway, unilaterally, outside of NAFTA. But Mexico would have done well to consider alternatives to liberalization, or at the very least, to ways they could make the United States pay for the policy changes. "Mexico lacked a negotiation strategy," said one Mexican negotiator. "We had people with Ph.D.s from Stanford who knew the issues, but had little experience. Although one believes in free trade, one has to know the protectionist arguments. There were many economists on our team who could not give the protectionist arguments."

The U.S. negotiators, in the view of their Mexican counterparts, were "the masters of timing. When you think the cake is cooked, they come up with 500 reasons to go on." Over and over, the U.S. negotiators would hunker down and say, "This just isn't enough; our industry won't accept it. You will have to do better.... Carla Hill's strategy all along was to let the negotiations drag out." An advisor to the Mexicans said, "They [the Mexicans] always underestimated the amount of time it would take to do a deal. This underestimation occurred because Mexico got caught up in their own story of trade liberalization. As a result they accepted a more comprehensive negotiation than they could manage." A Mexican negotiator reinforced this point:"We Mexicans did not have a good sense of timing. We were in a hurry from Dallas onward. The US was in a hurry in July and August, at the end. Canada was never in a hurry."

Canada had an attractive alternative to the NAFTA; indeed, Canadian negotiators were mainly at the table to prevent any erosion of the benefits of the hard-won Canada-U.S. FTA and to improve its terms where possible. Canada's position was the source of some frustration for the U.S. negotiators, one of whom said the Canadians treated the FTA like a sacred text. Even Canadian negotiators admitted they had to push the government to think of NAFTA as more than "just adding Mexico" to the FTA.

The attractiveness of nonagreement alternatives shapes the bargaining process by influencing the patterns of delayed mutual responsiveness in which concessions are made or withheld. A negotiator who attaches a lower subjective utility to the nonagreement alternative is more likely to perceive an agreement in terms of gains over that alternative, to be risk averse for the sure outcome available in a negotiated agreement, and to offer concessions in the threshold-adjustment process.

A review of the NAFTA negotiation process supports these hypotheses. The United States began the negotiations playing hard to get, evincing disinterest in securing an agreement, and emphasizing the importance of the MTN. Over time, however, especially after the Dunkel Text was negotiated in Geneva, the subjective utility that U.S. negotiators attached to a world without the NAFTA began to decline. By the very end of the negotiation process, President Bush's desire to wrap up the negotiations in time to showcase the deal at the Republican convention made the U.S. negotiators abandon their game of hard to get, and some degree of role reversal occurred, as the Canadians proved to be the party most willing to put an agreement at risk by withholding concessions in the end game.

In fact, the Canadians were in an enviable bargaining position throughout much of the negotiation. Their nonagreement alternative, the Canada-U.S. FTA provided a clear yardstick by which to measure progress in the negotiations. The fact that the Canadian negotiators attached a high level of subjective utility to the Canada-U.S. FTA made them, in the eyes of the Mexican and U.S. negotiators, less than creative in their strategies, but they were clearly willing to place the agreement at risk by withholding concessions at a number of key moments in the threshold-adjustment process—as the record of their bargaining in agriculture, autos, Chapter Nineteen, culture, and textiles shows.

The Mexican negotiators clearly assigned very low subjective utility to nonagreement and therefore, were most averse to putting the agreement at risk by withholding concessions. Mexico had no attractive alternative to NAFTA, and for reasons that would only become apparent after the negotiations were over, the very foundations of the Mexican political system were beginning to crumble under the Salinas government. As a result, the Mexicans were unwilling to put NAFTA at risk by withholding concessions, and time and again they acceded to American demands in the threshold-adjustment process.

In the end, however, the Mexicans secured the agreement they wanted so desperately to achieve, a result that would justify their actions, and as NAFTA entered into force, Mexican hopes for entry into the First World were high. The tragic events that coincided with the onset of the agreement offered further insight into the reasons why Mexico was prepared to go so far to make a deal, but they left many Mexicans with a bitter NAFTA aftertaste. Nevertheless, the die had been cast for Mexico, just as it had for Canada five years earlier. North American free trade will change Mexico and its relations with its northern neighbors in fundamental ways as it experiences the effects, for good and for ill, of trilateral integration and reform of its domestic political economy.

# Key Concepts

Anarchy    Politics without government.

Asymmetry    Differences in power capabilities.

Discount rate    The factor that determines the present value of future gain. Negotiators, like all people, tend to discount the value of things in the future, and differences in discount rates can drive the results of a negotiation. A person who discounts the future will be more impatient to reach an agreement soon, and this provides an advantage to the adversary who can threaten to drag out the negotiations knowing that time is more costly to the other player than to himself or herself.

Institutions    Rules and enforcement mechanisms that shape the interaction between individuals. Institutions have a pervasive influence on human activity because they structure the incentives that shape behavior. Moreover, institutions reduce uncertainty by creating a framework of greater predictability in social interaction. Institutions may be formal and explicit, such as religious edicts or municipal ordinances, or informal and tacit, such as linguistic conventions or cultural mores. Formal institutions are often reinforced by informal ones.

International regimes    Implicit or explicit principles, norms, rules, and decision-making procedures around which actors' expectations converge in a given area of international relations (Krasner cited in Keohane [1984, 57]).

Neoliberal institutionalism    A theory of international politics that accepts the state as the principal unit of analysis but argues that cooperation is possible for mutual gain. International institutions, such as regimes, can play a key role in fostering cooperation by providing a framework of legal liability, providing information, and reducing transaction costs. States, especially hegemonic states, may create regimes in order to overcome failures of coordination.

Neorealism   A theory of international politics that argues the state is the principal unit of analysis. Domestic forces play a secondary role in shaping states' foreign policy objectives because of the anarchic structure of the international system that compels states to preserve themselves before engaging in other ventures that might be mutually beneficial. The distinction between domestic and international politics is that the domestic political structure is defined in terms of the ordering principle of hierarchy, whereas the international structure is anarchic.

Nonagreement alternative   The course of action that a negotiator will follow in the event that it is not possible to reach an agreement. The more attractive a nonagreement alternative, the more willing a negotiator will be to hold out for a favorable deal—or, alternatively, walk away from any offer that does not improve on the nonagreement alternative.

Risk averse   Willing to offer concessions to increase the certainty of a negotiated settlement.

Risk orientation   Attitudes toward the acceptance or avoidance of risk (in this case, willingness to put an agreement at risk).

Risk prone   Willing to put agreement at risk by withholding concessions.

Subjective utility   The value attached by a negotiator to an agreement versus its alternatives.

Threshold adjustment   The point where perceived differences in the relative negotiating positions of parties are deemed to be sufficient to warrant a response.

Win-set   The set of all possible agreements that would win in an up-or-down vote.

# Structure and Personnel of Negotiating Teams

## Canada

NOTE: The Canadian model was the most complex of the three countries. The assistant chief negotiators handled whole sectors, with assistant negotiators serving as working group heads and reporting to the assistant chief negotiators. In addition, there was a unit, the Office of Trilateral Trade Negotiations (OTTN), that provided administrative coordination. Home departments are indicated.

Minister for International Trade: Michael Wilson
Chief Negotiator: John Weekes, Department of External Affairs
Deputy Chief Negotiator: Bob Clark, External Affairs
Chief Legal Counsel: Jonathan Fried, External Affairs
Assistant Chief Negotiators: Market access—Kevin Gore, External Affairs; Investment—Alan Nymark, Industry; Services—Meriel Bradford, External Affairs; Trade rules—Doug Wadell, External Affairs; Agriculture—Mike Gifford, Agriculture.
Office of Trilateral Trade Negotiations: Director, Keith Christie, External Affairs
Assistant Negotiators, Working Group Heads: Services—Pierre Sauvé, External Affairs; Rules of Origin—Sandy Moroz, External Affairs; Tariffs—Patricia Close, Finance; Procurement—Victor Lonmo, External Affairs; Intellectual Property Rights—John Gero, External Affairs; Financial Services—Frank Swedlove, Finance; Trade Remedies—David Iwassa, Fi-

nance; Investment—Emmy Verdun, Investment Canada; Agriculture—Phil Stone, Agriculture; Telecommunications—Michael Tiger, Communications; Standards—Bertin Coté, External Affairs; Energy—Michael Cleland, Energy, Mines, and Resources; Textiles—Tom MacDonald, External Affairs; Temporary Entry—Brian Grant, Immigration; Automobiles—Slawek Skorupinski, Industry.

## Mexico

Secretary of Trade and Industrial Development: Jaime Serra
Chief Negotiator: Herminio Blanco, Secretariat of Trade and Industrial Development (SECOFI) Deputy Chief Negotiator: Jaime Zabludovsky, SECOFI
Chief Legal Counsel: Guillermo Aguilar, SECOFI
Working Group Heads: Rules of Origin—Aslan Cohen, Federal Competition Commission; Market Access—Raúl Ramos, SECOFI; Automobiles—Israel Gutiérrez, SECOFI; Textiles—Enrique Espinoza, on secondment from the Banco Nacional de México; Agriculture—Eduardo Solís Sánchez, SECOFI, and Luis Téllez, Agriculture; Energy—José Alberro, PEMEX, and Jesús Flores, SECOFI; Procurement—Héctor Olea, SECOFI; Investment—Fernando Heftye Etienne, SECOFI; Standards—Agustín Portal Ariosa, SECOFI; Dispute Resolution—Alvaro Baillet, SECOFI; Intellectual Property Rights—Roberto Villareal, SECOFI; Services—Fernando de Mateo, SECOFI; Financial Services—Fernando Salas, SECOFI, and José Angel Gurría and Guillermo Ortiz, Finance; Transportation—Alejandro Peniche, Land Transportation; Telecommunications—Jorge Gurría, Communications and Transport.

## United States

U.S. Trade Representative: Carla Hills
Chief Negotiator: Jules Katz, Office of the U.S. Trade Representative (USTR)
Deputy Chief Negotiator: Charles Roh, USTR
General counsel: Josh Bolten, USTR
Working group heads: Rules of Origin—John Simpson, Treasury; Agriculture—Richard Schroeter, Agriculture; Investment—Bill Barreda, Treasury; Temporary Entry—Robert Bostick, Labor; Standards—Dan Brinza, USTR; Industrial Standards—John Donaldson, Commerce; Subsidies and Trade Remedies—Alan Dunn, Commerce; Tariffs and Nontariff Barriers—Robert Fisher, USTR; Dispute Settlement—Ken Frieberg, USTR; Au-

tomobiles—Ann Hughes, Commerce; Telecommunications—David Long, USTR; Land Transportation—Nancy MacRae, Transportation; Procurement—Gene McAllister, State; Financial Services—Patrick Pascoe, Treasury, and Olin Weddington, Treasury; Safeguards—Jorge Lopez, Labor; Services—Holly Hammonds, USTR; Intellectual Property Rights—Emory Simon, USTR; Textiles—Ron Sorini, USTR; Energy—William Ramsay, State.

# NOTES

## Chapter 1. Northern Reflections

1. The logic of Salinas's position was outlined later in 1990 in his speech to the Mexican Senate, which organized a forum to consult on Mexico's trade relations with the world in response to the administration's free trade initiative. See Salinas de Gortari (1990); see also Serra Puche (1990).

2. The Rivera family is a fictitious composite based on a variety of narratives, both written and directly observed, including those by Cobb (1990), Hellman (1993), and Hermosillo et al. (1995).

3. Larry Rohter, "Free-Trade Talks with US Set off Debate in Mexico," *New York Times*, March 29, 1990, A3.

4. Martha Brant, "Power Player," *Newsweek*, November 16, 1998, 16.

5. There was some irony in the fact that Government Research Corporation was owned by Toronto-based Public Affairs Resource Group, which would soon be taken over by the American consulting conglomerate Hill & Knowlton.

6. *Globe and Mail*, June 10, 1991, B4.

7. In fact, Don Campbell had participated in meetings with Blanco and Katz during the period when the United States was waiting for Congress to grant fast-track negotiating authority to the administration (see Chapter 4).

8. *Globe and Mail*, June 10, 1991, B1.

9. See Chapter 8 in Doern and Tomlin (1991).

## Chapter 2. Understanding International Negotiation

1. See also Bacharach and Lawler (1986).

2. Miguel Ángel Valverde Loya undertook a serious effort to apply two-level game theory to provide an understanding of the bargaining behavior of one NAFTA country (the United States). After outlining Putnam's theory, Valverde Loya (1997, 382) noted Keo-

hane's observation that a powerful but fragmented government could be outnegotiated by a weaker but more unified adversary. However, he found little evidence to support Keohane's hypothesis in the NAFTA negotiations and considerable evidence to the contrary. Valverde Loya argued that U.S. Presidents Bush and Clinton made side payments to domestic groups and legislators to increase their domestic win-sets. The Mexican president, operating with fewer domestic constraints, also made concessions in order to broaden the domestic U.S. coalition supporting NAFTA. Thus, unified government was a disadvantage for a weaker state in negotiating with a divided government in a stronger state.

3. The phrase "three amigos" was used by Canadian Prime Minister Jean Chrétien to describe the triumvirate.

### Chapter 3. Assessing the NAFTA Bargain

1. The overview of the contents of the NAFTA is based on an examination of the agreement itself, plus a number of detailed descriptions of the contents, including Appleton (1994), Hufbauer and Schott (1992, 1994), Johnston (1994), and Trebilcock and Howse (1995).

### Chapter 4. Getting to the Table

1. The prenegotiation analytical framework and concepts are drawn from Tomlin (1989, 256–62).
2. *New York Times*, November 24, 1988, D1.
3. *New York Times*, October 2, 1989, A6.
4. *New York Times*, October 4, 1989, D6.
5. *New York Times*, October 19, 1989, D9.
6. *Economist*, February 10, 1990, 48.
7. The most powerful private pressures in favor of free trade came from multinational enterprises (mainly U.S.-owned ones) that had become more export oriented as a result of the collapse of the Mexican market in the 1980s. They were followed by large domestic firms often associated with multinational corporations. Coordinadora de Organismos Empresariales de Comercio (COECE) was modeled on the Canadian system of International Trade Advisory Committees (ITAC) and Sectoral Advisory Groups on International Trade (SAGITs), but as Gustavo del Castillo (1995, 42) noted, "COECE was to serve as a buffer organization whose primary task was to help define a unified (nonoppositional) stance within the private sector with regard to the government's decision to negotiate free trade. In an early meeting of the economic cabinet in Mexico, it is reported that the decision was taken that: '. . . no opposition or discussion would be tolerated with respect to the decision to seek a free trade agreement with the United States. There would be no debate as was the case of Mexico's joining the GATT in 1979' " (del Castillo 1995, 42). Del Castillo (1995, 42–43) went on to observe, "The Mexican political system has been characterized by the centralization of functions, and in this respect it should not surprise anyone that free trade, just like any other issue and because of its importance, would be handled by the *camarillas* (cliques) which centralize decision making."
8. Hermann von Bertrab (1997, 2), who headed up a special Mexican office in Washington during the NAFTA negotiations, described the conversion in more dramatic, even Dickensian, terms, with Salinas coming, in his nightshirt, to Serra's hotel room during the night to pose the U.S. free trade question.

9. The problems that would be created for Canada in the hub-and-spoke model had been identified by Canadian economists Richard Lipsey (1990) and Ronald Wonnacott (1990).

10. In a statement from Mexico City, President Salinas indicated that he had sent Serra to Canada "to create the conditions for a greater dialogue with the objective of establishing a free-trade agreement with Canada" (*Calgary Herald*, June 14, 1990, F20).

11. *Toronto Star*, June 13, 1990, A3.

12. U.S. officials also had reservations about Canadian participation, which largely were concerned with the time constraints imposed on the negotiations by the 1992 U.S. elections and the possibility that Canada might slow down the process. Washington observers suggested that Mulroney's unwavering support for Bush during the Persian Gulf War now paid dividends, convincing Bush to override these reservations (*Globe and Mail*, January 12, 1991, B1).

13. The significance of fast track may be lost on non-cognoscenti. The procedure is deemed to be essential to provide American trade negotiators with the power to deliver on their commitments. Otherwise, foreign governments would be unable or unwilling to negotiate seriously with the U.S. administration, since Congress could always renege on commitments made by American negotiators (and, in fact, had done so on occasion before the fast-track procedure was established).

14. Although Dan Rostenkowski opposed an early start to NAFTA talks, an aide stated that Rostenkowski was not "prepared to fall on his sword over the issue" (*Wall Street Journal*, August 31, 1990, A12).

15. Hills and Katz had miscalculated seriously on the multilateral trade negotiations (MTN), which did not conclude until December 1993.

16. The timelines in the 1988 act were based on the expectation that the Uruguay Round would conclude by the end of 1990. Provision for an extension was included to allow for the possibility of a stalemate, which in fact occurred.

17. The 1988 act also gave Congress the power to derail already authorized agreements from the fast track, although this would require the concurrence of both houses of Congress (Koh 1992, 151).

18. The dual requirement's effect of providing a second front on which the Democratic Congress could battle the administration on trade policy was inadvertent. That the extension would apply to NAFTA as well as the MTN was not considered when the 1988 act was passed, since members were not then contemplating free trade with Mexico (Destler 1992, 99).

19. *Inside US Trade*, November 2, 1990, 8.

20. The unexpected delay in the MTN and Mexico's desire to blunt U.S. trade remedy actions subsequently would undo this particular decision.

21. On August 4, 1990, Iraq invaded Kuwait. Subsequently, the United Nations Security Council authorized an international coalition of forces, led by the United States, to expel Iraq from Kuwait. On January 16, 1991, the Persian Gulf War began with a coalition attack on Iraqi forces.

22. The general fast-track extension would apply to NAFTA too, even though Bush's September 1990 request for fast-track authority for negotiations with Mexico had not yet been acted on by the Senate and House committees.

23. There was one independent member in the House, plus three vacant seats.

24. Destler also indicated that the speaker of the house rejected proposals to uncouple the MTN and NAFTA for purposes of a vote, again out of a commitment to the integrity of the procedures governing fast-track authorization. Florida Democrat Sam Gibbons, chair of the trade subcommittee of the House Ways and Means Committee, and a committed free trader, was inclined differently, however. Commenting on the prospect that the disapproval resolution might be bottled up in committee so that it never reached a

vote in the House, Gibbons said of members, "They'd be complaining on the floor and thanking me in the cloakroom for not making them vote. Deep down in their bellies, they know free trade is the right thing." See *New York Times*, April 9, 1991, D5.

25. *Wall Street Journal*, April 25, 1991, A16.

26. Gephardt was labeled a protectionist during his 1988 presidential bid.

27. *Wall Street Journal*, May 9, 1991, A2.

28. However, Gephardt's support was hedged in two respects. First, he promised to introduce a resolution in the House urging the administration to be mindful of potential job losses and of environmental damage in Mexico. Second, he suggested that the House could force changes in any agreement negotiated with Mexico, by altering the fast-track legislation or amending implementing legislation, if the administration failed to keep its promise to protect jobs and the environment.

29. An AFL-CIO official would later state, "It's very difficult to win a vote against the House leadership" (*Wall Street Journal*, May 24, 1991, A3).

30. While the labor movement remained united in its opposition to NAFTA, the environmental movement was split by the administration's assurances of action on the environment. Some, like the Friends of the Earth, remained opposed, while others, like the National Wildlife Federation, accepted the administration's assurances, muted their opposition, and then used the negotiations to advance their concerns.

31. One hundred seventy of 261 Democrats voting supported the resolution. In contrast, the Republicans were not nearly so divided, with only 13 percent (21 of 161 Republicans voting) supporting disapproval in opposition to their own leadership.

32. *Wall Street Journal*, May 24, 1991, A3. The House vote on the Gephardt-Rostenkowski resolution was 329 to 85.

33. However, Democrats in the Senate were sharply divided, with 57 percent (31 of 54 Democrats voting) supporting disapproval in opposition to their own leadership. As in the House, only 12 percent of voting Republicans did so.

34. Super 301 requires the U.S. trade representative to establish a "Priority Watch List" of country practices that impede U.S. exports or, in the case of intellectual property, fail to protect rights (Special 301).

35. Wilson replaced John Crosbie as trade minister early in 1991.

36. *Financial Post*, April 26, 1991, 1.

37. Elements of the 1965 Canada-U.S. Automobile Products Trade Agreement (Auto Pact) were entrenched in the Free Trade Agreement (FTA).

38. *Miami Herald*, May 24, 1991, 5.

39. Houston was chosen for the meeting because Katz had a daughter living there.

### Chapter 5. Opening Rounds

1. *Duty drawbacks* are import duties that are repaid when the imported goods are re-exported or used in the manufacture of exported goods.

2. Ford and Chrysler were demanding up to an 80 percent rule of content; General Motors was willing to accept a lower-content rule.

3. PEMEX (Petroleos Mexicanos) for petroleum and CFE (Comisión Federal de Electricidad) for electricity are Mexico's major state-owned energy operators.

4. For example, the Office of the U.S. Trade Representative used a tariff line questionnaire to ask for responses on import sensitivities and export opportunities. The results were entered into a database at the Department of Commerce, and based on this, negotiators were able to identify areas, like lumber and paper, that were export opportunities Mexico was resisting, or footwear, where Mexico wanted access, but the United States had

to resist. Several tariff phaseout schedules were designed to look like what were referred to as kinky curves, where up-front cuts are followed by a freeze and then a resumption of cuts, in an effort to placate sensitive industries.

5. For a description of the production of the run-on, and then the composite texts, see Grayson (1995, 86–90).

6. The Mexicans had set up a study group on financial services during the fast-track debate, before the negotiations began.

7. The ministers generally met every two months, and the chiefs every month. When the chiefs met, they would bring in their assistant negotiators only as needed to provide briefings on progress. After each meeting of a working group, the host of the meeting would draft a summary report of the discussions. This was circulated for corrections and then given to the chief negotiators. Where the chiefs identified problems from these summaries, they called in the assistant negotiators to deal with them.

8. The Calvo clause stipulates that foreign investors cannot turn to their home governments to support their claims against the Mexican government.

### Chapter 6. The Dallas Jamboree

1. U.S. Department of Commerce, *Automotive Issues in the NAFTA*, mimeograph, October 29, 1991.

2. Both Guillermo Ortiz and José Angel Gurría became cabinet officials in the administration of Ernesto Zedillo.

### Chapter 7. Heavy Slogging after Dallas

1. The position of director general is equivalent to a U.S. assistant undersecretary and a Canadian assistant deputy minister.

2. U.S. Department of Commerce, *Automotive Working Group: Issues for the Ministerial*, mimeograph, October 23, 1991.

3. Tariff rate quotas (TRQs) determine a numerical volume of exports eligible to receive duty-free access to the other country's market for products that do not meet NAFTA rules of origin: products within the quota receive NAFTA's preferential tariffs; volumes over the quota receive most-favored-nation treatment.

4. Bristol-Myers, Squibb, DuPont, FMC Corporation, General Electric, Hewlett-Packard, IBM, Johnson & Johnson, Merck, Monsanto, Pfizer, Procter & Gamble, Rockwell International, and Time Warner.

5. "Pipeline protection" means the United States wanted innovations created before NAFTA was negotiated to be covered by the agreement.

### Chapter 8. End Game at the Watergate

1. The phrase "great curvaceous hulks" was used by critics to describe the "architectural extravaganza" constructed in the 1960s on a ten-acre industrial site once occupied by a gasworks (Scott and Lee 1993, 213).

2. The Nixon administration's infamous "plumbers," the code name for the group assigned to break into the Democratic Party's headquarters in 1972, led to the original Watergate scandal that brought Nixon down. The negotiations were held in the hotel in the Watergate complex.

3. The agreement also would have to be ratified subsequently by the U.S. Congress.

4. *Wall Street Journal*, July 21, 1992, A3.

5. U.S. negotiators were particularly concerned because House Majority Leader Gephardt had launched an attack on the agreement on July 27, 1992, complaining that it failed to adequately address concerns about labor and environmental standards.

6. The agreement would prevent Mexico from importing cheap foreign sugar for re-export into the United States, where it could be sold at a higher price sustained by U.S. government price supports. Any increase in Mexico's quota that resulted from efficiency increases by Mexican producers (or a reduction in consumption of domestic production) would simply reduce U.S. purchases from other foreign sugar producers.

7. Significant increases in exports of Canadian-made wool suits had been achieved by Quebec-based Peerless Clothing.

8. The threshold for defining a "major" takeover was scheduled in the FTA to rise in four steps to Can$150 million by 1992.

9. *Globe and Mail*, August 5, 1992, B5.

10. *Globe and Mail*, August 6, 1992, B1.

11. *Globe and Mail*, August 7, 1992, B6.

12. Bilateral discussions over a substitute system had been halted by 1991, after it became clear that there was no basis for an agreement between the two countries.

13. Hills signaled the probability of continuation into a second week when she canceled an appearance before the Senate Finance Committee, scheduled for Monday, August 10, providing an indication that there would be no agreement to discuss with the committee by then.

14. Apparently Wilson and the other negotiators were unaware of the laundry services available at the hotel!

15. Keith Bradsher in *New York Times*, August 11, 1992, D3.

16. *Globe and Mail*, August 8, 1992, B3.

17. *Globe and Mail*, August 8, 1992, B3.

18. In fact, the chiefs, especially Katz and Weekes, worked hard to limit the substantive involvement of the ministers, for fear that they would upset the delicate balance that they, the chief negotiators, were constructing around the issues.

19. At the time, Legault was senior assistant deputy minister for the United States and coordinator of the FTA in the Department of External Affairs.

20. U.S. officials indicated that General Motors really did not care as much about the issue and simply went along to present a united front among the producers.

21. At the top of the curve, risk aversion kicks in.

22. Even then, the lawyers could not leave the text alone. Not until late the next month would the final text of the agreement be ready to be initialed formally by officials from the three countries.

23. *New York Times*, August 13, 1992, A1.

### Chapter 9. Another End Game

1. By notifying Congress of plans to sign NAFTA, the Bush administration gave itself ninety days to develop legislation to present to Congress. As soon as the president signs an agreement, he thereby officially starts the timetable for consideration by Congress, which has ninety *legislative* days to debate whether to approve the implementing legislation necessary to bring the agreement into force.

2. As noted previously, work on the NAFTA text continued for more than a month after the conclusion of negotiations at the Watergate Hotel in August, in fact right up to

the initialing that took place in San Antonio. One Canadian official recalled, "The Challenger jet was waiting at the airport to take the NAFTA text (in French and English) to San Antonio for the initialing. [Jon] Fried [Canada's chief NAFTA lawyer] was working on changes right up to the initialing" and even called the printers to change part of the text. When he was told it was too late, Fried said, "That's not good enough, I'm calling [Canada's deputy chief negotiator] Bob Clark." But it was too late and the final text went to San Antonio without Fried's revisions.

3. *Inside US Trade*, October 10, 1992.

4. *New York Times*, October 20, 1992, A21.

5. *Trade News Bulletin*, June 30 1993.

6. The phrase "the spirit of Houston" was coined after a meeting in that city between Salinas and Bush when both were presidents-elect.

7. *El Financiero International*, December 7, 1992, 4.

8. *Inside US Trade*, March 5, 1993.

9. *Trade News Bulletin*, June 7, 1993.

10. *Inside US Trade*, April 30, 1993.

11. R. W. Apple Jr. wrote that "the private judgement of most senior members of the White House staff was that the president should abandon the trade accord." *Gazette*, (Montreal), November 18, 1993, D14.

12. *El Financiero International*, May 10, 1993, 1, 4.

13. *Trade News Bulletin*, May 24, 1993.

14. *Financial Post*, June 5, 1993.

15. The governor general is representative of the Queen of England, Canada's head of state.

16. *Trade News Bulletin*, July 1, 1993.

17. *Trade News Bulletin*, July 2, 1993.

18. *Trade News Bulletin*, July 13, 1993.

19. *El Financiero International*, July 26, 1993, 1, 3.

20. *Trade News Bulletin*, June 24, 1993.

21. In a strange development that coincided with the late July negotiations, Mickey Kantor flew to Mexico City to meet with Salinas in a rather unusual effort to gain additional protection in NAFTA for the Florida fruit and vegetable lobby and for U.S. sugar producers. He failed to consult in detail with his own domestic lobbies, however, and even the Department of Agriculture was not informed of Kantor's "personal quest" to seek last-minute changes in NAFTA. The lack of seriousness in Kantor's actions suggested to some observers that they were designed to impress domestic lobbies rather than achieve real results. Actually, even that may ascribe more reason to the initiative than it deserves. Recall that during the Watergate end game, Jules Katz and John Weekes worked to limit the damage that their ministers might do to the negotiations. Apparently, their problems were nothing compared to the challenge faced by Yerxa and Weekes in their efforts to limit collateral damage from the actions of Kantor and Hockin. While in Mexico, Kantor met with Mexican trade, labor, and environment ministers as well as the president.

22. *Inside US Trade*, August 13, 1993.

23. *Globe and Mail*, August 13, 1993, B1.

24. *Trade News Bulletin*, June 21, 1993.

25. *Trade News Bulletin*, July 28, 1993.

26. The Center for Public Integrity, *The Trading Game*, 1993, 17.

27. *Trade News Bulletin*, May 20, 1993.

28. After the United States and Mexico made it clear that they would not entertain any reopening of negotiations, the Chrétien government was forced to accept a face-saving exit from its demand, agreeing to the establishment of a NAFTA working group on subsi-

dies and dumping, coupled with a declaration that Canada would retain control of its sovereignty over energy in the event of a crisis.

29. *Globe and Mail*, November 19, 1993, A2.

30. *Toronto Star*, November 18, 1993, A1, A4.

## Chapter 10. A Mexican Tragedy

1. For a vivid account of the New Year's Eve party in Los Pinos, see Oppenheimer (1996, 6–15).

2. These numbers come from President Zedillo's 1995 address to the nation. "La ciudadanía, motor del avance político: Zedillo," *La Jornada*, September 2, 1995.

3. See Table 9 in Sachs et al. (1995), based on Bank of Mexico data.

4. One aspect of Mexico's informal rules, the *camarilla* system, is described in earlier chapters on the negotiation process.

5. For a biting analysis of the complexities of international solidarity with the Chiapas guerrillas, see Hellman (1999).

6. The facility (fund) was never actually used.

7. *Wall Street Journal*, March 28, 1994, A6.

8. The "*pactos*" were corporatist associations involving business, government, and labor representatives.

9. *Wall Street Journal*, June 14, 1994, 1.

10. *Business Week*, "Special 1994 Business Issue," January 24, 1995, 41.

11. Tim Loughran, "Mexican Ruling Party Closes Office of Dissidents," *Bloomberg Business News*, September 24, 1996; L. Ian MacDonald, "If Mexico's PRI Would Only RIP," *Gazette* (Montreal), March 29, 1999.

12. Treviño changed his testimony so many times it is hard to know what to believe, but at one point he insisted in writing, in an account that was published in *Time* magazine, that Massieu was killed because he knew that the decision to kill Colosio was made by the president and his immediate advisors. "Confessed Mexican Killer Implicates Ex-president," Reuters, January 29, 1999, and "Twists and Turns Continue in Mexico's Sensational Murder Case," Reuters, January 30, 1999.

13. This section draws on Cameron and Aggarwal (1996) and Cameron (1995).

14. Embassy of Canada, Mexico City, *Unclassified Report*, March 3, 1995.

15. *New York Times*, February 3, 1995, A1, A6.

16. International Monetary Fund, "IMF Approves US \$17.8 Billion Stand-By Credit for Mexico," Press release no. 95-10 (February 1, 1995).

17. The five major domestic financial groups were Banamex; Bancomer, which bought up Promex and Union; Serfin, which joined with the Hong Kong and Shanghai Banking Corporation (HSBC); Bital, which bought Atlantico; and Banorte, which bought Banpaís and Bancen.

18. Banco Bilbao Vizcaya (BBV) bought Proborsa, Oriente, and Cremi; Nova Scotia has the option to buy Inverlat; Santander bought Mexicano; Citibank bought Confia; and a German group is buying Bancrecer and Banoro.

19. Aurora Berdejo Arvizu, "Bancos ricos y bancos pobres, historia de la soberanía perdida," *Excelsior*, May 11, 1998, <http://www.excelsior.com.mx/9805/980511/exe10.html>.

20. For a representative example, see Carlos Acosta Córdova, "La mitad del Fobaproa en el 0.13% de los créditos de banqueros a parientes, amigos, socios y ellos mismos," *Proceso*, No. 1125 (May 24, 1998), 6–10.

21. A notorious example of the cozy connections between the Salinas clan and the private sector was a banquet held on February 23, 1993, when Salinas invited thirty of the

nation's businessmen to a dinner and asked them each to donate $25 million to the presidential campaign of the ruling party. Raúl was deeply involved in such fund raising. Quoted in PBS, "Frontline," Air date: April 8, 1997 (Show 1510), "Murder, Money & Mexico: The Rise and Fall of the Salinas Brothers." Available on the Internet at <http://www.pbs.org/wgbh/pages/frontline/shows/mexico/etc/script.html>.

22. Carlos Salinas de Gortari, "The Exile Speaks Out," *Newsweek*, November 16, 1998, 18.

23. Raymundo Riva Palacio, "Las uvas de la ira," *Milenio*, 73 (January 25, 1999), 31–2.

### Chapter 11. Conclusions

1. See United Nations Development Programme (1998, 128, 176, 200).

2. The Office of Deregulation introduced the "*semaforo fiscal*" (the tax streetlight) at customs in order to reduce the discretionary power of border officials.

3. According to a Canadian negotiator: "Canada learned from the experience of the FTA and the way the Trade Negotiation Office [the agency in charge of the FTA negotiations] was organized. It is not good to have everything centralized. The OTTN [the agency within the trade ministry that coordinated the NAFTA negotiations] learned from this experience with [FTA Chief Negotiator Simon] Reisman. Weekes sought to bring in more people from other agencies. His style was very different from Reisman's. At one point in the FTA negotiations, Pat Carney [minister of trade] said to Reisman in a fight: 'Don't forget, you work for me.' To which Reisman replied, 'Madame, I work for the Prime Minister.' That sort of thing did not happen under Weekes."

4. Ottawa had to mount another fight with U.S. legislators and the Clinton administration over last-minute congressional amendments to NAFTA's implementing legislation that would have altered U.S. trade law on countervailing duties, and could have undermined the functioning of binational panels. Another change would have allowed the appeal of panel decisions in U.S. courts (*Financial Post*, October 29, 1993).

# BIBLIOGRAPHY

Aggarwal, Vinod K. 1996. *Debt Games: Strategic Interaction in International Debt Rescheduling.* New York: Cambridge University Press.

Appleton, Barry. 1994. *Navigating NAFTA: A Concise User's Guide to the North American Free Trade Agreement.* Toronto: Carswell.

Axelrod, Robert. 1997. *The Complexity of Cooperation.* Princeton: Princeton University Press.

———. 1984. *The Evolution of Cooperation.* New York: Basic Books.

Axelrod, Robert, and Robert O. Keohane. 1996. "Achieving Cooperation under Anarchy: Strategies and Institutions." In *Cooperation under Anarchy*, edited by Kenneth A. Oye. Princeton: Princeton University Press.

Bachrach, S., and E. Lawler. 1986. "Power Dependence and Power Paradoxes in Bargaining." *Negotiation Journal* 2, no. 2: 167–74.

Baker, James, III. 1988. "The Geopolitical Implications of the US-Canada Trade Pact." *International Economy* 2, no. 1: 34–41.

Bazerman, M., and J. Carroll. 1987. "Negotiator Cognition." In *Research in Organizational Behavior*, edited by L. Cummings and B. Staw. New York: JAI Press.

Bensusán, Graciela. 1994. "Entre candados y dientes: La agenda laboral del TLCAN," *Perfiles Latinoamericanos* 3, no. 4: 109–41.

Bertraub, Hermann von. 1997. *Negotiating NAFTA: A Mexican Envoy's Account.* Washington Papers No. 173. Published with the Center for Strategic and International Studies. Westport, Conn.: Praeger.

Black, Gordon S., and Benjamin D. Black. 1994. *The Politics of American Discontent.* New York: John Wiley.

Blumenthal, Sidney. 1993. "The Making of a Machine." *New Yorker* 69 (November 29): 80, 89–93.

Borja Tamayo, Arturo, and Brian J.R. Stevenson. 1996. "Introducción: La teoría realista y los estudios internacionales." In *Regionalismo y poder en América: los límites del neorealismo*, edited by Arturo Borja Tamayo, Guadalupe González, and Brian J. R. Stevenson. Mexico City: CIDE.

———. 1996. "Los patrones históricos del continente americano y las limitaciones del realismo estructural." In *Regionalismo y poder en América: Los límites del neorealismo*, edited by Arturo Borja Tamayo, Guadalupe González, and Brian J. R. Stevenson. Mexico City: CIDE.

———. 1996. "Resumen y conclusiones." In *Regionalismo y poder en América: Los límites del neorealismo*, edited by Arturo Borja Tamayo, Guadalupe González, and Brian J. R. Stevenson. Mexico City: CIDE.

Cameron, Maxwell A. 1997. "North American Trade Negotiations: Liberalization Games between Asymmetric Players." *European Journal of International Relations* 3, no.1: 105–39.

———. 1995. "Crisis or Crises in Mexico?" *Third World Resurgence* 57 (December): 19–21.

———. 1991. "North American Free Trade, Public Goods, and Asymmetrical Bargaining: The Strategic Choices for Canada." *Frontera Norte* 3, no. 6: 47–64.

Cameron, Maxwell A., and Vinod K. Aggarwal. 1996. "Mexican Meltdown: States, Markets and Post-NAFTA Financial Turmoil." *Third World Quarterly* 17, no. 5: 957–87.

Camp, Roderic. 1990. "Camarillas in Mexican Politics: The Case of the Salinas Cabinet" *Mexican Studies* 6, no. 1: 85–108.

Canada Department of Finance. 1995. *Canada-Mexico Finance Executive Seminar: Summary Notes*. Ottawa: National Arts Centre.

Canada House of Commons Standing Committee on Foreign Affairs and International Trade. 1995. Report on the Issues of International Financial Institutions Reforms for the Agenda of the June 1995 G-7 Halifax Summit 1995. *From Bretton Woods to Halifax and Beyond: Towards a 21st Summit for the 21st Century Challenge*. Ottawa: House of Commons.

Castañeda, Jorge. 1995. *The Mexican Shock*. New York: New Press.

Centeno, Miguel Ángel. 1994. *Democracy within Reason: Technocratic Revolution in Mexico*. University Park: Pennsylvania State University Press.

Chabat, Jorge. 1996. "La integración de México al mundo de la posguerra fría: Del nacionalismo a la interdependencia imperfecta." In *Regionalismo y poder en América: Los límites del neorealismo*, edited by Arturo Borja Tamayo, Guadalupe González, and Brian J. R. Stevenson. Mexico City: CIDE.

Cobb, Charles E., Jr. 1990. "Mexico's Bajío—The Heartland." *National Geographic* 178, no. 6: 122–44.

Davey, William J. 1996. *Pine and Swine: Canada-United States Trade Dispute Settlement— The FTA Experience and NAFTA Prospects*. Ottawa: Centre for Trade Policy and Law, Carleton University.

del Castillo Gustavo, V. 1995. "Private Sector Trade Advisory Groups in North America: A Comparative Perspective." In *The Politics of Free Trade in North America*, edited by Gustavo del Castillo V and Gustavo Vega Cánovas. Ottawa: Centre for Trade Policy and Law, Carleton University.

Destler, I. M. 1992. *American Trade Politics*, Second Edition. Washington, D.C., and New York: Institute for International Economics and the Twentieth Century Fund.

Doern, Bruce, and Brian Tomlin. 1991. *Faith and Fear: The Free Trade Story*. Toronto: Stoddard.

Dominguez, Jorge I. 1998. "Ampliando hoizontes: Aproximaciones teóricas para el estudio de las relaciones México-Estados-Unidos." In *Nueva agenda bilateral en la relación México-Estados Unidos*, edited by Mónica Verea Campos, Rafael Fernández de Castro, and Sidney Weintraub. Mexico City: Fondo de Cultura Económica.

Druckman, D. 1993. "The Situational Levers of Negotiating Flexibility." *Journal of Conflict Resolution* 37, no. 2: 236–76.

———. 1986. "Stages, Turning Points, and Crises." *Journal of Conflict Resolution* 30, no. 2: 327–60.

Druckman, D., and R. Harris. 1990. "Alternative Models of Responsiveness in International Negotiations." *Journal of Conflict Resolution* 34, no. 2: 234–51.

Druckman, D., J. Husbands, and K. Johnston. 1991. "Turning Points in the INF Negotiations." *Negotiation Journal* 7, no. 1: 55–67.

Dryden, S. 1995. *Trade Warriors: USTR and the American Crusade for Free Trade.* New York: Oxford University Press.

Economist Intelligence Unit. 1991. *EIU Country Report: Mexico.* No. 3. New York: Economist Intelligence Unit.

Evans, Peter. 1993. "Building an Integrative Approach to International and Domestic Politics: Reflections and Projections." In *Double-Edged Diplomacy: International Bargaining and Domestic Politics*, edited by Peter B. Evans, Harold K. Jacobson, and Robert D. Putnam. Berkeley: University of California Press.

Farber, H., and H. Katz. 1979. "Interest Arbitration, Outcomes and the Incentives to Bargain." *Industrial and Labour Relations Review* 33: 55–63.

Faux, Jeff. 1993. "The Politics of NAFTA." An April 30 memorandum sent to Joan Baggett, Paul Begala, James Carville, Rahm Emanuel, Stanley Greenberg, Frank Greer, George Stephanopoulos, and David Wilhelm. Economic Policy Institute, Washington, D.C.

Fernández de Castro, Rafael. 1998. "La institucionalización de la relación inter-gubermental: Una forma de explicar la cooperación." In *Nueva agenda en la relación México-Estados Unidos*, edited by Mónica Verea Campos, Rafael Fernández de Castro, and Sidney Weintraub. Mexico City: Fondo de Cultura Económica.

Grayson, George W. 1995. *The North American Free Trade Agreement: Regional Community and the New World Order.* Lanham, Md.: University Press of America.

———. 1984. *The United States and Mexico: Patterns of Influence.* New York: Praeger.

Grieco, Joseph M. 1996. "Institucionalización económica regional: La experiencia de América en una perspectiva comparativa." In *Regionalismo y poder en América: Los límites del neorealismo*, edited by Arturo Borja Tamayo, Guadalupe González, and Brian J. R. Stevenson. Mexico City: CIDE.

Grinspun, Ricardo, and Maxwell A. Cameron. 1996 "NAFTA and the Political Economy of Mexico's External Relations." *Latin American Research Review* 313: 161–88.

Hart, Michael. 1990. *A North American Free Trade Agreement: The Strategic Implications for Canada.* Ottawa: Centre for Trade Policy and Law, Carleton University.

Hawes, Michael K. 1996. "Cambio estructural, realismo político, y el nuevo regionalismo: El TLCAN y las nuevas realidades estructurales." In *Regionalismo y poder en América: Los límites del neorealismo*, edited by Arturo Borja Tamayo, Guadalupe González, and Brian J. R. Stevenson. Mexico City: CIDE.

Helleiner, Gerald K. 1993. "Considering U.S.-Mexico Free Trade." In *The Political Economy of North American Free Trade*, edited by Ricardo Grinspun and Maxwell A. Cameron. New York: St. Martin's Press.

Hellman, Judith Adler. 1999. "Real and Virtual Chiapas: Magical Realism and the Left." In *Socialist Register 2000*, edited by Leo Panitch and Colin Leys. New York: Monthly Review Press.

———. 1993. "Mexican Perceptions of Free Trade: Support and Opposition to NAFTA." In *The Political Economy of North American Free Trade*, edited by Ricardo Grinspun and Maxwell A. Cameron. New York: St. Martin's Press.

Hermosillo, Paulina, Hortensia Sierra, and Elizabeth Luis Diaz. 1995 "Testimonies." In *First World, Ha ha ha! The Zapatista Challenge*, edited by Elaine Katzenberger. San Francisco: City Lights Books.

Herzenberg, Stephen. n.d. "A Tale of Two Countries." Unpublished paper. Office of Technology Assessment, Congress of the United States, Washington, D.C.

Howlett, Michael P. and P. Ramesh. 1995. *Studying Public Policy: Policy Cycles and Policy Subsytems.* Don Mills, Ontario: Oxford University Press.

Hufbauer, Gary Clyde, and Jeffrey J. Schott. 1992. *North American Free Trade: Issues and Recommendations.* Washington, D.C.: Institute for International Economics.

——. 1993. *NAFTA: An Assessment.* Washington, D.C.: Institute for International Economics.

Jackson, Robert J., and Doreen Jackson. 1990. *Politics in Canada: Culture, Institutions, Behaviour and Public Policy.* (Second edition). Scarborough, Ontario: Prentice-Hall.

Johnston, Jon R. 1994. *The North American Free Trade Agreement: A Comprehensive Guide.* Aurora, Ontario: Canadian Law Book.

Kahneman, D., and A. Tversky. 1979. "Prospect Theory: An Analysis of Decision under Risk." *Econometrica* 47 (March): 263–91.

Kaufman, Robert R. 1998. "Attitudes toward Economic Reform in Mexico: The Role of Political Orientations." *American Political Science Review* 92, no. 2: 359–75.

Keohane, Robert O. 1990. "El concepto de interdependencia y el análisis de las relaciones asimétricas." In *Interdependencia: ¿Un enfoque útil para análisis de las relaciones México-Estados Unidos?*, edited by Blanca Torres. Mexico City: Colegio de México.

——. 1989. *International Institutions and State Power: Essays in International Relations Theory.* Boulder: Westview Press.

——, ed. 1986. *Neorealism and Its Critics.* New York: Columbia University Press.

——. 1984. *After Hegemony: Cooperation and Discord in the World Political Economy.* Princeton: Princeton University Press.

Keohane, Robert O., and Joseph Nye. 1977. *Power and Interdependence: World Politics in Transition.* Boston: Little, Brown.

Koh, H. 1992. "The Fast Track and United States Trade Policy." *Brooklyn Journal of International Law* 18, no. 1: 143–89.

Krasner, Stephen D. 1993. "Bloques económicos regionales y el fin de la guerra fría." In *Liberación Económica y Libre Comercio en América del Norte*, edited by Gustavo Vega. Mexico City: Colegio de México.

——. 1990. "Interdependencia simple y obstáculos para la cooperación entre México y Estados Unidos." In *Interdependencia: ¿Un enfoque útil para análisis de las relaciones México-Estados Unidos?*, edited by Blanca Torres. Mexico City: Colegio de México.

——. 1985. *Structural Conflict: The Third World Against Global Liberalism.* Berkeley: University of California Press.

——. 1976. "State Power and the Structure of International Trade." *World Politics* 28, no. 3: 317–43.

Kratochwil, Friedrich V. 1989. *Rules, Norms, and Decisions: On the Conditions of Practical and Legal Reasoning in International Relations and Domestic Affairs.* Cambridge: Cambridge University Press.

Lax, D., and J. Sebenius. 1985. "The Power of Alternatives or the Limits to Negotiation." *Negotiation Journal* 1, no. 2: 163–79.

——. 1986. *The Manager as Negotiator.* New York: Free Press.

Levi, Margaret. 1988. *Of Rule and Revenue.* Berkeley: University of California Press.

Lipsey, Richard G. 1990. "Canada at the U.S.-Mexico Free Trade Dance: Wallflower or Partner?" *Commentary* 20. Toronto: C.D. Howe Institute.

Lustig, Nora. 1992. *Mexico, the Remaking of an Economy.* Washington, D.C.: Brookings Institution.

Mares, David. 1987. "Mexico's Challenges: Sovereignty and National Autonomy under Interdependence." *Third World Quarterly* 9, no. 3: 788–803.

Mastanduno, M. 1988. "Trade as a Strategic Weapon: American and Alliance Export Control Policy in the Early Postwar Period." In *The State and American Foreign Economic Policy*, edited by John Ikenberry, David Lake, and Michael Mastanduno. Ithaca: Cornell University Press.

Maxfield, Sylvia, and Adam Shapiro. 1998. "Assessing the NAFTA Negotiations." In *The Post-NAFTA Political Economy: Mexico and the Western Hemisphere*, edited by Carol Wise. University Park: Pennsylvania State University Press.

Mayer, Frederick W. 1998. *Interpreting NAFTA: The Science and Art of Political Analysis*. New York: Columbia University Press.

Milner, Helen. 1991. "The Assumption of Anarchy in International Relations Theory: A Critique." *Review of International Studies* 17: 67–85.

Moravcsik, Andrew. 1997. "Taking Preferences Seriously: A Liberal Theory of International Politics." *International Organization* 15, no. 4: 513–53.

——. 1993. "Introduction: Integrating International and Domestic Theories of International Bargaining." In *Double-Edged Diplomacy: International Bargaining and Domestic Politics*, edited by Peter B. Evans, Harold K. Jacobson, and Robert D. Putnam. Berkeley: University of California Press.

Neale, M., and M. Bazerman. 1985. "Perspectives for Understanding Negotiation." *Journal of Conflict Resolution* 29, no. 1: 33–55.

Onuf, Nicholas Greenwood. 1989. *Worlds of Our Making: Rules and Rule in Social Theory and International Relations*. Columbia: University of South Carolina Press.

Oppenheimer, Andreas. 1996. *Bordering on Chaos: Guerrillas, Stockbrokers, Politicians, and Mexico's Road to Prosperity*. Boston: Little, Brown.

Oye, Kenneth A. 1996. "Explaining Cooperation under Anarchy: Hypotheses and Strategies." In *Cooperation under Anarchy*, edited by Kenneth A. Oye. Princeton: Princeton University Press.

Pastor, Manual, and Carol Wise. 1998. "Mexican-Style Neoliberalism: State Policy and Distributional Stress." In *The Post-NAFTA Political Economy: Mexico and the Western Hemisphere*, edited by Carol Wise. University Park: Pennsylvania State University Press.

——. 1994. "The Origins and Sustainability of Mexico's Free Trade Policy." *International Organization* 48, no. 3: 459–89.

Pomper, Gerald M. 1993. *The Election of 1992: Reports and Interpretations*. Chatham, N.J.: Chatham House Publishers.

Putnam, Robert D. 1993. "Diplomacy and Domestic Politics: The Logic of Two-Level Games." In *Double-Edged Diplomacy: International Bargaining and Domestic Politics*, edited by Peter B. Evans, Harold K. Jacobson, and Robert D. Putnam. Berkeley: University of California Press.

Reynolds, Clark W. 1991. "North American Interdependence: Mexico's New Paradigm for the 1990s." In *Mexico's External Relations in the 1990s*, edited by Riorden Roett. Boulder: Lynne Rienner.

Ritter, A., and D. Pollock. 1986 "The International Debt Crisis: Towards Resolution?" In *Canada among Nations: The Conservative Agenda*, edited by M. Molot and B. Tomlin. Toronto: James Lorimer.

Ros, Jaime. 1994. "Mexico and NAFTA: Economic Effects and the Bargaining Process." In *Mexico and the North American Free Trade Agreement: Who Will Benefit?*, edited by Victor Bulmer-Thomas, Nikki Craske, and Monica Serrano. New York: St. Martin's Press.

Rubio, Luis. 1998. "Coping with Political Change." In *Mexico under Zedillo*, edited by Susan Kaufman Purcell and Luis Rubio. Boulder: Lynne Rienner.

Sachs, Jeffrey, Aaron Tornell, and Andrés Velasco. 1995. "The Collapse of the Peso: What

Have We Learned?" *Working Paper Series*. Cambridge, Mass.: Center for International Affairs, Harvard University.

Salinas de Gortari, Carlos. 1990. "Cinco premisas sobre las relaciones comerciales con el exterior." *Comercio Exterior* 40, no. 6: 524–25.

Saunders, H. 1985. "We Need a Larger Theory of Negotiation: The Importance of Pre-negotiating Phases." *Negotiation Journal* 1, no. 3: 249–62.

Schott, Jeffrey. 1989. *More Free Trade Areas?* Washington, D.C.: Institute for International Economics.

Scott, Pamela, and Antoinette J. Lee. 1993. *Buildings of the District of Columbia*. New York: Oxford University Press.

Serra Puche, Jaime. 1990. "Lineamientos para una estrategia comercial." *Comercio Exterior* 40, no. 6: 526–30.

Smith, Peter H. 1999. "Semiorganized International Crime: Drug Trafficking in Mexico." In *Transnational Crime in the Americas*, edited by Tom Farer. New York: Routledge.

Stein, Janice Gross. 1989. "Getting to the Table: The Triggers, Stages, Functions, and Consequences of Prenegotiation." In *Getting to the Table: The Processes of International Prenegotiation*, edited by Janice Gross Stein. Baltimore: Johns Hopkins University Press.

Story, Dale. 1986. *Industry, the State, and Public Policy in Mexico*. Austin: University of Texas Press.

Téllez Kuenzler, Luis. 1994. *La modernización del sector agropecuario y forestal. Una visión de la modernización de México*. Mexico City: Fondo de Cultura Económica.

Tomlin, Brian. 1989. "The Stages of Prenegotiation: The Decision to Negotiate North American Free Trade." In *Getting to the Table: The Processes of International Prenegotiation*, edited by Janice Gross Stein. Baltimore: Johns Hopkins University Press.

Torres, Blanca. 1998. "La Cooperación Bilateral Para la Protección del Medio Ambiente." In *Nueva agenda bilateral en la relación México-Estados Unidos*, edited by Mónica Verea Campos, Rafael Fernández de Castro, and Sidney Weintraub. Mexico City: Fondo de Cultura Económica.

Trebilcock, Michael, and Robert Howse. 1995. *The Regulation of International Trade*. London: Routledge.

United Nations Development Programme. 1998. *Human Development Report 1998*. New York: Oxford University Press.

Valverde Loya, Miguel Ángel. 1997. "Vinculación entre política interna y política exterior en los Estados Unidos: La negociación del Tratado de Libre Comercio de América del Norte." *Política y Gobierno* 4, no. 2: 377–403.

Waltz, Kenneth. 1979. *Theory of International Politics*. Reading, Mass.: Addison-Wesley.

Weaver, Kent R. 1997. "El manejo de una interdependencia compleja: Los efectos transfronterizos de las estructuras políticas internas de Canadá y Estados Unidos." In *México-Estados Unidos-Canadá, 1995–1996*, edited by G. Vega and F. Alba. Mexico City: Colegio de México.

Weintraub, Sidney, Luis F. Rubio, and Alan D. Jones. 1991. *U.S.-Mexican Industrial Integration: The Road to Free Trade*. Boulder: Westview.

Wendt, Alexander. 1994. "Collective Identity Formation and the International State." *American Political Science Review* 88, no. 2: 384–96.

———. 1992. "Anarchy Is What States Make of It: The Social Construction of Power Politics." *International Organization* 46, no. 2: 395–421.

Wonnacott, Ronald. 1990 "U.S. Hub-and-Spoke Bilaterals and the Multilateral Trading System." *Commentary* 23. Toronto: C.D. Howe Institute.

Zeuthen, F. 1930. *Problems of Monopoly and Economic Welfare*. London: Routledge.

# INDEX

Krasner, Stephen, 17–19, 51, 226, 229, 237
Kuwait, 71

Labastida Ochoa, Francisco, 223
Labor, 5, 11, 21, 32, 67, 69, 71–72, 74–76, 180–86, 188–92, 195–208
Lacondón jungle, 211
Lax, David, 26–27
Legault, Len, 170
Less-developed country (LDC), 105, 226
Levin, Sander, 189
Liberalization, 2–3, 6, 40, 59–60, 94, 98, 101, 105, 110–11, 123, 132–33, 135, 144–47, 193, 210–11, 219, 225, 228, 234
Liberal Party, 203
López Portillo, Hank, 57, 58
Los Pinos, 121, 198, 208, 211
Lozano Gracia, Antonio, 219

MacDonald, Tom, 138
MacGraw, Dan, 186
MacRae, Nancy, 144
Madison Hotel, 196
de la Madrid Hurtado, Miguel, 57
Major League Baseball All-Star Game, 151
Mancera Aguayo, Miguel, 213, 217
Marcos, Sub-comandante, 212
Mares, David, 227
Mayer, Frederick W., 14
McKennirey, John, 186
Meech Lake Accord, 66
Merkin, Bill, 13, 163–64
Mexico City, 1–2, 4–5, 9, 13, 64, 107, 121, 130, 143, 152–53, 184, 186, 190, 198, 208, 212, 216, 219, 221
Meyer, Lorenzo, 4, 18
Mitchell, George, 76
Monopolies, 34, 45, 46
Monterrey, 71
Moravcsik, Andrew, 23
Mosbacher, Robert, 61, 69–70
Most-Favoured Nation principle, 42
Motion Picture Association of America (MPAA), 173
Mulroney, Brian, 6, 7, 59, 64, 66–68, 71, 181, 185, 193
Multilateralism, 6, 18–19, 228
Multilateral Trade Negotiations (MTN), 8–10, 37–39, 42, 46–47, 68–69, 71–72, 96, 104, 106, 131, 140–43, 173, 226, 235
Muñoz Ledo, Porfirio, 221
Muñoz Rocha, Manuel, 216, 219, 223
Murphy, Peter, 9

Nacional Financiera, 212
Nader, Ralph, 194

NAFTA Secretariat, 48
National Association of Manufacturers, 75
National Audubon Society, 191
National College of Economists, 58
National Economic Council, 183–84, 191
National Environmental Policy Act, 194
National Resources Defense Council, 191
National Wildlife Federation, 191
National Treatment, 34, 43–44, 98–99, 114–15, 124, 152
Nature Conservancy, 191
Negotiations, 1, 5–6, 8–11, 13–19, 23, 25–26, 28, 32, 35, 37–40, 42–43, 45–49, 52–53, 55, 59–61, 63–82, 88–89, 92–101, 104–7, 110–17, 120–24, 126, 130–34, 137–48, 150–52, 159–68, 170–75, 178–79, 182–86, 188–201, 204–5, 212, 223, 225–35, 237
Neoliberal institutionalism, 20, 25, 29, 237
Neorealism, 29, 226–27, 237
Newsweek, 5
New York, 70, 202, 217–18
New York Times, 4, 13, 59–61, 178, 180, 218
Nissan, 134–35
Non-agreement alternatives, 15–17, 27–29, 175, 178, 233, 235
North America, 36, 90, 130, 134–35, 138, 153, 159, 184, 232
North American Commission on the Environment (NACE), 188, 192–94
Nye, Joseph, 19
Nymark, Alan, 239

Office of Deregulation, 227
Omnibus Trade and Competitiveness Act, 5, 69, 77
Oñate, Santiago, 186
Organization for Economic Cooperation and Development (OECD), 209
Ortiz, Guillermo, 113–14, 212–13, 216–18
Otero, Joaquin ("Jack"), 183, 197
Ottawa, 9–10, 12, 77, 88, 190, 192, 195, 198

Pacto Economico, 213, 217
Pairwise bargaining, 38
Panetta, Leon, 192
Partido de la Revolución Democrática (PRD), 214
Partido Revolucionario Institucional (PRI), 6
Party of the Mexican Revolution (PRM), 210
Peerless Clothing, 139
Pemex (Petroleos Mexicanos), 39, 93, 116, 152, 160–61, 171–72, 175, 230
Peniche, Alejandro, 143
Peres, Shimon, 61
Perot, Ross, 40, 180, 189, 203, 213
Persian Gulf War, 71, 81